W9-DGQ-519

THE ANCIENT WISDOM

THE ANCIENT WISDOM

THE
ANCIENT WISDOM

An Outline of
Theosophical Teachings

by

ANNIE BESANT

1969

THE THEOSOPHICAL PUBLISHING HOUSE
ADYAR, MADRAS 20, INDIA
Wheaton, Illinois 60187, U.S.A.
68, Great Russell St., London W.C.I., England

© The Theosophical Publishing House, Adyar, 1939.

First Printed		1897
First Adyar Edition		1939
Second ,,	,,	1946
Third ,,	,,	1949
Fourth ,,	,,	1951
Fifth ,,	,,	1954
Sixth ,,	,,	1959
Seventh ,,	,,	1966
Eighth ,,	,,	1969

PRINTED IN INDIA

At the Vasanta Press, The Theosophical Society,
Adyar, Madras 20

DEDICATED

WITH GRATITUDE, REVERENCE, AND LOVE

TO

H. P. BLAVATSKY

WHO SHOWED ME THE LIGHT

PREFACE

This book is intended to place in the hands of the general reader an epitome of Theosophical teachings, sufficiently plain to serve the elementary student, and sufficiently full to lay a sound foundation for further knowledge. It is hoped that it may serve as an introduction to the profounder works of H. P. Blavatsky, and be a convenient stepping-stone to their study.

Those who have learned a little of the Ancient Wisdom know the illumination, the peace, the joy, the strength, its lessons have brought into their lives. That this book may win some to con its teachings, and prove for themselves their value, is the prayer with which it is sent forth into the world.

August, 1897

Annie Besant

CONTENTS

CONTENTS

INTRODUCTION

THE UNITY UNDERLYING ALL RELIGIONS

RIGHT thought is necessary to right conduct, right understanding to right living, and the Divine Wisdom—whether called by its ancient Sanskrit name of Brahma Vidyā, or its modern Greek name of Theosophia, Theosophy—comes to the world as at once an adequate philosophy and an all-embracing religion and ethic. It was once said of the Christian Scriptures by a devotee that they contained shallows in which a child could wade and depths in which a giant must swim. A similar statement might be made of Theosophy, for some of its teachings are so simple and so practical that any person of average intelligence can understand and follow them, while others are so lofty, so profound, that the ablest strains his intellect to contain them and sinks exhausted in the effort.

In the present volume an attempt will be made to place Theosophy before the reader simply and clearly, in a way which shall convey its general principles and truths as forming a coherent conception of the universe, and shall give such detail as is necessary for the understanding of their relations to each other. An elementary textbook cannot pretend to give the fullness of knowledge that may be obtained from abstruser works, but it should leave the student with clear fundamental ideas on his subject, with much indeed to add by future study but with little to unlearn. Into the outline given by such a book the student should be able to paint the details of further research.

It is admitted on all hands that a survey of the great religions of the world shows that they hold in common many religious, ethical, and philosophical ideas. But while the fact is universally granted, the explanation of the fact is a matter of dispute. Some allege that religions have grown up on the soil of human ignorance tilled by imagination, and have been gradually elaborated from crude forms of animism and fetishism; their likenesses are referred to universal natural phenomena imperfectly observed and fancifully explained, solar and star worship being the universal key for one school, phallic worship the equally universal key for another; fear, desire, ignorance, and wonder led the primitive man to personify powers of Nature, and priests played upon his terrors and his hopes, his misty fancies, and his bewildered questionings; myths became scriptures and symbols facts, and as their basis was universal the likeness of the products was inevitable.

Thus speak the doctors of " Comparative Mytho-
logy ", and plain people are silenced but not convinced under the rain of proofs; they cannot deny
the likenesses, but they dimly feel: Are all man's
dearest hopes and loftiest imaginings really nothing
more than the outcome of savage fancies and of
groping ignorance? Have the great leaders of the
race, the martyrs and heroes of humanity, lived,
wrought, suffered and died deluded, for the mere
personifications of astronomical facts and for the
draped obscenities of barbarians?

The second explanation of the common property
in the religions of the world asserts the existence of
an original teaching in the custody of a Brotherhood of great spiritual Teachers, who—Themselves
the outcome of past cycles of evolution—acted as
the instructors and guides of the child humanity of
our planet, imparting to its races and nations in
turn the fundamental truths of religion in the form
most adapted to the idiosyncrasies of the recipients.
According to this view, the Founders of the great
religions are members of the one Brotherhood, and
were aided in Their mission by many other members,
lower in degree than themselves, Initiates and disciples of various grades, eminent in spiritual insight,
in philosophic knowledge, or in purity of ethical
wisdom. These guided the infant nations, gave
them their polity, enacted their laws, ruled them as

kings, taught them as philosophers, guided them as priests; all the nations of antiquity looked back to such mighty men, demigods and heroes, and they left their traces in literature, in architecture, in legislation.

That such men lived it seems difficult to deny in the face of universal tradition, of still existing Scriptures, and of prehistoric remains for the most part now in ruins, to say nothing of other testimony which the ignorant would reject. The sacred books of the East are the best evidence for the greatness of their authors; for who in later days or in modern times can even approach the spiritual sublimity of their religious thought, the intellectual splendour of their philosophy, the breadth and purity of their ethic? And when we find that these books contain teachings about God, man, and the universe identical in substance under much variety of outer appearance, it does not seem unreasonable to refer them to a central primary body of doctrine. To that body we give the name of the Divine Wisdom, in its Greek form: THEOSOPHY.

As the origin and basis of all religions, it cannot be the antagonist of any; it is indeed their purifier, revealing the valuable inner meaning of much that has become mischievous in its external presentation by the perverseness of ignorance and the accretions of superstition; but it recognizes and defends itself in each, and seeks in each to unveil its hidden wisdom. No man in becoming a Theosophist need cease to be a Christian, a Buddhist, a Hindu; he will but acquire a deeper insight into his own faith, a firmer hold on its spiritual truths, a broader understanding of its sacred teachings. As Theosophy of old gave birth to religions, so in modern times does it justify and defend them. It is the rock whence all of them were hewn, the hole of the pit whence all were dug. It justifies at the bar of intellectual criticism the deepest longings and emotions of the human heart; it verifies our hopes for man; it gives us back ennobled our faith in God.

The truth of this statement becomes more and more apparent as we study the various world-Scriptures, and but a few selections from the wealth of material available will be sufficient to establish the fact, and to guide the student in his search for further verification. The main spiritual verities of religion may be summarized thus:

i. One eternal infinite incognizable real Existence.

ii. From THAT, the manifested God, unfolding from unity to duality, from duality to trinity.

iii. From the manifested Trinity many spiritual Intelligences, guiding the cosmic order.

iv. Man a reflection of the manifested God and therefore a trinity fundamentally, his inner and real Self being eternal, one with the Self of the universe.

v. His evolution by repeated incarnations, into which he is drawn by desire, and from which he is set free by knowledge and sacrifice, becoming divine in potency as he had ever been divine in latency.

China, with its now fossilized civilization, was peopled in old days by the Turanians, the fourth subdivision of the great Fourth Race, the race which inhabited the lost continent of Atlantis, and spread its offshoots over the world. The Mongolians, the last subdivision of that same race, later reinforced its population, so that in China we have traditions from ancient days, preceding the settlement of the Fifth, or Aryan Race in India. In the *Ching Chang Ching*, or *Classic of Purity*, we have a fragment of an ancient Scripture of singular beauty, breathing out the spirit of restfulness and peace so characteristic of the " original teaching ". Mr. Legge says in the introductory note to his translation [1] that the treatise—

Is attributed to Ko Yüan (or Hsüan), a Tāoist of the Wū dynasty (A.D. 222-227), who is fabled to have attained to the state of an Immortal, and is generally so denominated. He is represented as a worker of miracles; as addicted to intemperance, and very eccentric in his ways. When shipwrecked on one

[1] *The Sacred Books of the East*, vol. xl.

occasion, he emerged from beneath the water with his clothes unwet, and walked freely on its surface. Finally he ascended to the sky in bright day. All these accounts may safely be put down as the figments of a later time.

Such stories are repeatedly told of Initiates of various degrees, and are by no means necessarily "figments", but we are more interested in Ko Yŭan's own account of the book:

When I obtained the true Tāo, I had recited this Ching [book] ten thousand times. It is what the Spirits of Heaven practise and had not been communicated to scholars of this lower world. I got it from the Divine Ruler of the Eastern Hwa; he received it from the Divine Ruler of the Golden Gate; he received it from the Royal-mother of the West.

Now the "Divine Ruler of the Golden Gate" was the title held by the Initiate who ruled the Toltec empire in Atlantis, and its use suggests that the *Classic of Purity* was brought thence to China when the Turanians separated off from the Toltecs. The idea is strengthened by the contents of the brief treatise; which deals with Tāo—literally "the Way"—the name by which the One Reality is indicated in the ancient Turanian and Mongolian religion. We read:

The Great Tāo has no bodily form, but It produced and nourishes heaven and earth. The Great Tāo has no passions, but It causes the sun and moon to revolve as they do. The Great Tāo has no name, but It effects the growth and maintenance of all things (i, 1).

2

This is the manifested God as unity, but duality supervenes:

Now the Tāo (shows itself in two forms), the Pure and the Turbid, and has (the two conditions of) Motion and Rest. Heaven is pure and earth is turbid; heaven moves and the earth is at rest. The masculine is pure and the feminine is turbid; the masculine moves and the feminine is still. The radical (Purity) descended, and the (turbid) issue flowed abroad, and thus all things were produced (i, 2).

This passage is particularly interesting from the allusion to the active and receptive sides of Nature, the distinction between Spirit, the generator, and matter, the nourisher, so familiar in later writings.

In the *Tāo Teh Ching* the teaching as to the Unmanifested and the Manifested comes out very plainly:

The Tāo that can be trodden is not the enduring and unchanging Tāo. The name that can be named is not the enduring and unchanging name. Having no name, it is the Originator of heaven and earth; having a name, it is the Mother of all things. . . Under these two aspects it is really the same; but as development takes place it receives the different names. Together we call them the Mystery (i, 1, 2, 4).

Students of the Kabalah will be reminded of one of the Divine Names, " the Concealed Mystery ". Again:

There was something undefined and complete, coming into existence before heaven and earth. How still it was and formless, standing alone and undergoing no change, reaching everywhere and in no danger (of

being exhausted). It may be regarded as the Mother
of all things. I do not know its name, and I give it
the designation of the Tāo. Making an effort to give it
a name, I call it the Great. Great, it passes on (in
constant flow). Passing on, it becomes remote.
Having become remote, it returns (xxv, 1-3).

Very interesting it is to see here the idea of the
forthgoing and the returning of the One Life, so
familiar to us in Hindu literature. Familiar also
seems the verse:

All things under heaven sprang from It as existent
(and named); that existence sprang from It as non-
existent (and not named) (xl, 2).

That a universe might become, the Unmanifest
must give forth the One from whom duality and
trinity proceed:

The Tāo produced One; One produced Two; Two
produced Three; Three produced all things. All things
leave behind them the Obscurity (out of which they
have come), and go forward to embrace the Brightness
(into which they have emerged), while they are
harmonized by the Breath of Vacancy (xlii, 1).

"Breath of Space" would be a happier translation. Since all is produced from It, It exists
in all:

All-pervading is the great Tāo. It may be found
on the left hand and on the right. . . It clothes all
things as with a garment, and makes no assumption of
being their lord;—It may be named in the smallest
things. All things return (to their root and disappear),
and do not know that it is It which presides over their

doing so;—It may be named in the greatest things
(xxxiv, 1, 2).

Chwang-ze (fourth century B.C.) in his presentation of the ancient teachings, refers to the spiritual
Intelligences coming from the Tāo:

It has Its root and ground (of existence) in Itself.
Before there were heaven and earth, from of old, there
It was securely existing. From It came the mysterious
existence of spirits, from It the mysterious existence of
God (Bk. vi. Pt. i, Sec. vi, 7).

A number of the names of these Intelligences
follow, but such beings are so well known to play a
great part in the Chinese religion that we need not
multiply quotations about them.

Man is regarded as a trinity. Tāoism, says
Mr. Legge, recognizes in him the spirit, the mind,
and the body. This division comes out clearly in
the *Classic of Purity*, in the teaching that man must
get rid of desire to reach union with the One:

Now the spirit of man loves purity, but his mind
disturbs it. The mind of man loves stillness, but his
desires draw it away. If he could always send his desires
away, his mind would of itself become still. Let his mind
be made clean, and his spirit of itself becomes pure. . .
The reason why men are not able to attain to this is
because their minds have not been cleansed, and their
desires have not been sent away. If one is able to send
the desires away, when he then looks in at his mind
it is no longer his; when he looks out at his body it is
no longer his; and when he looks farther off at external
things, they are things which he has nothing to do
with (i, 3, 4).

Then, after giving the stages of indrawing to " the condition of perfect stillness ", it is asked:

In that condition of rest independently of place, how can any desire arise? And when no desire any longer arises there is the true stillness and rest. That true (stillness) becomes (a) constant quality, and responds to external things (without error); yea, that true and constant quality holds possession of the nature. In such constant response and constant stillness there is the constant purity and rest. He who has this absolute purity enters gradually into the (inspiration of the) True Tāo (i, 5).

The supplied words " inspiration of " rather cloud than elucidate the meaning, for entering into the Tāo is congruous with the whole idea and with other Scriptures.

On putting away of desire is laid much stress in Tāoism; a commentator on the *Classic of Purity* remarks that understanding the Tāo depends on absolute purity, and

The acquiring of this Absolute Purity depends entirely on the putting away of Desire, which is the urgent practical lesson of the Treatise.

The *Tāo Teh Ching* says:

Always without desire we must be found,
If its deep mystery we would sound;
But if desire always within us be,
Its outer fringe is all that we shall see (i, 3).

Reincarnation does not seem to be so distinctly taught as might have been expected, although passages are found which imply that the main idea was taken for granted and that the entity was considered as ranging through animal as well as human births. Thus we have from Chwang-ze the quaint and wise story of a dying man, to whom his friend said:

" Great indeed is the Creator! What will He now make you to become? Where will He take you to? Will He make you the liver of a rat or the arm of an insect?" Szelaiz replied, "Wherever a parent tells a son to go, east, west, south, or north, he simply follows the command. . . . Here now is a great founder, casting his metal. If the metal were to leap up (in the pot) and say, ' I must be made into a (sword like the) Moysh,' the great founder would be sure to regard it as uncanny. So, again, when a form is being fashioned in the mould of the womb, if it were to say, ' I must become a man, I must become a man,' the Creator would be sure to regard it as uncanny. When we once understand that heaven and earth are a great melting-pot and the Creator a great founder, where can we have to go to that shall not be right for us? We are born as from a quiet sleep and we die to a calm awaking " (Bk. vi. Pt. i, Sec. vi).

Turning to the Fifth, the Aryan Race, we have the same teachings embodied in the oldest Aryan religion—the Brāhmanical. The eternal Existence is proclaimed in the *Chhāndogyopanishad* as " One only, without a second ", and it is written:

It willed I shall multiply for the sake of the universe (*vi*, ii, 1, 3).

The Supreme Logos, Brahman, is threefold—
Being, Consciousness, Bliss, and it is said:

> From This arise life, mind, and all the senses, ether,
> air, fire, water, earth the support of all (*Mundakopani-*
> *shad*, ii, 3).

No grander description of Deity can be found
anywhere than in the Hindu Scriptures, but they
are becoming so familiar that brief quotations will
suffice. Let the following serve as specimens of
their wealth of gems.

> Manifest, near, moving in the secret place, the great
> abode, herein rests all that moves, breathes, and shuts
> the eyes. Know That is to be worshipped, being and
> non-being, the best, beyond the knowledge of all crea-
> tures. Luminous, subtler than the subtle, in which
> the worlds and their denizens are infixed. That this
> imperishable Brahman; That also life and voice and
> mind. . . . In the golden highest sheath is spotless,
> partless Brahman; That the pure Light of lights,
> known by the knowers of the Self . . . That
> deathless Brahman is before, Brahman behind, Brah-
> man to the right and to the left, below, above, pervad-
> ing; this Brahman truly is the all. This the best
> (*Mundakopanishad*, II, ii, 1, 2, 9, 11).

> Beyond the universe, Brahman, the Supreme, the
> great, hidden is all beings according to their bodies,
> the one Breath of the whole universe, the Lord, whom
> knowing (men) become immortal, I know that mighty
> Spirit, the shining sun beyond the darkness . . . I
> know Him the unfading, the ancient, the Soul of all,
> omnipresent by His nature, whom the Brahman-
> knowers call unborn, whom they call eternal (*Shvetāsh-*
> *vataropanishad*, iii, 7, 8, 21).

When there is no darkness, no day nor night, no
being nor non-being (there is) Shiva even alone; That
the indestructible, That is to be worshipped by Savitri,
from That came forth the ancient wisdom.   Not above
nor below, nor in the midst, can He be comprehended.
Nor is there any similitude for Him whose name is
infinite glory.   Not with the sight is established His
form, none may by the eye behold Him; they who know
Him by the heart and by the mind, dwelling in the
heart, become immortal (*ibid.*, iv. 18-20).

That man in his inner Self is one with the Self
of the universe—" I am That "—is an idea that so
thoroughly pervades all Hindu thought that man is
often referred to as the " divine town of Brahman ",[1]
the " town of nine gates ",[2] God dwelling in the
cavity of his heart.[3]

In one manner is to be seen (the Being) which cannot be proved, which is eternal, without spot, higher
than the ether, unborn, the great eternal Soul . . .
This great unborn Soul is the same which abides as
the intelligent (soul) in all living creatures, the same
which abides as ether in the heart:[4] in him it sleeps;
it is the Subduer of all, the Ruler of all, the sovereign
Lord of all; it does not become greater by good works
nor less by evil works.   It is the Ruler of all, the
sovereign Lord of all beings, the Preserver of all beings,
the Bridge, the Upholder of the worlds, so that they
fall not to ruin (*Brihadāranyakopanishad*, IV, iv, 20, 22,
Trs. by Dr. E. Röer).

[1] *Mundakopanishad*, II, ii, 7.

[2] *Shvetāshvataropanishad*, iii, 14.

[3] *Ibid.*, ii.

[4] The " ether in the heart " is a mystical phrase used to indicate
the One, who is said to dwell therein.

When God is regarded as the evolver of the universe, the three-fold character comes out very clearly as Shiva, Vishnu, and Brahma, or again as Vishnu sleeping on the waters, the Lotus springing from Him, and in the Lotus Brahma. Man is likewise threefold, and in the *Māndūkyopanishad* the Self is described as conditioned by the physical body, the subtle body, and the mental body, and then rising out of all into the One " without duality ". From the Trimūrti (Trinity) come many Gods, connected with the administration of the universe, as to whom it is said in the *Brihadāranyakopanishad*:

Adore Him, ye Gods, after whom the year by rolling days is completed, the Light of lights, as the immortal Life (IV, iv, 16).

It is hardly necessary to even mention the presence in Brāhmanism of the teaching of reincarnation, since its whole philosophy of life turns on this pilgrimage of the Soul through many births and deaths, and not a book could be taken up in which this truth is not taken for granted. By desires man is bound to this wheel of change, and therefore by knowledge, devotion, and the destruction of desires, man must set himself free. When the Soul knows God it is liberated.[1] The intellect purified by knowledge beholds Him.[2] Knowledge joined to

---

[1] *Shvetāsh.*, i, 8.

[2] *Mund.*, III, i, 8.

devotion finds the abode of Brahman.[1] Whoever knows Brahman becomes Brahman.[2] When desires cease the mortal becomes immortal and obtains Brahman.[3]

Buddhism, as it exists in its northern form, is quite at one with the more ancient faiths, but in the southern form it seems to have let slip the idea of the LOGOIC Trinity as of the One Existence from which They come forth. The LOGOS in His triple manifestation is: the First LOGOS, Amitābha, the Boundless Light; the Second, Avalokiteshvara, or Padmapāni (Chenresi); the Third, Manjusri—" the representative of creative wisdom, corresponding to Brahma ".[4] Chinese Buddhism apparently does not contain the idea of a primordial Existence, beyond the LOGOS, but Nepalese Buddhism postulates Ādi-Buddha, from whom Amitābha arises. Padmapāni is said by Eitel to be the representative of compassionate Providence and to correspond partly with Shiva, but as the aspect of the Buddhist Trinity that sends forth incarnations He appears rather to represent the same idea as Vishnu, to whom He is allied by bearing the Lotus (fire and water, or Spirit and Matter as the primary

[1] *Mund.*, III, ii, 4.
[2] *Ibid.*, III, ii, 9.
[3] *Katho.*, vi, 14.
[4] Eitel's *Sanskrit-Chinese Dictionary, sub voce.*

constituents of the universe). Reincarnation and Karma are so much the fundamentals of Buddhism that it is hardly worth while to insist on them save to note the way of liberation, and to remark that as the Lord Buddha was a Hindu preaching to Hindus, Brāhmanical doctrines are taken for granted constantly in His teaching, as matters of course. He was a purifier and a reformer, not an iconoclast, and struck at the accretions due to ignorance, not at fundamental truths belonging to the Ancient Wisdom:

Those beings who walk in the way of the law that has been well taught, reach the other shore of the great sea of birth and death, that is difficult to cross (*Udāna-varga*, xxix, 37).

Desire binds man, and must be got rid of:

It is hard for one who is held by the fetters of desire to free himself of them, says the Blessed One. The steadfast, who care not for the happiness of desires, cast them off and do soon depart (to Nirvāna). . . . Mankind has no lasting desires; they are impermanent in them who experience them; free yourselves then from what cannot last, and abide not in the sojourn of death (*ibid.*, ii, 6, 8).

He who has destroyed desires for (worldly) goods, sinfulness, the bonds of the eye of the flesh, who has torn up desire by the very root, he, I declare, is a Brāhmana (*ibid.*, xxxiii, 68).

And a Brāhmana is a man " having his last body ", [1] and is defined as one,

[1] *Udānavarga*, xxxiii, 41.

Who, knowing his former abodes (existences) per-
ceives heaven and hell, the Muni, who has found the
way to put an end to birth (*ibid*, xxxiii, 55).

In the exoteric Hebrew Scriptures, the idea of a
Trinity does not come out strongly, though duality
is apparent, and the God spoken of is obviously the
LOGOS, not the One Unmanifest:

I am the Lord and there is none else. I form the
light and create darkness; I make peace and create evil;
I am the Lord that doeth all these things (*Isa.*, xlvii, 7).

Philo, however, has the doctrine of the LOGOS
very clearly, and it is found in the Fourth Gospel:

In the beginning was the Word [Logos] and the
Word was with God and the Word was God. . . . All
things were made by Him, and without Him was not
anything made that was made (*S. John* i, 1, 3).

In the Kabalah the doctrine of the One, the
Three, the Seven, and then the many, is plainly
taught:

The Ancient of the Ancients, the Unknown of the
Unknown, has a form, yet also has not any form. It
has a form through which the universe is maintained.
It also has not any form, as It cannot be compre-
hended. When It first took this form [Kether, the
Crown, the First Logos] It permitted to proceed from
It nine brilliant Lights [Wisdom and the Voice, forming
with Kether the Triad, and then the seven lower
Sephiroth]. . . . It is the Ancient of the Ancients, the
Mystery of the Mysteries, the Unknown of the Un-
known. It has a form which appertains to It, since
It appears (through it) to us, as the Ancient Man Above
All, as the Ancient of the Ancients, and as that which

there is the Most Unknown among the Unknown. But under that form by which It makes Itself known, It however still remains the Unknown (Isaac Myer's *Qabbalah*, from the *Zohar*, pp. 274, 275).

Myer points out that the " form " is " not ' the Ancient of ALL the Ancients ', who is the Ain Soph ".

Again:

Three Lights are in the Holy Upper which unite as One; and they are the basis of the Thorah, and this opens the door to all . . . Come, see the mystery of the word. These are three degrees and each exists by itself, and yet all are One and are knotted in One, nor are they separated one from another. . . . Three come out from One, One exists in Three, it is the force between Two, Two nourish One, One nourishes many sides, thus All is One (*ibid.*, 373, 375, 376).

Needless to say that the Hebrews held the doctrine of many Gods—" Who is like unto Thee, O Lord, among the Gods? " [1]—and of multitudes of subordinate ministrants, the " Sons of God ", the " Angels of the Lord ", the " Ten Angelic Hosts ".

Of the commencement of the universe, the *Zohar* teaches:

In the beginning was the Will of the King, prior to any existence which came into being through emanation from his Will. It sketched and engraved the forms of all things that were to be manifested from concealment into view, in the supreme and dazzling light of the Quadrant [the sacred Tetractys] (Myer's *Qabbalah*, pp. 194, 195).

[1] *Exod.* xv, ii.

Nothing can exist in which the Deity is not immanent, and with regard to Reincarnation it is taught that the Soul is present in the divine Idea ere coming to earth; if the Soul remained quite pure during its trial it escaped rebirth, but this seems to have been only a theoretical possibility, as it is said:

All souls are subject to revolution (metempsychosis, a'leen o'gilgoolah), but men do not know the ways of the Holy One; blessed be It! they are ignorant of the way they have been judged in all time, and before they came into this world and when they have quitted it (*ibid.*, p. 198).

Traces of this belief occur both in the Hebrew and Christian exoteric Scriptures, as in the belief that Elijah would return, and later that he had returned in John the Baptist.

Turning to glance at Egypt, we find there from hoariest antiquity its famous Trinity, Ra, Osiris-Isis as the dual Second Logos, and Horus. The great hymn to Amun-Ra will be remembered:

The Gods bow before Thy Majesty by exalting the Souls of That which produceth them . . . and say to Thee: Peace to all emanations from the unconscious Father of the conscious Fathers of the Gods. . . . Thou Producer of beings, we adore the Souls which emanate from Thee. Thou begettest us, O Thou Unknown, and we greet Thee in worshipping each God-Soul which descendeth from Thee and liveth in us (quoted in *Secret Doctrine*, iii, 485, 1893 Edn.; v, 463, Adyar Edn.).

The "conscious Fathers of the Gods" are the LOGOI, the "unconscious Father" is the One Existence, unconscious not as being less but as being infinitely more than what we call consciousness, a limited thing.

In the fragments of the *Book of the Dead* we can study the conceptions of the reincarnation of the human Soul, of its pilgrimage towards and its ultimate union with the LOGOS. The famous papyrus of "the scribe Ani, triumphant in peace", is full of touches that remind the reader of the Scriptures of other faiths; his journey through the underworld, his expectation of re-entering his body (the form taken by reincarnation among the Egyptians), his identification with the LOGOS:

Saith Osiris Ani: I am the great One, son of the great One; I am Fire, the son of Fire. . . . I have knit together my bones, I have made myself whole and sound; I have become young once more; I am Osiris, the Lord of eternity (xliii, 1, 4).

In Pierret's recension of the *Book of the Dead* we find the striking passage:

I am the being of mysterious names who prepares for himself dwelling for millions of years (p. 22). Heart, that comest to me from my mother, my heart necessary to my existence on earth. . . . Heart, that comest to me from my mother, heart that is necessary to me for my transformation (pp. 113, 114).

In Zoroastrianism we find the conception of the One Existence, imaged as Boundless Space, whence arises the LOGOS, the creator Aūharmazd:

> Supreme in omniscience and goodness, and unrivalled in splendour: the region of light is the place of Aūharmazd (*The Bundahis, Sacred Books of the East,* v. 3, 4: v. 2).

To him in the *Yasna*, the chief liturgy of the Zarathustrians, homage is first paid:

> I announce and I (will) complete (my Yasna [worship]) to Ahura Mazda, the Creator, the radiant and glorious, the greatest and the best, the most beautiful (?) (to our conceptions), the most firm, the wisest, and the one of all whose body is most perfect, who attains his ends the most infallibly, because of His righteous order, to Him who disposes our minds aright, who sends His joy-creating grace afar; who made us and has fashioned us, and who has nourished and protected us, who is the most bounteous Spirit (*Sacred Books of the East,* xxxi, pp. 195, 196).

The worshipper then pays homage to the Ameshaspends and other Gods, but the supreme manifested God, the LOGOS is not here presented as triune. As with the Hebrews, there was a tendency in the exoteric faith to lose sight of this fundamental truth. Fortunately we can trace the primitive teaching, though it disappeared in later times from the popular belief. Dr. Haug, in his *Essays on the Parsis* (translated by Dr. West and forming vol. v of Trübner's Oriental Series) states that Ahuramazda—

Aūharmazd or Hormazd—is the Supreme Being, and that from him were produced

Two primeval causes, which, though different, were united and produced the world of material things as well as that of the spirit (p. 303).

These were called twins and are everywhere present, in Ahuramazda as well as in man. One produces reality, the other non-reality, and it is these who in later Zoroastrianism became the opposing Spirits of good and evil. In the earlier teachings they evidently formed the Second Logos, duality being his characteristic mark.

The " good " and " bad " are merely Light and Darkness, Spirit and Matter, the fundamental " twins " of the Universe, the Two from the One. Criticizing the later idea, Dr. Haug says:

Such is the original Zoroastrian notion of the two creative Spirits, who form only two parts of the Divine Being. But in the course of time this doctrine of the great founder was changed and corrupted, in consequence of misunderstandings and false interpretations. Spentōmainyush [the " good spirit "] was taken as a name of Ahuramazda Himself, and then of course Angrōmainyush [the " evil spirit "], by becoming entirely separated from Ahuramazda, was regarded as the constant adversary of Ahuramazda; thus the Dualism of God and Devil arose (p. 205).

Dr. Haug's view seems to be supported by the *Gātha Ahunavaiti*, given with the other Gāthas by " the archangels " to Zoroaster or Zarathustra:

3

In the beginning there was a pair of twins, two spirits, each of a peculiar activity; these are the good and the base. . . . And these two spirits united created the first (the material things); one the reality, the other the non-reality. . . . And to succour this life (to increase it) Armaiti came with wealth, the good and true mind; she the everlasting one, created the material world. . . . All perfect things are garnered up in the splendid residence of the Good Mind, the Wise and the Righteous, who are known as the best beings (*Yas.*, xxx, 3, 4, 7, 10; Dr. Haug's Trans., pp 149-151).

Here the three Logoi are seen, Ahuramazda the first, the supreme Life; in and from him the " twins ", the Second Logos; then Armaiti the Mind, the Creator of the Universe, the Third Logos.[1] Later Mithra appears, and in the exoteric faith clouds the primitive truth to some extent; of him it is said:

Whom Ahura Mazda has established to maintain and look over all this moving world; who, never sleeping, wakefully guards the creation of Mazda (*Mihir Yast.*, xxvii, 103; *Sacred Books of the East*, xviii).

He was a subordinate God, the Light of Heaven, as Varuna was the Heaven itself, one of the great ruling Intelligences. The highest of these ruling Intelligences where the six Ameshaspends, headed by the Good Thought of Ahuramazda, Vohūman—

Who have charge of the whole material creation (*Sacred Books of the East*, v, p. 10, note).

[1] Armaiti was at first Wisdom and the Goddess of Wisdom. Later, as the Creator, She became identified with the earth, and was worshipped as the Goddess of Earth.

Reincarnation does not seem to be taught in the books which, so far, have been translated, and the belief is not current among modern Parsis. But we do find the idea of the Spirit in man as a spark that is to become a flame and to be reunited to the Supreme Fire, and this must imply a development for which rebirth is a necessity. Nor will Zoroastrianism ever be understood until we recover the *Chaldæan Oracles* and allied writings, for there is its real root.

Travelling westward to Greece, we meet with the Orphic system, described with such abundant learning by Mr. G. R. S. Mead in his work *Orpheus*. The Ineffable Thrice-unknown Darkness was the name given to the One Existence.

According to the theology of Orpheus, all things originate from an immense principle, to which through the imbecility and poverty of human conception we give a name, though it is perfectly ineffable, and in the reverential language of the Egyptians is a *thrice unknown darkness* in contemplation of which all knowledge is refunded into ignorance (Thomas Taylor, quoted in *Orpheus*, p. 93).

From this the " Primordial Triad ", Universal Good, Universal Soul, Universal Mind, again the LOGIC Trinity. Of this Mr. Mead writes:

The first Triad, which is manifestable to intellect, is but a reflection of, or substitute for the Unmanifestable, and its hypostases are: (*a*) the Good, which is super-essential; (*b*) Soul (the World Soul), which is a self-motive essence; (c) Intellect (or the Mind), which is an impartible, immovable essence (ibid., p. 94).

After this, a series of ever-descending Triads, showing the characteristics of the first in diminishing splendour until man is reached, who

> Has in him potentially the sum and substance of the universe. . . . "The race of men and gods is one" (Pindar, who was a Pythagorean, quoted by Clemens, Strom., v, p. 709) . . . Thus man was called the microcosm or little world, to distinguish him from the universe or great world (ibid., p. 271).

He has the Nous, or real mind, the Logos or rational part, the Alogos or irrational part, the two latter again forming a Triad, and thus presenting the more elaborate septenary division. The man was also regarded as having three vehicles, the physical and subtle bodies and the luciform body or augoeides, that

> Is the " causal body," or karmic vesture of the soul, in which its destiny, or rather all the seeds of past causation are stored. This is the " thread-soul," as it is sometimes called, the " body " that passes over from one incarnation to another (ibid., p. 284).

As to reincarnation:

> Together with all the adherents of the Mysteries in every land the Orphics believed in reincarnation (ibid., p. 292).

To this Mr. Mead brings abundant testimony, and he shows that it was taught by Plato, Empedocles,

Pythagoras, and others. Only by virtue could men escape from the life-wheel.

Taylor, in his notes to the *Select Works of Plotinus*, quotes from Damascius as to the teachings of Plato on the One beyond the One, the unmanifest Existence:

> Perhaps, indeed, Plato leads us ineffably through *the one* as a medium to the ineffable beyond *the one* which is now the subject of discussion; and this by an ablation of *the one* in the same manner as he leads to *the one* by an ablation of other things. . . . That which is beyond *the one* is to be honoured in the most perfect silence. . . . *The one* indeed wills to be by itself, but with no other; but the unknown beyond *the one* is perfectly ineffable, which we acknowledge we neither know, nor are ignorant of, but which has about itself *super-ignorance*. Hence by proximity to this *the one* itself is darkened; for being near to the immense principle, if it be lawful so to speak, it remains as it were in the adytum of the truly mystic silence. . . . The first is above *the one* and *all things*, being more simple than either of these (pp. 341-343).

The Pythagorean, Platonic, and Neo-Platonic schools have so many points of contact with Hindu and Buddhist thought that their issue from one fountain is obvious. R. Garbe in his work, *Die Sāmkhya Philosophie* (iii, pp. 85 to 105) presents many of these points, and his statement may be summarized as follows:

The most striking is the resemblance—or more correctly the identity—of the doctrine of the One and Only in the Upanishads and the Eleatic school. Xenophanes' teaching of the unity of God and the Kosmos and of the changelessness of the One, and even more that of Parmenides, who held that reality is ascribable only to the One unborn, indestructible and omnipresent, while all that is manifold and subject to change is but an appearance, and further that Being and Thinking are the same—these doctrines are completely identical with the essential contents of the Upanishads and of the Vedāntic philosophy which springs from them. But even earlier still the view of Thales, that all that exists has sprung from Water, is curiously like the Vaidic doctrine that the Universe arose from the waters. Later on Anaximander assumed as the basis ($\mathring{a}\rho\chi\acute{\eta}$) of all things an eternal, infinite, and indefinite Substance, from which all definite substances proceed and into which they return—an assumption identical with that which lies at the root of the Sāmkhya, *viz.*, the Prakriti from which the whole material side of the universe evolved. And his famous saying $\pi\acute{a}\nu\tau a$ $\mathring{\rho}\epsilon\hat{\iota}$ (panta rhei) expresses the characteristic view of the Sānkhya that all things are ever changing under the ceaseless activity of the three gunas. Empedocles again taught theories of transmigration and evolution practically the same as those of the Sānkhyas, while his theory that nothing can come into being which does not already exist is even more closely identical with a characteristically Sānkhyan doctrine.

Both Anaxagoras and Democritus also present several points of close agreement, especially the latter's view as to the nature and position of the Gods, and the same applies, notably in some curious matters of detail, to Epicurus. But it is, however, in the teachings of Pythagoras that we find the closest and most frequent identities of teachings and argumentation, explained as due to Pythagoras himself having visited India and learnt his philosophy there, as tradition asserts. In later centuries we find some peculiarly Sānkhyan and Buddhist ideas playing a prominent part in Gnostic thought. The following quotation from Lassen, cited by Garbe on p. 97, shows this very clearly:

Buddhism in general distinguishes clearly between Spirit and Light, and does not regard the latter as immaterial; but a view of Light is found among them which is closely related to that of the Gnostics. According to this, Light is the manifestation of Spirit in matter; the intelligence thus clothed in Light comes into relation with matter, in which the Light can be lessened and at last quite obscured, in which case the Intelligence falls finally into complete unconsciousness. Of the highest Intelligence it is maintained that it is neither Light nor Not-Light, neither Darkness nor Not-Darkness, since all these expressions denote relations of the Intelligence to the Light, which indeed in the beginning was free from these connections, but later on encloses the Intelligence and mediates its connection with matter. It follows from this that the Buddhist view ascribes to the highest Intelligence the power to produce light from itself, and that in this respect also there is an agreement between Buddhism and Gnosticism.

Garbe here points out that, as regards the features alluded to, the agreement between Gnosticism and the Sānkhya is very much closer than that with Buddhism; for while these views as to the relations between Light and Spirit pertain to the later phases of Buddhism, and are not at all fundamental to, or characteristic of it as such, the Sānkhya teaches clearly and precisely that Spirit *is* Light. Later still the influence of the Sānkhya thought is very plainly evident in the Neo-Platonic writers; while the doctrine of the LoGos or Word, though not of Sānkhyan origin, shows even in its details that it has been derived from India, where the conception of Vāch, the Divine Word, plays so prominent a part in the Brāhmanical system.

Coming to the Christian religion, contemporaneous with the Gnostic and Neo-Platonic systems, we shall find no difficulty in tracing most of the same fundamental teachings with which we have now become so familiar. The threefold LoGos appears as the Trinity: the First LoGos, the fount of all life, being the Father; the dual-natured Second LoGos the Son, God-man; the Third, the creative Mind, the Holy Ghost, whose brooding over the waters of Chaos brought forth the worlds.

Then come " the seven Spirits of God "[1] and the hosts of archangels and angels. Of the One Existence from which all comes and into which all returns, but little is hinted, the Nature that by searching cannot be found out; but the great doctors of the Church Catholic always posit the unfathomable Deity, incomprehensible, infinite, and therefore necessarily but One and partless. Man is made in the " image of God ", [2] and is consequently triple in his nature—Spirit and Soul and body; [3] he is a " habitation of God ", [4] the " temple of God ", [5] the " temple of the Holy Ghost ", [6]—phrases that exactly echo the Hindu teaching. The doctrine of reincarnation is rather taken for granted in the *New Testament* than distinctly taught; thus Jesus, speaking of John the Baptist, declares that he is Elias " which was for to come ", [7] referring to the words of Malachi, " I will send you Elijah the prophet "; [8] and again, when asked as to Elijah coming before the Messiah, He answered that " Elias is come already and they knew him not "; [9] so again

[1] *Rev.* iv, 5.
[2] *Gen.* i, 26, 27.
[3] *I Thess.* v, 23.
[4] *Eph.* ii, 22.
[5] *I Cor.* iii, 16.
[6] *I Cor.* vi, 19.
[7] *Matt.* xi, 14.
[8] *Mal.* iv, 5.
[9] *Matt.* xvii, 12.

we find the disciples taking reincarnation for granted in asking whether blindness from birth was a punishment for a man's sin, and Jesus in answer not rejecting the possibility of ante-natal sin, but only excluding it as causing the blindness in the special instance.[1] The remarkable phrase applied to " him that overcometh " in *Rev.* iii, 12, that he shall be " a pillar in the temple of my God, and he shall go no more out," has been taken as signifying escape from rebirth. From the writings of some of the Christian Fathers a good case may be made out for a current belief in reincarnation; some argue that only the pre-existence of the Soul is taught, but this view does not seem to me supported by the evidence.

The unity of moral teaching is not less striking than the unity of the conceptions of the universe and of the experiences of those who rose out of the prison of the body into the freedom of the higher spheres. It is clear that this body of primeval teaching was in the hands of definite custodians, who had schools, in which they taught, disciples who studied their doctrines. The identity of these schools and of their discipline stands out plainly when we study the moral teaching, the demands made on the pupils, and the mental and spiritual states to which they were raised. A caustic division

---

[1] *John*, ix, 1-13.

is made in the *Tāo Teh Ching* of the types of scholars:

Scholars of the highest class, when they hear about the Tāo, earnestly carry it into practice. Scholars of the middle class, when they have heard about it, seem now to keep it and now to lose it. Scholars of the lowest class, when they have heard about it, laugh greatly at it (*Sacred Books of the East*, xxxix, *op. cit.*, xli, 1).

In the same book we read:

The sage puts his own person last, and yet it is found in the foremost place; he treats his person as if it were foreign to him, and yet that person is preserved. Is it not because he has no personal and private ends that therefore such ends are realized? (vii, 2). He is free from self-display, and therefore he shines; from self-assertion, and therefore he is distinguished; from self-boasting, and therefore his merit is acknowledged; from self-complacency, and therefore he acquires superiority. It is because he is thus free from striving that therefore no one in the world is able to strive with him (xxii, 2). There is no guilt greater than to sanction ambition; no calamity greater than to be discontented with one's lot; no fault greater than the wish to be getting (xlvi, 2). To those who are good (to me) I am good; and to those who are not good (to me) I am also good; and thus (all) get to be good. To those who are sincere (with me) I am sincere; and to those who are not sincere (with me) I am also sincere; and thus (all) get to be sincere (xlix, 1). He who has in himself abundantly the attributes (of the Tāo) is like an infant. Poisonous insects will not sting him; fierce beasts will not seize him; birds of prey will not strike him (lv, 1). I have three precious things which I prize and hold fast. The first is gentleness; the second is economy; the third is shrinking from taking precedence of others.

. . . . Gentleness is sure to be victorious, even in battle, and firmly to maintain its ground. Heaven will save its possessor, by his (very) gentleness protecting him (lxvii, 2, 4).

Among the Hindus there were selected scholars deemed worthy of special instruction to whom the Guru imparted the secret teachings, while the general rules of right living may be gathered from Manu's *Ordinances*, the *Upanishads*, the *Mahābhārata* and many other treatises:

Let him say what is true, let him say what is pleasing, let him utter no disagreeable truth, and let him utter no agreeable falsehood; that is the eternal law (*Manu*, iv, 138). Giving no pain to any creature, let him slowly accumulate spiritual merit (iv, 238). For that twice-born man, by whom not the smallest danger even is caused to created beings, there will be no danger from any (quarter) after he is freed from his body (vi, 40). Let him patiently bear hard words, let him not insult anybody, and let him not become anybody's enemy for the sake of this (perishable) body. Against an angry man let him not in return show anger, let him bless when he is cursed (vi, 47, 48). Freed from passion, fear and anger, thinking on Me, taking refuge in Me, purified in the fire of wisdom, many have entered My Being (*Bhagavad Gita*, iv, 10). Supreme joy is for this Yogi whose Manas is peaceful, whose passion-nature is calmed, who is sinless and of the nature of Brahman (vi, 27). He who beareth no ill-will to any being, friendly and compassionate, without attachment and egoism, balanced in pleasure and pain, and forgiving, ever content, harmonious, with the self controlled, resolute, with Manas and Buddhi dedicated to Me, he, My devotee, is dear to Me (xii, 13, 14).

If we turn to the Buddha, we find Him with His Arhats, to whom His secret teachings were given; while published we have:

The wise man through earnestness, virtue, and purity makes himself an island which no flood can submerge (*Udānavarga*, iv, 5). The wise man in this world holds fast to faith and wisdom, these are his greatest treasures; he casts aside all other riches (x, 9). He who bears ill-will to those who bear ill-will can never become pure; but he who feels no ill-will pacifies those who hate; as hatred brings misery to mankind, the sage knows no hatred (xiii, 12). Overcome anger by not being angered; overcome evil by good; overcome avarice by liberality; overcome falsehoods by truth (xx, 18).

The Zoroastrian is taught to praise Ahuramazda, and then:

What is fairest, what pure, what immortal, what brilliant, all that is good. The good spirit we honour, the good kingdom we honour, and the good law, and the good wisdom (*Yasna*, xxxvii). May there come to this dwelling contentment, blessing, guilelessness, and wisdom of the pure (*Yasana*, lix). Purity is the best good. Happiness, happiness is to him: namely, to the best pure in purity (*Ashem-vohu*). All good thoughts, words, and works are done with knowledge. All evil thoughts, words, and works are not done with knowledge (*Mispa Kumata*). (Selected from the *Avesta* in *Ancient Iranian and Zoroastrian Morals*, by Dhunjibhoy Jamsetjee Medhora).

The Hebrew had his " schools of the prophets " and his Kabalah, and in the exoteric books we find the accepted moral teachings:

Who shall ascend into the hill of the Lord and who stand in His holy place? He that hath clean hands

and a pure heart; who hath not lifted up his soul unto
vanity, nor sworn deceitfully (*Ps.* xxiv, 3, 4). What
doth the Lord require of thee but to do justly, and to
love mercy, and to walk humbly with thy God?
(*Micah*. vi, 8). The lip of truth shall be established
for ever; but a lying tongue is but for a moment (*Prov.*
xii, 19). Is not this the fast that I have chosen? to
loose the bands of wickedness, to undo the heavy burdens, and to let the oppressed go free, and that ye
break every yoke? Is it not to deal thy bread to the
hungry and that thou bring the poor that are cast
out to thy house? When thou seest the naked that
thou cover him, and that thou hide not thyself from
thine own flesh? (*Is.* lviii, 6, 7).

The Christian Teacher had His secret instructions
for His disciples,[1] and He bade them:

> Give not that which is holy unto the dogs, neither
cast ye your pearls before swine (*Matt*. vii, 6).

For public teaching we may refer to the beati-
tudes in the Sermon on the Mount, and to such
doctrines as:

> I say unto you, love your enemies, bless them that
curse you, do good to them that hate you, and pray
for them which despitefully use you and persecute you
. . . . Be ye therefore perfect, even as your
Father which is in heaven is perfect (*Matt*. v, 44, 48).
He that findeth his life shall lose it; and he that loseth
his life for my sake shall find it (x, 39). Whosoever
shall humble himself as this little child, the same is
greatest in the kingdom of heaven (xviii, 4). The
fruit of the Spirit is love, joy, peace, long-suffering,
gentleness, goodness, faith, meekness, temperance;
against such there is no law (*Gal.*, v, 22, 23). Let

[1] *Matt.* xiii, 10-17.

us love one another; for love is of God; and everyone that loveth is born of God and knoweth God
(I *John* iv, 7).

The school of Pythagoras and those of the Neo-
Platonists kept up the tradition for Greece, and we
know that Pythagoras gained some of his learning
in India, while Plato studied and was initiated in
the schools of Egypt. More precise information
has been published of the Grecian schools than of
others; the Pythagorean had pledged disciples as
well as an outer discipline, the inner circle passing
through three degrees during five years of probation.
(For details see G. R. S. Mead's *Orpheus*, pp. 268
et. seq.) The outer discipline he describes as
follows:

We must first give ourselves up entirely to God.
When a man prays he should never ask for any particular benefit, fully convinced that that will be given
which is right and proper, and according to the
wisdom of God and not the subject of our own selfish
desires (Diod. Sic., ix, 41). By virtue alone does man
arrive at blessedness, and this is the exclusive privilege
of a rational being (Hippodamu, *De Felicitate*, ii, Orelli,
Opusc. Grǣcor Sent. et Moral., ii, 284). In himself, of
his own nature, man is neither good nor happy,
but he may become so by the teaching of the true
doctrine (μαθήσιος καί προνοίας ποτιδέεται)—(Hippo.
ibid.). The most sacred duty is filial piety. "God
showers blessings on him who honours and reveres the
author of his days," says Pampelus (*De Parentibus*,
Orelli, *op. cit.*, ii, 345). Ingratitude towards one's
parents is the blackest of all crimes, writes Perictione
(*ibid.*, p. 350), who is supposed to have been the mother

of Plato. The cleanliness and delicacy of all Pythagorean writings were remarkable ('Œlian, *Hist. Var.*,
xiv, 19). In all that concerns chastity and marriage
their principles are of the utmost purity. Everywhere
the great teacher recommends chastity and temperance; but at the same time he directs that the married
should first become parents before living a life of
absolute celibacy, in order that children might be born
under favourable conditions for continuing the holy
life and succession of the Sacred Science (Iamblichus,
Vit. Pythag., and Hierocl., ap. Stob. *Serm.* xlv, 14).
This is exceedingly interesting, for it is precisely the
same regulation that is laid down in the *Mānava
Dharma Shāstra*, the great Indian Code. . . . Adultery
was most sternly condemned (Iamb., *ibid.*). Moreover,
the most gentle treatment of the wife by the husband
was enjoined, for had he not taken her as his companion
" before the Gods "? (See Lascaulx, *Zur Geschichte der
Ehe bei den Griechen*, in the *Mém. de l'Acad. de Bavière*,
vii, 107, *sq.*).

Marriage was not an animal union, but a spiritual
tie. Therefore, in her turn, the wife should love her
husband even more than herself, and in all things be
devoted and obedient. It is further interesting to
remark that the finest characters among women with
which ancient Greece presents us were formed in the
school of Pythagoras, and the same is true of the men.
The authors of antiquity are agreed that this discipline
had succeeded in producing the highest examples not
only of the purest chastity and sentiment, but also a
simplicity of manners, a delicacy, and a taste for
serious pursuits which was unparalleled. This is
admitted even by Christian writers (see Justin, xx, 4).
. . . Among the members of the school the idea of
justice directed all their acts, while they observed the
strictest tolerance and compassion in their mutual
relationships. For justice is the principle of all virtue,
as Polus (ap. Stob., *Serm.*, viii, ed. Schow, p. 232)

teaches: 'tis justice which maintains peace and balance in the soul; she is the mother of good order in all communities, makes concord between husband and wife, love between master and servant.

The word of a Pythagorean was also his bond. And finally a man should live so as to be ever ready for death (Hippolytus, *Philos.*, vi,) (*Ibid.*, pp. 263-276).

The treatment of the virtues in the Neo-Platonic schools is interesting, and the distinction is clearly made between morality and spiritual development, or, as Plotinus put it, " The endeavour is not to be without sin, but to be a God ".[1] The lowest stage was the becoming without sin by acquiring the " political virtues " which made a man perfect in conduct (the physical and ethical being below these), the reason controlling and adorning the irrational nature. Above these were the cathartic, pertaining to reason alone, which liberated the Soul from the bonds of generation; the theoretic, lifting the Soul into touch with natures superior to itself; and the paradigmatic, giving it a knowledge of true being:

Hence he who energizes according to the practical virtues is *a worthy man*; but he who energizes according to the cathartic virtues is *a demonical man*, or is also *a good demon*.[2] He who energizes according to the intellectual virtues alone is *a God*. But he who energizes

[1] *Select Works of Plotinus*, trans. by Thomas Taylor, ed. 1895, p. 11.

[2] A good spiritual intelligence, as the daimon of Socrates.

4

according to the paradigmatic virtues is *the Father of the Gods*. (Note on Intellectual Prudence, pp. 325-332.)

By various practices the disciples were taught to escape from the body, and to rise into higher regions. As grass is drawn from a sheath, the inner man was to draw himself from his bodily casing. The "body of light" or "radiant body" of the Hindus is the "luciform body" of the Neo-Platonists, and in this the man rises to find the Self:

> Not grasped by the eye, nor by speech, nor by the other senses (*lit.*, Gods), nor by austerity, nor by religious rites; by serene wisdom, by the pure essence only, doth one see the partless One in meditation. This subtle Self is to be known by the mind in which the fivefold life is sleeping. The mind of all creatures is instinct with [these] lives; in this, purified, manifests the Self (*Mundakopanishad*, III, ii, 8, 9).

Then alone can man enter the region where separation is not, where "the spheres have ceased". In G. R. S. Mead's Introduction to Taylor's *Plotinus* he quotes from Plotinus a description of a sphere which is evidently the Turīya of the Hindus:

> They likewise see all things, not those with which generation, but those with which essence is present. And they perceive themselves in others. For all things there are diaphanous; and nothing is dark and resisting but everything is apparent to every one internally and throughout. For light everywhere meets with light; since everything contains all things in itself and again

---

[1] *Kathopanishad*, vi, 17.

sees all things in another. So that all things are everywhere and all is all. Each thing likewise is everything. And the splendour there is infinite. For everything there is great, since even that which is small is great. The sun too which is there is all the stars; and again each star is the sun and all the stars. In each, however, a different property predominates, but at the same time all things are visible in each. Motion likewise there is pure; for the motion is not confounded by a mover different from it (p. lxxiii).

A description which is a failure, because the region is one above describing by mortal language, but a description that could only have been written by one whose eyes had been opened.

A whole volume might easily be filled with the similarities between the religions of the world, but the above imperfect statement must suffice as a preface to the study of Theosophy, to that which is a fresh and fuller presentment to the world of the ancient truths on which it has ever been fed. All these similarities point to a single source, and that is the Brotherhood of the White Lodge, the Hierarchy of Adepts who watch over and guide the evolution of humanity, and who have preserved these truths unimpaired; from time to time, as necessity arose, reasserting them in the ears of men. From other worlds, from earlier humanities, They came to help our globe, evolved by a process comparable to that now going on with ourselves, and that will be more intelligible when we have completed our present study than it may now appear; and They have afforded this help, reinforced by the flower of our own humanity, from the earliest times until to-day. Still They teach eager pupils, showing the path and guiding the disciple's steps; still They may be reached by all who seek Them, bearing in their hands the sacrificial fuel of love, of devotion, of unselfish longing to know in order to serve; still They carry out the ancient discipline, still unveil the ancient Mysteries. The two pillars of Their Lodge gateway are Love and Wisdom, and through its strait portal can only pass those from whose shoulders has fallen the burden of desire and selfishness.

A heavy task lies before us, and beginning on the physical plane we shall climb slowly upwards, but a bird's-eye view of the great sweep of evolution and of its purpose may help us, ere we begin our detailed study in the world that surrounds us. A Logos, ere a system has begun to be, has in His mind the whole, existing as idea—all forces, all forms, all that in due process shall emerge into objective life. He draws the circle of manifestation within which He wills to energize, and circumscribes Himself to be the life of His universe. As we watch, we see strata appearing of successive densities, till seven vast regions are apparent, and in these centres of energy appear whirlpools of matter that separate from each other, until when the processes of separation and of condensation are over—so far as we are here concerned—we see a central sun, the physical symbol of the LOGOS, and seven great planetary Chains, each Chain consisting of seven globes. Narrowing down our view to the Chain of which our globe is one, we see life-waves sweep round it, forming the Kingdoms of Nature, the three elemental, the mineral, vegetable, animal, human. Narrowing down our view still further to our own globe and its surroundings, we watch human evolution, and see man developing self-consciousness by a series of many life-periods; then centering on a single man we trace his growth and see that each life-period has a threefold division, that each is linked to all life-periods behind it, reaping their results, and to all life-periods before it, sowing their harvests, by a law that cannot be broken; that thus man may climb upwards with each life-period adding to his experience, each life-period lifting him higher in purity, in devotion, in intellect, in power of usefulness, until at last he stands where They stand who are now the Teachers, fit to pay to his younger brothers the debt he owes to Them.

CHAPTER I

THE PHYSICAL PLANE

WE have just seen that the source from which a universe proceeds is a manifested Divine Being, to whom in the modern form of the Ancient Wisdom the name LOGOS, or Word, has been given. The name is drawn from Greek philosophy, but perfectly expresses the ancient idea, the Word which emerges from the Silence, the Voice, the Sound, by which the worlds come into being. We must now trace the evolution of spirit-matter, in order that we may understand something of the nature of the materials with which we have to deal on the physical plane, or physical world. For it is in the potentialities wrapped up, involved, in the spirit-matter of the physical world that lies the possibility of evolution. The whole process is an unfolding, self-moved from within and aided by intelligent beings without, who can retard or quicken evolution, but cannot transcend the capacities inherent in the materials. Some idea of these earliest stages of the world's " becoming " is therefore necessary, although any attempt to go into minute details would carry us far beyond the limits of such an elementary treatise as the present. A very cursory sketch must suffice.

Coming far from the depths of the One Existence, from the ONE beyond all thought and all speech, a LOGOS, by imposing on Himself a limit, circumscribing voluntarily the range of His own Being, becomes the manifested God, and tracing the limiting sphere of His activity thus outlines the area of His universe. Within that sphere the universe is born, is evolved, and dies; it lives, it moves, it has its being in Him; its matter is His emanation; its forces and energies are currents of His life; He is immanent in every atom, all-pervading, all-sustaining, all-evolving; He is its source and its end, its cause and its object, its centre and circumference; it is built on Him as its sure foundation, it breathes in Him as its encircling space; He is in everything and everything in Him. Thus have the Sages of the Ancient Wisdom taught us of the beginning of the manifested worlds.

From the same source we learn of the Self-unfolding of the LOGOS into a threefold form; the First LOGOS, the Root of all Being; from Him the Second, manifesting the two aspects of Life and Form, the primal duality, making the two poles of Nature between which the web of the universe is to be woven—Life-Form, Spirit-Matter, Positive-Negative,

Active-Receptive, Father-Mother of the worlds.
Then the Third Logos, the Universal Mind, that in
which all archetypally exists, the source of beings,
the fount of fashioning energies, the treasure-house
in which are stored up all the archetypal forms
which are to be brought forth and elaborated in
lower kinds of matter during the evolution of the
universe. These are the fruits of past universes,
brought over as seeds for the present.

The phenomenal spirit and matter of any universe
are finite in their extent and transitory in their
duration, but the roots of spirit and matter are
eternal. The root of matter [1] has been said by a
profound writer to be visible to the Logos as a veil
thrown over the One Existence, the supreme
Brahman [2]—to use the ancient name.

It is this " veil " which the Logos assumes for the
purpose of manifestation, using it for the self-
imposed limit which makes activity possible. From
this He elaborates the matter of His universe, being
Himself its informing, guiding, and controlling life.[3]

Of what occurs on the two higher planes of the
universe, the seventh and the sixth, we can form

[1] Mūlaprakriti.

[2] Parabrahman.

[3] Hence He is called " The Lord of Māyā " in some Eastern
Scriptures, Māyā, or illusion, being the principle of form; form
is regarded as illusory, from its transitory nature and perpetual
transformations, the life which expresses itself under the veil of
form being the reality.

but the haziest conception. The energy of the
Logos as whirling motion of inconceivable rapidity
" digs holes in space " in this root of matter, and
this vortex of life encased in a film of the root of
matter is the primary atom; these and their aggregations, spread throughout the universe, form all
the subdivisions of spirit-matter of the highest or
seventh plane. The sixth plane is formed by some
of the countless myriads of these primary atoms,
setting up a vortex in the coarsest aggregations of
their own plane, and this primary atom enwalled
with spiral strands of the coarsest combinations of
the seventh plane becomes the finest unit of spirit-
matter, or atom, of the sixth plane. These sixth
plane atoms and their endless combinations form
the subdivisions of the spirit-matter of the sixth
plane. The sixth plane atom, in its turn, sets up a
vortex in the coarsest aggregations of its own plane,
and with these coarsest aggregations as a limiting
wall, becomes the finest unit of spirit-matter, or
atom, of the fifth plane. Again, these fifth plane
atoms and their combinations form the subdivisions
of the spirit-matter of the fifth plane. The process
is repeated to form successively the spirit-matter of
the fourth, the third, the second, and the first planes.
These are the seven great regions of the universe, so
far as their material constituents are concerned.
A clearer idea of them will be gained by analogy

when we come to master the modifications of the spirit-matter of our own physical world.[1]

The word " spirit-matter " is used designedly. It implies the fact that there is no such thing as " dead " matter; all matter is living, the tiniest particles are lives. Science speaks truly in affirming: " No force without matter, no matter without force." They are wedded together in an indissoluble marriage throughout the ages of the life of a universe, and none can wrench them apart. Matter is form, and there is no form which does not express a life; spirit is life, and there is no life that is not limited by a form. Even the Logos, the Supreme Lord, has during manifestation the universe as His form, and so down to the atom.

This involution of the life of the Logos as the ensouling force in every particle, and its successive enwrapping in the spirit-matter of every plane, so that the materials of each plane have within them in a hidden, or latent condition, all the form- and force-possibilities of all the planes above them as well as those of their own—these two facts make

[1] The student may find the conception clearer if he thinks of the fifth plane atoms as Ātmā; those of the fourth plane as Ātmā enveloped in Buddhi-matter; those of the third plane as Ātmā enveloped in Buddhi- and Manas-matter; those of second as Ātmā enveloped in Buddhi-, Manas- and Kāma-matter; those of the lowest as Ātmā enveloped in Buddhi-, Manas-, Kāma- and Sthūla-matter. Only the outermost is active in each, but the inner are there, though latent, ready to come into activity on the upward arc of evolution.

evolution certain and give to the very lowest particle the hidden potentialities which will render it fit—as they become active powers—to enter into the forms of the highest beings. In fact, evolution may be summed up in a phrase: it is latent potentialities becoming active powers.

The second great wave of evolution, the evolution of form, and the third great wave, the evolution of self-consciousness, will be dealt with later on. These three currents of evolution are distinguishable on our earth in connection with humanity: the making of the materials, the building of the house, and the growing of the tenant of the house; or, as said above, the evolution of spirit-matter, the evolution of form, the evolution of self-consciousness. If the reader can grasp and retain this idea, he will find it a helpful clue to guide him through the labyrinth of facts.

We can now turn to the detailed examination of the physical plane, that on which our world exists and to which our bodies belong.

Examining the materials belonging to this plane, we are struck by their immense variety, the innumerable differences of constitution in the objects around us, minerals, vegetables, animals, all differing in their constituents; matter hard and soft, transparent and opaque, brittle and ductile, bitter and sweet, pleasant and nauseous, coloured and colourless. Out of this confusion three subdivisions of matter emerge as a fundamental classification: matter is solid, liquid, and gaseous. Further examination shows that these solids, liquids, and gases are made up by combinations of much simpler bodies, called by chemists " elements ", and that these elements may exist in a solid, liquid or gaseous condition without changing their respective natures. Thus the chemical element, oxygen, is a constituent of wood, and in combination with other elements forms the solid wood fibres; it exists in the sap with another element, yielding a liquid combination as water; and it exists also in it by itself as gas. Under these three conditions it is oxygen. Further, pure oxygen can be reduced from a gas to a liquid, and from a liquid to a solid, remaining pure oxygen all the time; and so with other elements. We thus obtain as three subdivisions, or conditions, of matter on the physical plane, solid, liquid, gas. Searching further, we find a fourth condition, ether, and minuter search reveals that this ether exists in four conditions as well defined as those of solid, liquid, and gas; to take oxygen again as an example: as it may be reduced from the gaseous condition to the liquid and the solid, so it may be raised from the gaseous through four etheric stages, the last of which consists of the ultimate physical atom, the disintegration of the atom taking the matter out of the physical plane altogether, and into the next plane above. In the annexed plate three gases are shown in the gaseous and four etheric states; it will be observed that the structure of the ultimate physical atom is the same for all, and that the variety of the " elements " is due to the variety of ways in which these ultimate physical atoms combine. Thus the seventh subdivision of physical spirit-matter is composed of homogeneous atoms; the sixth is composed of fairly simple heterogeneous combinations of these, each combination behaving as a unit; the fifth is composed of more complex combinations, and the fourth of still more complex ones, but in all cases these combinations act as units; the third subdivision consists of yet more complicated combinations, regarded by the chemist as gaseous atoms or " elements ", and on this subdivision many of the combinations have received special names, oxygen, hydrogen, nitrogen, chlorine, etc., and each newly-discovered combination now receives its name; the second subdivision consists of combinations in the liquid condition, whether regarded as elements such as bromine, or as combinations such as water or alcohol; the first subdivision is composed of all solids, again whether regarded as elements, such as iodine, gold, lead, etc., or as compounds, such as wood, stone, chalk, and so on.

The physical plane may serve the student as a model from which by analogy he may gain an idea

of the subdivisions of the spirit-matter of other
planes. When a Theosophist speaks of a plane, he
means a region throughout which spirit-matter
exists, all whose combinations are derived from a
particular set of atoms; these atoms, in turn, are
units possessing similar organizations, whose life is
the life of the Logos veiled in fewer or more cover-
ings according to the plane, and whose form consists
of the solid, or lowest subdivision of matter of the
plane, immediately above. A plane is thus a division
in Nature, as well as a metaphysical idea.

Thus far we have been studying the results in
our own physical world of the evolution of spirit-
matter in our division of the first or lowest plane of
our system. For countless ages the fashioning of
materials has been going on, the current of the
evolution of spirit-matter, and in the materials of
our globe we see the outcome at the present time.
But when we begin to study the inhabitants of the
physical plane, we come to the evolution of form,
the building of organisms out of these materials.

When the evolution of materials had reached a
sufficiently advanced state, the second great life-
wave from the Logos gave the impulse to the
evolution of form, and He became the organizing
force [1] of His universe, countless hosts of entities,

---

[1] As Ātmā-Buddhi, indivisible in action, and therefore spoken
of as the Monad. All *forms* have Ātmā-Buddhi as controlling life.

entitled Builders,[1] taking part in the building up of forms out of combinations of spirit-matter. The life of the LOGOS abiding in each form is its central, controlling, and directing energy. This building of forms on the higher planes cannot here be conveniently studied in detail; it may suffice to say that all forms exist as Ideas in the Mind of the LOGOS, and that in this second life-wave these were thrown outwards as models to guide the Builders. On the third and second planes the early spirit-matter combinations are designed to give it facility in assuming shapes organized to act as units, and gradually to increase its stability when shaped into an organism. The process went on upon the third and second planes, in what are termed the three Elemental Kingdoms, the combinations of matter formed therein being called generally " elemental essence ", and this essence being moulded into forms by aggregation, the forms enduring for a time and then disintegrating. The outpoured life, or Monad, evolved through these kingdoms and reached in due course the physical plane, where it began to draw together the ethers and hold them in filmy shapes, in which life currents played and into which the denser materials were builded, forming the first minerals. In these are beautifully shown—as may

[1] Some are lofty spiritual Intelligences, but the name covers even the building nature-spirits. The subject is dealt with in Chapter XII.

be seen by reference to any book on crystallography
the numerical and geometrical lines on which forms
are constructed, and from them may be gathered
plentiful evidence that life is working in all minerals,
although much " cribbed, cabined, and confined ".
The fatigue to which metals are subject is another
sign that they are living things, but it is here enough
to say that the occult doctrine so regards them,
knowing the already-mentioned processes by which
life has been involved in them. Great stability of
form having been gained in many of the minerals,
the evolving Monad elaborated greater plasticity of
form in the vegetable kingdom, combining this with
stability of organization. These characteristics found
a yet more balanced expression in the animal world,
and reached their culmination of equilibrium in
man, whose physical body is made up of constituents
of most unstable equilibrium, thus giving great
adaptability, and yet held together by a combining
central force which resists general disintegration
even under the most varied conditions.

Man's physical body has two main divisions: the
dense body, made of constituents from the three
lower levels of the physical plane, solids, liquids,
and gases; and the *etheric double*, violet-grey or
blue-grey in colour, interpenetrating the dense body
and composed of materials drawn from the four
higher levels. The general function of the physical

body is to receive contacts from the physical world, and send the report of them inwards, to serve as materials from which the conscious entity inhabiting the body is to elaborate knowledge. Its etheric portion has also the duty of acting as a medium through which the life-currents poured out from the sun can be adapted to the uses of the denser particles. The sun is the great reservoir of the electrical, magnetic, and vital forces for our system, and it pours out abundantly these streams of life-giving energy. They are taken in by the etheric doubles of all minerals, vegetables, animals, and men, and are by them transmuted into the various life-energies needed by each entity.[1] The etheric doubles draw in, specialize, and distribute them over their physical counterparts. It has been observed that in vigorous health much more of the life-energies are transmuted than the physical body requires for its own support, and that the surplus is rayed out and is taken up and utilized by the weaker. What is technically called the health aura is the part of the etheric double that extends a few inches from the whole surface of the body and shows radiating lines, like the radii of a sphere, going outwards in all directions. These lines droop when vitality is

[1] When thus appropriated the life is called Prāna, and it becomes the life-breath of every creature. Prāna is but a name for the universal life while it is taken in by an entity and is supporting its separated life.

diminished below the point of health, and resume their radiating character with renewed vigour. It is this vital energy, specialized by the etheric double, which is poured out by the mesmerizer for the restoration of the weak and for the cure of disease, although he often mingles with it currents of a more rarefied kind. Hence the depletion of vital energy shown by the exhaustion of the mesmerizer who prolongs his work to excess.

Man's body is fine or coarse in its texture according to the materials drawn from the physical plane for its composition. Each subdivision of matter yields finer or coarser materials; compare the bodies of a butcher and of a refined student; both have solids in them, but solids of such different qualities. Further, we know that a coarse body can be refined, a refined body coarsened. The body is constantly changing; each particle is a life, and the lives come and go. They are drawn to a body consonant with themselves, they are repelled from one discordant with themselves. All things live in rhythmical vibrations, all seek the harmonious and are repelled by dissonance. A pure body repels coarse particles because they vibrate at rates discordant with its own; a coarse body attracts them because their vibrations accord with its own. Hence if the body changes its rates of vibrations, it gradually drives out of it the constituents that cannot fall into the new rhythm, and fills up their places by drawing in from external Nature fresh constituents that are harmonious. Nature provides materials vibrating in all possible ways, and each body exercises its own selective action.

In the earlier building of human bodies this selective action was due to the Monad of form, but now that man is a self-conscious entity he presides over his own building. By his thoughts he strikes the keynote of his music, and sets up the rhythms that are the most powerful factors in the continual changes in his physical and other bodies. As his knowledge increases he learns how to build up his physical body with pure food, and so facilitates the tuning of it. He learns to live by the axiom of purification: " Pure food, a pure mind, and constant memory of God." As the highest creature living on the physical plane, he is the vicegerent of the LoGos thereon, responsible, so far as his powers extend, for its order, peace, and good government; and this duty he cannot discharge without these three requisites.

The physical body, thus composed of elements drawn from all the subdivisions of the physical plane, is fitted to receive and to answer impressions from it of every kind. Its first contacts will be of the simplest and crudest sorts, and as the life within it thrills out in answer to the stimulus from without, throwing its molecules into responsive vibrations, there is developed all over the body the sense of touch, the recognition of something coming into contact with it. As specialized sense-organs are developed to receive special kinds of vibrations, the value of the body increases as a future vehicle for a conscious entity on the physical plane. The more impressions it can answer to, the more useful does it become; for only those to which it can answer can reach the consciousness. Even now there are myriads of vibrations pulsing around us in physical Nature from the knowledge of which we are shut out because of the inability of our physical vehicle to receive and vibrate in accord with them. Un-imagined beauties, exquisite sounds, delicate subtleties, touch the walls of our prison-house and pass on unheeded. Not yet is developed the perfect body that shall thrill to every pulse in Nature as the æolian harp to the zephyr.

The vibrations that the body is able to receive it transmits to physical centres, belonging to its highly complicated nervous system. The etheric vibrations which accompany all the vibrations of the denser physical constituents are similarly received by the etheric double, and transmitted to its corresponding centres. Most of the vibrations in the dense matter are changed into chemical heat, and other forms of physical energy; the etheric give rise to magnetic and electric action, and also pass on the vibrations to the astral body, whence, as we shall see later, they reach the mind. Thus information about the external world reaches the conscious entity enthroned in the body, the Lord of the body, as he is sometimes called. As the channels of information develop and are exercised, the conscious entity grows by the materials supplied to his thought by them, but so little is man yet developed that even the etheric double is not yet sufficiently harmonized to convey regularly to the man impressions received by it independently of its denser comrade, or to impress them on his brain. Occasionally it succeeds in doing so and then we have the lowest form of clairvoyance, the seeing of the etheric doubles of physical objects and of things that have etheric bodies as their lowest vesture.

Man dwells, as we shall see, in various vehicles, physical, astral, and mental, and it is important to know and remember that as we are evolving upwards, the lowest of the vehicles, the dense physical, is that which consciousness first controls and rationalizes. The physical brain is the instrument of consciousness in waking life on the physical plane, and consciousness works in it—in the undeveloped man—more effectively than in any other vehicle. Its potentialities are less than those of the subtler vehicles, but its actualities are greater, and the man knows

himself as " I " in the physical body ere he finds
himself elsewhere. Even if he be more highly developed than the average man, he can only show as
much of himself down here as the physical organism
permits, for consciousness can manifest on the physical
plane only so much as the physical vehicle can carry.

The dense and etheric bodies are not normally
separated during earth-life; they normally function
together, as the lower and higher strings of a single
instrument when a chord is struck, but they also
carry on separate though co-ordinated activities.
Under conditions of weak health or nervous excite-
ment the etheric double may in great part be
abnormally extruded from its dense counterpart;
the latter then becomes very dully conscious, or
entranced, according to the less or greater amount
of the etheric matter extruded. Anæsthetics drive
out the greater part of the etheric double, so that
consciousness cannot affect or be affected by the
dense body, its bridge of communication being
broken. In the abnormally organized persons
called mediums, dislocation of the etheric and
dense bodies easily occurs, and the etheric double,
when extruded, largely supplies the physical basis
for " materialization ".

In sleep, when the consciousness leaves the physical vehicle which it uses during waking life, the
dense and etheric bodies remain together, but in

the physical dream-life they function to some extent independently. Impressions experienced during waking life are reproduced by the automatic action of the body, and both the physical and etheric brains are filled with disjointed fragmentary pictures, the vibrations as it were, jostling each other, and causing the most grotesque combinations. Vibrations from outside also affect both, and combinations often set up during waking life are easily called into activity by currents from the astral world of like nature with themselves. The purity or impurity of waking thoughts will largely govern the pictures arising in dreams, whether spontaneously set up or induced from without.

At what is called death, the etheric double is drawn away from its dense counterpart by the escaping consciousness; the magnetic tie existing between them during earth-life is snapped asunder, and for some hours the consciousness remains enveloped in this etheric garb. In this it sometimes appears to those with whom it is closely bound up, as a cloudy figure, very dully conscious and speechless—the wraith. It may also be seen, after the conscious entity has deserted it, floating over the grave where its dense counterpart is buried, slowly disintegrating as time goes on.

When the time comes for rebirth, the etheric double is built in advance of the dense body, the

latter exactly following it in its ante-natal development. These bodies may be said to trace the
limitations within which the conscious entity will
have to live and work during his earth-life, a subject
that will be more fully explained in Chapter IX,
on Karma.

CHAPTER II

THE ASTRAL PLANE

THE astral plane is the region of the universe next to the physical, if the word "next" may be permitted in such a connection. Life is more active there than on the physical plane, and form is more plastic. The spirit-matter of that plane is more highly vitalized and finer than any grade of spirit-matter in the physical world. For, as we have seen, the ultimate physical atom, the constituent of the rarest physical ether, has for its sphere-wall innumerable aggregations of the coarsest astral matter. The word "next" is, however, inappropriate, as suggesting the idea that the planes of the universe are arranged as concentric circles, one ending where the next begins. Rather are they concentric interpenetrating spheres, not separated from each other by distance but by difference of constitution. As air permeates water, as ether permeates the densest solid, so does astral matter permeates all physical. The astral world is above us, below us, on every side of us, through us; we live and move in it, but it is intangible, invisible, inaudible, imperceptible, because the prison of the physical body shuts us away from it, the physical particles being too gross to be set in vibration by astral matter.

In this chapter we shall study the plane in its general aspects, leaving on one side for separate consideration those special conditions of life on the astral plane surrounding the human entities who are passing through it on their way from earth to heaven.[1]

The spirit-matter of the astral plane exists in seven subdivisions, as we have seen in the spirit-matter of the physical. There, as here, there are numberless combinations, forming the astral solids, liquids, gases, and ethers. But most material forms there have a brightness, a translucency, as compared to forms here, which have caused the epithet astral, or starry to be applied to them—an epithet which is on the whole, misleading, but is too firmly established by use to be changed. As there are no specific names for the subdivisions of astral spirit-matter, we may use the terrestrial designations. The main idea to be grasped is that astral objects are combinations of astral matter, as physical objects are combinations of physical matter, and that the

[1] Devachān, the happy or bright state, is the Theosophical name for heaven. Kāmaloka, the place of desire, is the name given to the conditions of intermediate life on the astral plane.

astral world scenery much resembles that of earth in consequence of its being largely made up of the astral duplicates of physical objects. One peculiarity, however, arrests and confuses the untrained observer; partly because of the translucency of astral objects, and partly because of the nature of astral vision—consciousness being less hampered by the finer astral matter than when encased in the terrestrial—everything is transparent, its back is as visible as its front, its inside as its outside. Some experience is needed, therefore, ere objects are correctly seen, and a person who has developed astral vision, but has not yet had much experience in its use, is apt to receive the most topsy-turvy impressions and to fall into the most astounding blunders.

Another striking and at first bewildering characteristic of the astral world is the swiftness with which forms—especially when unconnected with any terrestrial matrix—change their outlines.

An astral entity will change his whole appearance with the most startling rapidity, for astral matter takes form under every impulse of thought, the life swiftly remoulding the form to give itself new expression. As the great life-wave of the evolution of form passed downwards through the astral plane, and constituted on that plane the Third Elemental Kingdom, the Monad drew round itself combinations of astral matter, giving to these combinations

—entitled elemental essence—a peculiar vitality and the characteristic of responding to, and instantly taking shape under, the impulse of thought vibrations. This elemental essence exists in hundreds of varieties on every subdivision of the astral plane, as though the air became visible here—as indeed it may be seen in quivering waves under great heat— and were in constant undulatory motion with changing colours like mother-of-pearl. This vast atmosphere of elemental essence is ever answering to vibrations caused by thoughts, feelings, and desires, and is thrown into commotion by a rush of any of these like bubbles in boiling water.[1] The duration of the form depends on the strength of the impulse to which it owes its birth; the clearness of its outline depends on the precision of thinking, and the colour depends on the quality—intellectual, devotional, passional—of the thought.

The vague, loose thoughts which are so largely produced by undeveloped minds gather round themselves loose clouds of elemental essence when they arrive in the astral world, and drift about, attracted hither and thither to other clouds of similar nature, clinging round the astral bodies of persons whose magnetism attracts them—either good or evil—and after a while disintegrating, to again form part of the general atmosphere of

[1] C. W. Leadbeater, *Astral Plane*, p. 52.

elemental essence. While they maintain a separate existence they are living entities, with bodies of elemental essence and thoughts as the ensouling lives, and they are then called artificial elementals or thought-forms.

Clear, precise thoughts have each their own definite shapes, with sharp clean outlines, and show an endless variety of designs. They are shaped by vibrations set up by thought, just as on the physical plane we find figures which are shaped by vibrations set up by sound. " Voice-figures " offer a very fair analogy for " thought-figures ", for Nature, with all her infinite variety, is very conservative of principles, and reproduces the same methods of working on plane after plane in her realms. These clearly defined artificial elementals have a longer and much more active life than their cloudy brethren, exercising a far stronger influence on the astral bodies (and through them on the minds) of those to whom they are attracted. They set up in them vibrations similar to their own, and thus thoughts spread from mind to mind without terrestrial expression. More than this: they can be directed by the thinker towards any person he desires to reach, their potency depending on the strength of his will and the intensity of his mental power.

Among average people the artificial elementals created by feeling or desire are more vigorous and more definite than those created by thought. Thus an outburst of anger will cause a very definitely outlined and powerful flash of red, and sustained anger will make a dangerous elemental, red in colour, and pointed, barbed, or otherwise qualified to injure. Love, according to its quality, will set up forms more or less beautiful in colour and design, all shades of crimson to the most exquisite and soft hues of rose, like the palest blushes of the sunset or the dawn, clouds or tenderly strong protective shapes. Many a mother's loving prayers go to hover round her son as angel-forms, turning aside from him evil influences that perchance his own thoughts are attracting.

It is characteristic of these artificial elementals, when they are directed by the will towards any particular person, that they are animated by the one impulse of carrying out the will of their creator. A protective elemental will hover round its object, seeking any opportunity of warding off evil or attracting good—not consciously, but by a blind impulse, as finding there the line of least resistance. So also, an elemental ensouled by a malignant thought will hover round its victim seeking opportunity to injure. But neither the one nor the other can make any impression unless there be in the astral body of the object something akin to themselves, something that can answer accordantly to their vibrations, and thus enable them to attach themselves. If there be nothing in him of matter cognate to their own, then by a law of their nature they rebound from him along the path they pursued in going to him—the magnetic trace they have left —and rush to their creator with a force proportionate to that of their projection. Thus a thought of deadly hatred, failing to strike the object at which it was darted, has been known to slay its sender, while good thoughts sent to the unworthy return as blessings to him that poured them forth.

A very slight understanding of the astral world will thus act as a most powerful stimulus to right thinking, and will render heavy the sense of responsibility in regard to the thoughts, feelings, and desires that we let loose into this astral realm. Ravening beasts of prey, rending and devouring, are too many of the thoughts with which men people the astral plane. But they err from ignorance, they know not what they do. One of the objects of Theosophical teaching, partly lifting up the veil of the unseen world, is to give men a sounder basis for conduct, a more rational appreciation of the causes of which the effects only are seen in the terrestrial world. And few of its doctrines are more important in their ethical bearing than this of the creation and direction of thought-forms, or artificial elementals, for through it man learns that his mind does not concern himself alone, that his thoughts do not affect himself alone, but that he is ever sending out angels and devils into the world of men, for whose creation he is responsible, and for whose influence he is held accountable. Let men, then, know the law, and guide their thoughts thereby.

If, instead of taking artificial elementals separately, we take them in the mass, it is easy to realize the tremendous effect they have in producing national and race feelings, and thus in biassing and prejudicing the mind. We all grow up surrounded by an atmosphere crowded with elementals embodying certain ideas; national prejudices, national ways of looking at all questions, national types of feelings and thoughts, all these play on us from our birth, ay, and before. We see everything through this atmosphere, every thought is more or less refracted by it, and our own astral bodies are vibrating in accord with it. Hence the same idea will look quite different to a Hindu, an Englishman, a Spaniard, and a Russian; some conceptions easy to the one will be almost impossible to the other, customs instinctively attractive to the one are instinctively odious to the other. We are all dominated by our national atmosphere, *i.e.*, by that portion of the astral world immediately surrounding us. The thoughts of others, cast much in the same mould, play upon us and call out from us synchronous vibrations; they intensify the points in which we accord with our surroundings and flatten away the differences, and this ceaseless action upon us through the astral body impresses on us the national hall-mark and traces channels for mental energies into which they readily flow. Sleeping and waking, these currents play upon us, and our very unconsciousness of their action makes it the more effective. As most people are receptive rather than initiative in their nature, they act almost as automatic reproducers of the thoughts which reach them, and thus the national atmosphere is continually intensified.

When a person is beginning to be sensitive to astral influences, he will occasionally find himself suddenly overpowered or assailed by a quite in-explicable and seemingly irrational dread, which swoops down upon him with even paralyzing force. Fight against it as he may, he yet feels it, and perhaps resents it. Probably there are few who have not experienced this fear to some extent, the uneasy dread of an invisible something, the feeling of a presence of "not being alone". This arises partly from a certain hostility which animates the natural elemental world against the human, on account of the various destructive agencies devised by mankind on the physical plane and reacting on the astral, but is also largely due to the presence of so many artificial elementals of an unfriendly kind,

6

bred by human minds. Thoughts of hatred, jealousy, revenge, bitterness, suspicion, discontent, go out by millions crowding the astral plane with artificial elementals whose whole life is made of these feelings. How much also is there of vague distrust and suspicion poured out by the ignorant against all whose ways and appearance are alien and unfamiliar! The blind distrust of all foreigners, the surly contempt, extending in many districts even towards inhabitants of another county—these things also contribute evil influences to the astral world. There being so much of these things among us, we create a blindly hostile army on the astral plane, and this is answered in our own astral bodies by a feeling of dread, set up by the antagonistic vibrations that are sensed, but not understood.

Outside the class of artificial elementals, the astral world is thickly populated, even excluding, as we do for the present, all the human entities who have lost their physical bodies by death. There are great hosts of natural elementals, or nature-spirits, divided into five main classes—the elementals of the ether, the fire, the air, the water, and the earth; the last four groups have been termed, in mediæval occultism, the Salamanders, Sylphs, Undines, and Gnomes (needless to say there are two other classes, completing the seven, not concerning us here, as they are still unmanifested). These are the true elementals, or creatures of the elements, earth, water, air, fire, and ether, and they are severally concerned in the carrying on of the activities connected with their own element; they are the channels through which work the divine energies in these several fields, the living expressions of the law in each. At the head of each division is a great Being, the captain of a mighty host,[1] the directing and guiding intelligence of the whole department of Nature which is administered and energized by the class of elementals under his control. Thus Agni, the fire-God, is a great spiritual entity concerned with the manifestation of fire on all the planes of the universe, and carries on his administration through the hosts of fire-elementals. By understanding the nature of these, or knowing the methods of their control, the so-called miracles or magical feats are worked, which from time to time are recorded in the public press whether they are avowedly the results of magical arts, or are done by the aid of " spirits "— as in the case of the late Mr. Home, who could unconcernedly pick a red-hot coal out of a blazing fire with his fingers and hold it in his hand unhurt. Levitation (the suspension of a heavy body in the

---

[1] Called a Deva, or God, by the Hindus. The student may like to have the Sanskrit names of the five Gods of the manifested elements: Indra, lord of the Ākāsha, or ether of space; Agni, lord of fire; Pavana, lord of air; Varuna, lord of water; Kshiti, lord of earth.

air without visible support) and walking on the water have been done by the aid respectively of the elementals of the air and the water, although another method is more often employed.

As the elements enter into the human body, one or another predominating according to the nature of the person, each human being has relations with these elementals, the most friendly to him being those whose element is preponderant in him. The effects of this fact are often noted, and are popularly ascribed to " luck ". A person has " a lucky hand " in making plants grow, in lighting fires, in finding underground water, etc., etc. Nature is ever jostling us with her occult forces, but we are slow to take her hints. Tradition sometimes hides a truth in a proverb or a fable, but we have grown beyond all such " superstitions ".

We find also on the astral plane, nature-spirits— less accurately termed elementals—who are concerned with the building of forms in the mineral, vegetable, animal, and human kingdoms. There are nature-spirits who build up minerals, who guide the vital energies in plants, and who, molecule by molecule, form the bodies of the animal kingdom; they are concerned with the making of the astral bodies of minerals, plants, and animals, as well as with that of the physical. These are the fairies and elves of legends, the " little people " who play so large a part in the folk-lore of every nation, the charming irresponsible children of Nature, whom science has coldly relegated to the nursery, but who will be replaced in their own grade of natural order by the wiser scientists of a later day. Only poets and occultists believe in them just now, poets by the intuition of their genius, occultists by the vision of their trained inner sense. The multitude laugh at both, most of all at the occultists; but it matters not—wisdom shall be justified of her children.

The play of the life-currents in the etheric doubles of the forms in the mineral, vegetable, and animal kingdoms, awoke out of latency the astral matter involved in the structure of their atomic and molecular constituents. It began to thrill in a very limited way in the minerals, and the Monad of form, exercising his organizing power, drew in materials from the astral world, and these were built by the nature-spirits into a loosely constituted mass, the mineral astral body. In the vegetable world the astral bodies are a little more organized, and their special characteristic of " feeling " begins to appear. Dull and diffused sensations of well-being and discomfort are observable in most plants as the results of the increasing activity of the astral body. They dimly enjoy the air, the rain, and the sunshine, and gropingly seek them, while they shrink from noxious conditions. Some seek the light and some seek the darkness; they answer to stimuli, and adapt themselves to external conditions, some showing plainly a sense of touch. In the animal kingdom the astral body is more developed, reaching in the higher members of that kingdom a sufficiently definite organization to cohere for some time after the death of the physical body, and to lead an independent existence on the astral plane.

The nature-spirits concerned with the building of the animal and human astral bodies have been given the special name of desire-elementals,[1] because they are strongly animated by desires of all kinds, and constantly build themselves into the astral bodies of animals and men. They also use the varieties of elemental essence similar to that of which their own bodies are composed to construct the astral bodies of animals, those bodies thus acquiring, as interwoven parts, the centres of sensation and of the various passional activities. These centres are stimulated into functioning by impulses received by the dense physical organs, and transmitted by the etheric physical organs to the astral body. Not until the astral centre is reached does the animal feel pleasure or pain. A stone may be struck, but it will feel no pain; it has dense and etheric physical molecules, but its astral body is unorganized; the

[1] Kāmadevas, they are called, " desire-gods ".

animal feels pain from a blow because he possesses the astral centres of sensation, and the desire-elementals have woven into him their own nature.

As a new consideration enters into the work of these elementals with the human astral body, we will finish our survey of the inhabitants of the astral plane ere studying this more complicated astral form.

The desire-bodies,[1] or astral bodies, of animals are found, as has just been stated, to lead an independent though fleeting existence on the astral plane after death has destroyed their physical counterparts. In " civilized " countries these animal astral bodies add much to the general feeling of hostility which was spoken of above, for the organized butchery of animals in slaughter-houses and by sport sends millions upon millions of these annually into the astral world, full of horror, terror, and shrinking from men. The comparatively few creatures that are allowed to die in peace and quietness are lost in the vast hordes of the murdered, and from the currents set up by these there rain down influences from the astral world on the human and animal races which drive them yet farther apart and engender " instinctive " distrust and fear on the one side and lust of inflicting cruelty on the other.

[1] Kāmarūpa is the technical name for the astral body, from kāma, desire, and rūpa, form.

These feelings have been much intensified of late years by the coldly devised methods of the scientific torture called vivisection, the unmentionable barbarities of which have introduced new horrors into the astral world by their reaction on the culprits,[1] as well as having increased the gulf between man and his " poor relations ".

Apart from what we may call the normal population of the astral world, there are passing travellers in it, led there by their work, whom we cannot leave entirely without mention. Some of these come from our own terrestrial world, while others are visitors from loftier regions.

Of the former, many are Initiates of various grades, some belonging to the Great White Lodge —the Himālayan or Tibetan Brotherhood, as it is often called [2]—while others are members of different occult lodges throughout the world, ranging from white through all shades of grey to black.[3] All these are men living in physical bodies, who have

[1] See Chapter III, on Kāmaloka.

[2] It is to some members of this Lodge that the Theosophical Society owes its inception.

[3] Occultists who are unselfish and wholly devoted to the carrying out of the Divine Will, or who are aiming to attain these virtues, are called " white ". Those who are selfish and are working against the Divine purpose in the universe are called " black ". Expanding selflessness, love, and devotion are the marks of the one class; contracting selfishness, hatred, and harsh arrogance are the signs of the other. Between these are the classes whose motives are mixed and who have not yet realized that they must evolve towards the One Self or towards the separated selves;

learned to leave the physical encasement at will, and to function in full consciousness in the astral body. They are of all grades of knowledge and virtue, beneficent and maleficent, strong and weak, gentle and ferocious. There are also many younger aspirants, still uninitiated, who are learning to use the astral vehicle, and who are employed in works of benevolence or malevolence according to the path they are seeking to tread.

After these, we have psychics of varying degrees of development, some fairly alert, others dreamy and confused, wandering about while their physical bodies are asleep or entranced. Unconscious of their external surroundings, wrapped in their own thoughts, drawn as it were within their astral shell, are millions of drifting astral bodies inhabited by conscious entities, whose physical frames are sunk in sleep. As we shall see presently, the consciousness in its astral vehicle escapes when the body sinks into sleep, and passes on to the astral plane; but it is not conscious of its surroundings until the astral body is sufficiently developed to function independently of the physical.

Occasionally is seen on this plane a disciple [1] who has passed through death and is awaiting an

these I have called grey. Their members gradually drift into, or deliberately join, one of the two great groups with clearly marked aims.

[1] A chelā, the accepted pupil of an Adept.

almost immediate reincarnation under the direction of his Master. He is, of course, in the enjoyment of full consciousness, and is working like other disciples who have merely slipped off their bodies in sleep. At a certain stage [1] a disciple is allowed to reincarnate very quickly after death, and under these circumstances he has to await on the astral plane a suitable opportunity for rebirth.

Passing through the astral plane also are the human beings who are on their way to reincarnation; they will again be mentioned later on,[2] and they concern themselves in no way with the general life of the astral world. The desire-elementals, however, who have affinity with them from their past passional and sensational activities, gather round them, assisting in the building of the new astral body for the coming earth-life.

We must now turn to the consideration of the human astral body during the period of existence in this world, and study its nature and constitution as well as its relations with the astral realm. We will take the astral body of (a) an undeveloped man, (b) an average man, and (c) a spiritually developed man.

(a) An undeveloped man's astral body is a cloudy, loosely organized, vaguely outlined mass of astral

[1] See Chapter XI, on " Man's Ascent ".
[2] See Chapter VII, on " Reincarnation ".

spirit-matter, containing materials—both astral matter and elemental essence—drawn from all the subdivisions of the astral plane, but with a great predominance of substances from the lower, so that it is dense and coarse in texture, fit to respond to all the stimuli connected with the passions and appetites. The colours caused by the rates of vibration are dull, muddy, and dusky—browns, dull reds, dirty greens, are the predominant hues. There is no play of light or quickly changing flashing of colours through this astral body, but the various passions show themselves as heavy surges, or, when violent, as flashes; thus sexual passion will send a wave of muddy crimson, rage a flash of lurid red.

The astral body is larger than the physical, extending round it in all directions ten or twelve inches in such a case as we are considering. The centres of the organs of sense are definitely marked, and are active when worked on from without; but in quiescence the life-streams are sluggish, and the astral body stimulated neither from the physical nor mental worlds, is drowsy and indifferent.[1] It is a constant characteristic of the undeveloped state that activity is prompted from without rather than from the inner consciousness. A stone to be moved must be pushed; a plant moves under the

---

[1] The student will recognize here the predominance of the tāmasic guna, the quality of darkness or inertness in nature.

attractions of light and moisture; an animal becomes active when stirred by hunger; a poorly
developed man needs to be prompted in similar
ways. Not till the mind is partly grown does it
begin to initiate action. The centres of higher
activities,[1] related to the independent functioning
of the astral senses, are scarcely visible. A man at
this stage requires for his evolution violent sensations
of every kind, to arouse the nature and stimulate it
into activity. Heavy blows from the outer world,
both of pleasure and pain, are wanted to awaken
and spur to action. The more numerous and violent
the sensations, the more he can be made to feel, the
better for his growth. At this stage quality matters
little, quantity and vigour are the main requisites.
The beginnings of this man's morality will be in his
passions; a slight impulse of unselfishness in his relations to wife or child or friend, will be the first
step upwards, by causing vibrations in the finer
matter of his astral body and attracting into it more
elemental essence of an appropriate kind. The
astral body is constantly changing its materials
under this play of the passions, appetites, desires,
and emotions. All good ones strengthen the finer
parts of the body, shake out some of the coarser
constituents, draw into it the subtler materials, and

[1] The seven chakras, or wheels, so named from the whirling
appearance they present, like wheels of living fire when in activity.

attract round it elements of a beneficent kind who aid in the renovating process. All evil ones have diametrically opposite effects, strengthening the coarser, expelling the finer, drawing in more of the former, and attracting elementals who help in the deteriorating process. The man's moral and intellectual powers are so embryonic in the case we are considering that most of the building and changing of his astral body may be said to be done for him rather than by him. It depends more on his external circumstances than on his own will, for, as just said, it is characteristic of a low stage of development that a man is moved from without and through the body much more than from within and by the mind. It is a sign of considerable advance when a man begins to be moved by the will, by his own energy self-determined, instead of being moved by desire, *i.e.*, by a response to an external attraction or repulsion.

In sleep, the astral body, enveloping the consciousness, slips out of the physical vehicle, leaving the dense and etheric bodies to slumber. At this stage, however, the consciousness is not awake in the astral body, lacking the strong contacts that spur it while in the physical frame, and the only things that affect the astral body may be elementals of the coarser kinds, that may set up therein vibrations which are reflected in the etheric and dense brains, and induce dreams of animal pleasures. The astral body floats just over the physical, held by its strong attraction, and cannot go far away from it.

(b) In the average moral and intellectual man the astral body shows an immense advance on that just described. It is larger in size, its materials are more balanced in quality, the presence of the rarer kinds giving a certain luminous quality to the whole, while the expression of the higher emotions sends playing through it beautiful ripples of colour. Its outline is clear and definite, instead of vague and shifting, as in the former case, and it assumes the likeness of its owner. It is obviously becoming a vehicle for the inner man, with definite organization and stability, a body fit and ready to function, and able to maintain itself, apart from the physical. While retaining great plasticity, it yet has a normal form, to which it continually recurs when any pressure is removed that may have caused it to change its outline. Its activity is constant, and hence it is in perpetual vibration, showing endless varieties of changing hues; also the " wheels " are clearly visible though not yet functioning.[1] It responds quickly to all the contacts coming to it through the physical body, and is stirred by the influences rained on it from the conscious entity within, memory and

[1] Here the student will note the predominance of the rājasic guna, the quality of activity in nature.

imagination stimulating it to action, and causing it to become the prompter of the body to activity instead of only being moved by it. Its purification proceeds along the same lines as in the former case—the expulsion of lower constituents by setting up vibrations antagonistic to them and the drawing in of finer materials in their place. But now the increased moral and intellectual development of the man puts the building almost entirely under his own control, for he is no longer driven hither and thither by stimuli from external nature, but reasons, judges, and resists or yields as he thinks well. By the exercise of well-directed thought he can rapidly affect the astral body, and hence its improvement can proceed apace. Nor is it necessary that he should understand the *modus operandi* in order to bring about the effect, any more than that a man should understand the laws of light in order to see.

In sleep, this well-developed astral body slips, as usual, from its physical encasement, but is by no means held captive by it, as in the former case. It roams about in the astral world, drifted hither and thither by the astral currents, while the consciousness within it, not yet able to direct its movements, is awake, engaged in the enjoyment of its own mental images and mental activities, and able also to receive impressions through its astral covering, and to change them into mental pictures.

In this way a man may gain knowledge when out of the body, and may subsequently impress it on the brain as a vivid dream or vision, or without this link of memory it may filter through into the brain-consciousness.

(c) The astral body of a spiritually developed man is composed of the finest particles of each sub-division of astral matter, the higher kinds largely predominating in amount. It is therefore a beautiful object in luminosity and colour, hues not known on earth showing themselves under the impulses thrown into it by the purified mind. The wheels of fire are now seen to deserve their names, and their whirling motion denotes the activity of the higher senses. Such a body is, in the full sense of the words, a vehicle of consciousness, for, in the course of evolution it has been vivified in every organ and brought under the complete control of its owner. When in it he leaves the physical body there is no break of consciousness; he merely shakes off his heavier vesture, and finds himself unencumbered by its weight. He can move anywhere within the astral sphere with immense rapidity, and is no longer bound by the narrow terrestrial conditions. His body answers to his will, reflects and obeys his thought. His opportunities for serving humanity are thus enormously increased, and his powers are directed by his virtue and his beneficence. The absence of gross particles in his astral body renders it incapable of responding to the promptings of lower objects of desire, and they turn away from him as beyond their attraction. The whole body vibrates only in answer to the higher emotions, his love has grown into devotion, his energy is curbed by patience. Gentle, calm, serene, full of power, but with no trace of restlessness, such a man " all the Siddhis stand ready to serve ".[1]

The astral body forms the bridge over the gulf which separates consciousness from the physical brain. Impacts received by the sense-organs and transmitted, as we have seen, to the dense and etheric centres, pass thence to the corresponding astral centres; here they are worked on by the elemental essence and are transmuted into feelings, and are then presented to the inner man as objects of consciousness, the astral vibrations awakening corresponding vibrations in the materials of the mental body.[2] By these successive gradations in fineness of spirit-matter the heavy impacts of terrestrial objects can be transmitted to the conscious entity; and, in turn, the vibrations set up by his thoughts can pass along the same bridge to the physical brain and there induce physical vibrations

[1] Here the sāttvic guna, the quality of bliss and purity in nature, is predominant. Siddhis are superphysical powers.

[2] See Chapter IV, " The Mental Plane ".

corresponding to the mental. This is the regular normal way in which consciousness receives impressions from without, and in turn sends impressions outwards. By this constant passage of vibrations to and fro the astral body is chiefly developed; this current plays upon it from within and from without, evolves its organization and subserves its general growth. By this it becomes larger, finer in texture, more definitely outlined, and more organized interiorily. Trained thus to respond to consciousness, it gradually becomes fit to function as its separate vehicle, and to transmit to it clearly the vibrations received directly from the astral world. Most readers will have had some little experience of impressions coming into consciousness from without, that do not arise from any physical impact, and that are very quickly verified by some external occurrence. These are frequently impressions that reach the astral body directly, and are transmitted by it to the consciousness, and such impressions are often of the nature of previsions which very quickly prove themselves to be true. When the man is far progressed, though the stage varies much according to other circumstances, links are set up between the physical and the astral, the astral and the mental, so that consciousness works unbrokenly from one state to the other, memory having in it none of the lapses which in the ordinary man interpose a period of unconsciousness in passing from one plane to another. The man can then also freely exercise the astral senses while the consciousness is working in the physical body, so that these enlarged avenues of knowledge become an appanage of his waking consciousness. Objects which were before matters of faith become matters of knowledge, and he can personally verify the accuracy of much of the Theosophical teaching as to the lower regions of the invisible world.

* * * *

When man is analysed into "principles", *i.e.*, into modes of manifesting life, his four lower principles, termed the "Lower Quaternary", are said to function on the astral and physical planes. The fourth principle is Kāma, desire, and it is the life manifesting in the astral body and conditioned by it; it is characterized by the attribute of feeling, whether in the rudimentary form of sensation, or in the complex form of emotion, or in any of the grades that lie between. This is summed up as desire, that which is attracted or repelled by objects, according as they give pleasure or pain to the personal self. The third principle is Prāna, the life specialized for the support of the physical organism. The second principle is the etheric double, and the first is the dense body. These three function on the physical plane. In H. P. Blavatsky's later classifications she removed both Prāna and the dense physical body from the rank of principles, Prāna as being universal life, and the dense physical body as being the mere counterpart of the etheric, and made of constantly changing materials built into the etheric matrix. Taking this view, we have the grand philosophic conception of the One Life, the One Self, manifesting as man, and presenting varying and transitory differences according to the conditions imposed on it by the bodies which it vivifies; itself remaining the same in the centre, but showing different aspects when looked at from outside, according to the kinds of matter in one body or another. In the physical body it is Prāna, energizing, controlling, co-ordinating. In the astral body it is Kāma, feeling, enjoying, suffering. We shall find it in yet other aspects, as we pass to higher planes, but the fundamental idea is the same throughout, and it is another of those root-ideas of Theosophy, which, firmly grasped, serve as guiding clues in this most tangled world.

CHAPTER III

KĀMALOKA

KĀMALOKA, literally the place or habitat of desire, is, as has already been intimated, a part of the astral plane, not divided from it as a distinct locality, but separated off by the conditions of consciousness of the entities belonging to it.[1] These are human beings who have lost their physical bodies by the stroke of death, and have to undergo certain purifying changes before they can pass on to the happy and peaceful life which belongs to the man proper, to the human soul.[2]

This region represents and includes the conditions described as existing in the various hells, purgatories, and intermediate states, one or other of which

[1] The Hindus call this state Pretaloka, the habitat of Pretas. A Preta is the human being who has lost his physical body, but is still encumbered with the vesture of his animal nature. He cannot carry this on with him, and until it is disintegrated he is kept imprisoned by it.

[2] The soul is the human intellect, the link between the Divine Spirit in man and his lower personality. It is the Ego, the individual, the " I ", which develops by evolution. In Theosophical parlance, it is Manas, the Thinker. The mind is the energy of this, working within the limitations of the physical brain, or the astral and mental bodies.

is alleged by all the great religions to be the temporary dwelling-place of man after he leaves the
body and before he reaches "heaven". It does
not include any place of eternal torture, the endless
hell still believed in by some narrow religionists
being only a nightmare dream of ignorance, hate,
and fear. But it does include conditions of suffering, temporary and purificatory in their nature, the
working out of causes set going in his earth-life by
the man who experiences them. These are as
natural and inevitable as any effects caused in this
world by wrong-doing, for we live in a world of
law and every seed must grow up after its own kind.
Death makes no sort of difference in a man's moral
and mental nature, and the change of state caused
by passing from one world to another takes away his
physical body, but leaves the man as he was.

The kāmalokic condition is found on each subdivision of the astral plane, so that we may speak
of it as having seven regions, calling them the first,
second, third, up to the seventh, beginning from
the lowest and counting upwards.[1] We have
already seen that materials from each subdivision
of the astral plane enter into the composition of the
astral body, and it is a peculiar re-arrangement of

[1] Often these regions are reckoned the other way, taking the
first as the highest and the seventh as the lowest. It does not
matter from which end we count, and I am reckoning upwards
to keep them in accord with the planes and the principles.

these materials, to be explained in a moment, which separates the people dwelling in one region from those dwelling in another, although those in the same region are able to intercommunicate. The regions, being each a subdivision of the astral plane, differ in density, and the density of the external form of the kāmalokic entity determines the region to which he is limited; these differences of matter are the barriers that prevent passage from one region to another; the people dwelling in one can no more come into touch with people dwelling in another than a deep-sea fish can hold a conversation with an eagle—the medium necessary to the life of the one would be destructive to the life of the other.

When the physical body is struck down by death, the etheric body, carrying Prāna with it and accompanied by the remaining principles—that is, the whole man except the dense body—withdraws from the " tabernacle of flesh ", as the outer body is appropriately called. All the outgoing life-energies draw themselves inwards, and are " gathered up by Prāna ", their departure being manifested by the dullness that creeps over the physical organs of the senses. They are there, uninjured, physically complete, ready to act as they have always been; but the " Inner Ruler " is going, he who through them saw, heard, felt, smelt, tasted, and by themselves they are mere aggregations of matter, living indeed but without power of perceptive action. Slowly the lord of the body draws himself away, enwrapped in the violet-grey etheric body, and absorbed in the contemplation of the panorama of his past life, which in the death-hour unrolls before him, complete in every detail.   In that life-picture are all the events of his life, small and great; he sees his ambitions with their success or frustration, his efforts, his triumphs, his failures, his loves, his hatreds; the predominant tendency of the whole comes clearly out, the ruling thought of the life asserts itself, and stamps itself deeply into the soul, marking the region in which the chief part of his post-mortem existence will be spent. Solemn the moment when the man stands face to face with his life, and from the lips of his past hears the presage of his future. For a brief space he sees himself as he is, recognizes the purpose of his life, knows that the Law is strong and just and good. Then the magnetic tie breaks between the dense and etheric bodies, the comrades of a life-time are disjoined, and—save in exceptional cases—the man sinks into peaceful unconsciousness.

Quietness and devotion should mark the conduct of all who are gathered round a dying body, in order that a solemn silence may leave uninterrupted this review of the past by the departing man. Clamorous weeping, loud lamentations, can but jar and disturb the concentrated attention of the soul, and to break with the grief of a personal loss into the stillness which aids and soothes him is at once selfish and impertinent. Religion has wisely commanded prayers for the dying, for these preserve calm and stimulate unselfish aspirations directed to his helping, and these, like all loving thoughts, protect and shield.

Some hours after death—generally not more than thirty-six, it is said—the man draws himself out of the etheric body, leaving it in turn as a senseless corpse, and the latter, remaining near its dense counterpart, shares its fate. If the dense body be buried, the etheric double floats over the grave, slowly disintegrating, and the unpleasant feelings many experience in a churchyard are largely due to the presence of these decaying etheric corpses. If the body be burnt, the etheric double breaks up very quickly, having lost its nidus, its physical centre of attraction, and this is one among many reasons why cremation is preferable to burial as a way of disposing of corpses.

The withdrawal of the man from the etheric double is accompanied by the withdrawal from it of Prāna, which thereupon returns to the great reservoir of life universal, while the man, ready now to pass into Kāmaloka, undergoes a re-arrangement of his astral body, fitting it for submission to the purificatory changes which are necessary for the freeing of

the man himself.[1] During earth-life the various
kinds of astral matter intermingle in the formation
of the body, as do the solids, liquids, gases, and
ethers in the physical. The change in the arrangement of the astral body after death consists in the
separation of these materials, according to their
respective densities, into a series of concentric shells
—the finest within, the densest without—each shell
being made of the materials drawn from one subdivision only of the astral plane; the astral body
thus becomes a set of seven superimposed layers, or
a seven-shelled encasement of astral matter, in which
the man may not inaptly be said to be imprisoned,
as only the breaking of these can set him free. Now
will be seen the immense importance of the purification of the astral body during earth-life; the man
is retained in each subdivision of Kāmaloka so long
as the shell of matter pertaining to that subdivision
is not sufficiently disintegrated to allow of his escape
into the next. Moreover, the extent to which his
consciousness has worked in each kind of matter
determines whether he will be awake and conscious
in any given region, or will pass through it in
unconsciousness, " wrapped in rosy dreams ", and

---

[1] These changes result in the formation of what is called by
Hindus the Yātanā or suffering body, or in the case of very wicked
men, in whose astral bodies there is a preponderance of the coarsest
matter, the Dhruvam, or strong body.

merely detained during the time necessary for the process of mechanical disintegration.

A spiritually advanced man, who has so purified his astral body that its constituents are drawn only from the finest grade of each division of astral matter, merely passes through Kāmaloka without delay, the astral body disintegrating with extreme swiftness, and he goes on to whatever may be his bourne, according to the point he has reached in evolution. A less developed man, but one whose life has been pure and temperate and who has sat loosely on the things of earth, will wing a less rapid flight through Kāmaloka, but will dream peacefully, unconscious of his surroundings, as his mental body disentangles itself from the astral shells, one after the other, to awaken only when he reaches the heavenly places. Others, less developed still, will awaken after passing out of the lower regions, becoming conscious in the division which is connected with the active working of the consciousness during the earth-life, for this will be aroused on receiving familiar impacts, although these be received now directly through the astral body, without the help of the physical. Those who have lived in the animal passions will awake in their appropriate region, each man literally going " to his own place ".

The case of men struck suddenly out of physical life by accident, suicide, murder, or sudden death in

any form, differs from those of persons who pass
away by the failure of the life-energies through
disease or old age. If they are pure and spiritually-
minded they are specially guarded, and sleep out
happily the term of their natural life. But in other
cases they remain conscious—often entangled in the
final scene of earth-life for a time, and unaware that
they have lost the physical body—held in whatever
region they are related to by the outermost layer of
the astral body; their normal kāmalokic life does
not begin until the natural web of earth-life is
out-spun, and they are vividly conscious of both
their astral and physical surroundings. One man
who had committed an assassination and had
been executed for his crime was said, by one of
H. P. Blavatsky's Teachers, to be living through
the scenes of the murder and the subsequent events
over and over again in Kāmaloka, ever repeating
his diabolical act and going through the terrors of
his arrest and execution. A suicide will repeat
automatically the feelings of despair and fear which
preceded his self-murder, and go through the act
and the death-struggle, time after time, with ghastly
persistence. A woman, who perished in the flames
in a wild condition of terror and with frantic efforts
to escape, created such a whirl of passions that, five
days afterwards, she was still struggling desperately,
fancying herself still in the fire and wildly repulsing

all efforts to soothe her; while another woman who, with her baby on her breast, went down beneath the whirl of waters in a raging storm, with her heart calm and full of love, slept peacefully on the other side of death, dreaming of husband and children in happy life-like visions. In more ordinary cases, death by accident is still a disadvantage, brought on a person by some serious fault,[1] for the possession of full consciousness in the lower kāmalokic regions, which are closely related to the earth, is attended by many inconveniences and perils. The man is full of all the plans and interests that made up his life, and is conscious of the presence of the people and things connected with them; he is almost irresistibly impelled by his longings to try and influence the affairs to which his passions and feelings still cling, and is bound to the earth while he has lost all his accustomed organs of activity; his only hope of peace lies in resolutely turning away from earth and fixing his mind on higher things, but comparatively few are strong enough to make this effort, even with the help always offered them by workers on the astral plane, whose sphere of duty lies in helping and guiding those who have left this world.[2] Too often such sufferers, impatient

---

[1] Not necessarily a fault committed in the present life. The law of cause and effect will be explained in Chapter IX, on " Karma ".

[2] These workers are disciples of some of the great Teachers who guide and help humanity, and they are employed in this special duty of succouring souls in need of such assistance.

of their helpless inactivity, seek the assistance of sensitives, with whom they can communicate and so mix themselves up once more in terrestrial affairs; they sometimes seek even to obsess convenient mediums and thus to utilize the bodies of others for their own purposes, so incurring many responsibilities in the future. Not without occult reason have English churchmen been taught to pray: " From battle, murder, *and from sudden death*, Good Lord, deliver us."

We may now consider the divisions of Kāmaloka one by one, and so gain some idea of the conditions which the man has made for himself in the intermediate state by the desires which he has cultivated during physical life; it being kept in mind that the amount of vitality in any given " shell "—and therefore his imprisonment in that shell—depends on the amount of energy thrown during earth-life into the kind of matter of which that shell consists. If the lowest passions have been active, the coarsest matter will be strongly vitalized and its amount will also be relatively large. This principle rules through all kāmalokic regions, so that a man during earth-life can judge very fairly as to the future for himself that he is preparing immediately on the other side of death.

The first, or lowest, division is the one that contains the conditions described in so many Hindu and Buddhist Scriptures under the name of " hells " of various kinds. It must be understood that a man, in passing into one of these states, is not getting rid of the passions and vile desires that have led him thither; these remain, as part of his character, lying latent in the mind in a germinal state, to be thrown outwards again to form his passional nature when he is returning to birth in the physical world.[1] His presence in the lowest region of Kāmaloka is due to the existence in his kāmic body of matter belonging to that region, and he is held prisoner there until the greater part of that matter has dropped away, until the shell composed of it is sufficiently disintegrated to allow the man to come into contact with the region next above.

The atmosphere of this place is gloomy, heavy, dreary, depressing to an inconceivable extent. It seems to reek with all the influences most inimical to good, as in truth it does, being caused by the persons whose evil passions have led them to this dreary place. All the desires and feelings at which we shudder find here the materials for their expression; it is, in fact, the lowest slum, with all the horrors veiled from physical sight parading in their naked hideousness. Its repulsiveness is much increased by the fact that in the astral world character expresses itself in form, and the man who is full of

[1] See Chapter VII, on " Reincarnation ".

evil passions *looks* the whole of them; bestial appetites
shape the astral body into bestial forms, and repul-
sively human animal shapes are the appropriate
clothing of brutalized human souls. No man can
be a hypocrite in the astral world, and cloak foul
thoughts with a veil of virtuous seeming; whatever
a man *is* that he appears to be in outward form and
semblance, radiant in beauty if his mind be noble,
repulsive in hideousness if his nature be foul. It
will readily be understood, then, how such Teachers
as the Buddha—to whose unerring vision all worlds
lay open—should describe what was seen in these
hells in vivid language of terrible imagery, that
seems incredible to modern readers only because
people forget that, once escaped from the heavy
and unplastic matter of the physical world, all
souls appear in their proper likenesses and look just
what they are. Even in this world a degraded and
besotted ruffian moulds his face into most repellent
aspect; what then can be expected when the plastic
astral matter takes shape with every impulse of his
criminal desires, but that such a man should wear a
horrifying form, taking on changing elements of
hideousness?

For it must be remembered that the population—
if that word may be allowed—of this lowest region
consists of the very scum of humanity, murderers,
ruffians, violent criminals of all types, drunkards,

profligates, the vilest of mankind. None is here, with consciousness awake to its surroundings, save those guilty of brutal crimes, or of deliberate persistent cruelty, or possessed by some vile appetite. The only persons who may be of a better general type, and yet for a while be held here, are suicides, men who have sought by self-murder to escape from the earthly penalties of crimes they had committed, and who have but worsened their position by the exchange. Not all suicides, be it understood, for self-murder is committed from many motives, but only such as are led up to by crime and are then committed in order to avoid the consequences.

Save for the gloomy surroundings and the loathsomeness of a man's associates, every man here is the immediate creator of his own miseries. Unchanged, except for the loss of the bodily veil, men here show out their passions in all their native hideousness, their naked brutality, full of fierce unsatiated appetites, seething with revenge, hatred, longings after physical indulgences which the loss of physical organs incapacitates them from enjoying, they roam, raging and ravening, through this gloomy region, crowding round all foul resorts on earth, round brothels and gin-palaces, stimulating their occupants to deeds of shame and violence, seeking opportunities to obsess them, and so to drive them into worse excesses. The sickening atmosphere felt

round such places comes largely from these earth-
bound astral entities, reeking with foul passions, and
unclean desires. Mediums—unless of very pure
and noble character—are special objects of attack,
and too often the weaker ones, weakened still further
by the passive yielding of their bodies for the temporary habitation of other excarnate souls, are
obsessed by these creatures, and are driven into
intemperance or madness. Executed murderers,
furious with terror and passionate revengeful hatred,
acting over again, as we have said, their crime and
re-creating mentally its terrible results, surround
themselves with an atmosphere of savage thought-
forms, and, attracted to anyone harbouring revengeful and violent designs, they egg him on into the
actual commission of the deed over which he broods.
Sometimes a man may be seen constantly followed
by his murdered victim, never able to escape from
his haunting presence, which hunts him with a dull
persistency, try he never so eagerly to escape. The
murdered person, unless himself of a very base type,
is wrapped in unconsciousness, and this very unconsciousness seems to add a new horror to its
mechanical pursuit.

Here also is the hell of the vivisector, for cruelty
draws into the astral body the coarsest materials
and the most repulsive combinations of the astral
matter, and he lives amid the crowding forms of

his mutilated victims—moaning, quivering, howling (they are vivified, not by the animal souls but by elemental life), pulsing with hatred to the tormentor —rehearsing his worst experiments with automatic regularity, conscious of all the horror, and yet imperiously impelled to the self-torment by the habit set up during earth-life.

It is well once again to remember, ere quitting this dreary region, that we have here no arbitrary punishments inflicted from outside, but only the inevitable working out of the causes set going by each person. During physical life they yielded to the vilest impulses and drew into, built into, their astral bodies the materials which alone could vibrate in answer to those impulses; this self-built body becomes the prison-house of the soul, and must fall into ruins ere the soul can escape from it. As inevitably as a drunkard must live in his repulsive soddened physical body here, so must he live in his equally repulsive astral body there. The harvest sown is reaped after its kind. Such is the law in all the worlds, and it may not be escaped. Nor indeed is the astral body there more revolting and horrible than it was when the man was living upon earth and made the atmosphere around him fetid with his astral emanations. But people on earth do not generally recognize its ugliness, being astrally blind.

Further, we may cheer ourselves in contemplating these unhappy brothers of ours by remembering that their sufferings are but temporary, and are giving a much-needed lesson in the life of the soul. By the tremendous pressure of Nature's disregarded laws they are learning the existence of those laws, and the misery that accrues from ignoring them in life and conduct. The lesson they would not learn during earth-life, whirled away on the torrent of lusts and desires, is pressed on them here, and will be pressed on them in their succeeding lives, until the evils are eradicated and the man has risen into a better life. Nature's lessons are sharp, but in the long run they are merciful, for they lead to the evolution of the soul and guide it to the winning of its immortality.

Let us pass to a more cheerful region. The second division of the astral world may be said to be the astral double of the physical, for the astral bodies of all things and of many people are largely composed of the matter belonging to this division of the astral plane, and it is therefore more closely in touch with the physical world than any other part of the astral. The great majority of people make some stay here, and a very large proportion of these are consciously awake in it. These latter are folk whose interests were bound up in the trivial and petty objects of life, who set their hearts on trifles, as well as those who allowed their lower natures to rule them, and who died with the appetites still active and desirous of physical enjoyment. Having largely sent their life outwards in these directions, thus building their astral bodies largely of the materials that responded very readily to material impacts, they are held by these bodies in the neighbourhood of their physical attractions. They are mostly dissatisfied, uneasy, restless, with more or less of suffering according to the vigour of the wishes they cannot gratify; some even undergo positive pain from this cause, and are long delayed ere these earthly longings are exhausted. Many unnecessarily lengthen their stay by seeking to communicate with the earth, in whose interests they are entangled, by means of mediums, who allow them to use their physical bodies for this purpose, thus supplying the loss of their own. From them, comes most of the mere twaddle with which everyone is familiar who has had experience of public spiritualistic seances, the gossip and trite morality of the petty lodging-house and small shop —feminine, for the most part. As these earth-bound souls are generally of small intelligence, their communications are of no more interest (to those already convinced of the existence of the soul after death) than was their conversation when they were in the body, and—just as on earth—they are positive in proportion to their ignorance, representing the whole astral world as identical with their own very limited area. There as here:

> They think the rustic cackle of their burgh
> The murmur of the world.

It is from this region that people who have died with some anxiety on their minds will sometimes seek to communicate with their friends in order to arrange the earthly matter that troubles them; if they cannot succeed in showing themselves, or in impressing their wishes by a dream on some friend, they will often cause much annoyance by knockings and other noises directly intended to draw attention or caused unconsciously by their restless efforts. It is a charity in such cases for some competent person to communicate with the distressed entity and learn his wishes, as he may thus be freed from the anxiety which prevents him from passing onwards. Souls, while in this region, may also very easily have their attention drawn to the earth, even although they would not spontaneously have turned back to it, and this disservice is too often done to them by the passionate grief and craving for their beloved presence by friends left behind on earth. The thought-forms set up by these longings throng round them, beat against them, and oftentimes arouse them if they are peacefully sleeping, or violently draw their thoughts to earth if they are already conscious. It is especially in the former case that this unwitting selfishness on the part of friends on earth does mischief to their dear ones that they would themselves be the first to regret; and it may be that the knowledge of the unnecessary suffering thus caused to those who have passed through death may, with some, strengthen the binding force of the religious precepts which enjoin submission to the divine law and the checking of excessive and rebellious grief.

The third and fourth regions of the kāmalokic world differ but little from the second, and might almost be described as etherealized copies of it, the fourth being more refined than the third, but the general characteristics of the three subdivisions being very similar. Souls of somewhat more progressed types are found there, and although they are held there by the encasement built by the activity of their earthly interests, their attention is for the most part directed onwards rather than backwards, and, if they are not forcibly recalled to the concerns of earth-life, they will pass on without very much delay. Still, they are susceptible to earthly stimuli, and the weakening interest in terrestrial affairs may be reawakened by cries from below. Large numbers of educated and thoughtful people, who were chiefly occupied with worldly affairs during their physical lives, are conscious in these regions, and may be induced to communicate through mediums, and, more rarely, seek such communication themselves. Their statements are naturally of a higher type than those spoken of as coming from the second division, but are not marked by any characteristics that render them more valuable than similar statements made by persons still in the body. Spiritual illumination does not come from Kāmaloka.

The fifth subdivision of Kāmaloka offers many new characteristics. It presents a distinctly luminous and radiant appearance, eminently attractive to those accustomed only to the dull hues of earth, and justifying the epithet astral, starry, given to the whole plane. Here are situated all the materialized heavens which play so large a part in popular religions all the world over. The happy hunting-grounds of the Red Indian, the Valhalla of the Norsemen, the houri-filled paradise of the Muslim, the golden jewelled-gated New Jerusalem of the Christian, the lyceum-filled heaven of the material-istic reformer, all have here their places. Men and women who clung desperately to every " letter that killeth " have here the literal satisfaction of their cravings, unconsciously creating in astral matter by their powers of imagination, fed on the mere husks of the world's Scriptures, the cloud-built palaces whereof they dreamed. The crudest religious beliefs find here their temporary cloud-land realization,

and literalists of every faith, who were filled with
selfish longings for their own salvation in the most
materialistic of heavens, here find an appropriate,
and to them enjoyable home, surrounded by the
very conditions in which they believed. The religious and philanthropic busybodies, who cared more
to carry out their own fads and impose their own
ways on their neighbours than to work unselfishly
for the increase of human virtue and happiness, are
here much to the fore, carrying on reformatories,
refuges, schools, to their own great satisfaction, and
much delighted are they still to push an astral
finger into an earthly pie with the help of a sub-
servient medium whom they patronize with lofty
condescension. They build astral churches and
schools and houses, reproducing the materialistic
heavens they coveted; and though to keener vision
their erections are imperfect, even pathetically
grotesque, they find them all-sufficing. People of
the same religions flock together and co-operate
with each other in various ways, so that communities
are formed, differing as widely from each other as
do similar communities on earth. When they are
attracted to the earth they seek, for the most part,
people of their own faith and country, chiefly by
natural affinity, doubtless, but also because barriers
of language still exists in Kāmaloka, as may be
noticed occasionally in messages received in

spiritualistic circles. Souls from this region often take the most vivid interest in attempts to establish communication between this and the next world, and the " spirit-guides " of average mediums come, for the most part, from this and from the region next above. They are generally aware that there are many possibilities of higher life before them, and that they will, sooner or later, pass away into worlds whence communications with this earth will not be possible.

The sixth kāmalokic region resembles the fifth, but is far more refined, and is largely inhabited by souls of a more advanced type, wearing out the astral vesture in which much of their mental energies had worked while they were in the physical body. Their delay here is due to the larger part played by selfishness in their artistic and intellectual life, and to the prostitution of their talents to the gratification of the desire-nature in a refined and delicate way. Their surroundings are of the best that are found in Kāmaloka, as their creative thoughts fashion the luminous materials of their temporary home into fair landscapes and rippling oceans, snow-clad mountains and fertile plains, scenes that are of fairy-like beauty compared with even the most exquisite that earth can show. Religionists also are found here, of a slightly more progressed kind than those in the division immediately below, and with more definite views of their own limitations. They look forward more clearly to passing out of their present sphere and reaching a higher state.

The seventh, the highest, subdivision of Kāmaloka, is occupied almost entirely by intellectual men and women who were either pronouncedly materialistic while on earth, or who are so wedded to the ways in which knowledge is gained by the lower mind in the physical body that they continue its pursuit in the old ways, though with enlarged faculties. One recalls Charles Lamb's dislike of the idea that in heaven knowledge would have to be gained " by some awkward process of intuition " instead of through his beloved books. Many a student lives for long years, sometimes for centuries —according to H. P. Blavatsky—literally in an astral library, conning eagerly all books that deal with his favourite subject, and perfectly contented with his lot. Men who have been keenly set on some line of intellectual investigation, and have thrown off the physical body with their thirst for knowledge unslaked, pursue their object still with unwearied persistence, fettered by their clinging to the physical modes of study. Often such men are still sceptical as to the higher possibilities that lie before them, and shrink from the prospect of what is practically a second death—the sinking into unconsciousness ere the soul is born into the higher life of heaven. Politicians, statesmen, men of science, dwell for a while in this region, slowly disentangling themselves from the astral body, still held to the lower life by their keen and vivid interest in the movements in which they have played so large a part, and in the effort to work out astrally some of the schemes from which Death snatched them ere yet they had reached fruition.

To all, however, sooner or later—save to that small minority who during earth-life never felt one touch of unselfish love, of intellectual aspirations, of recognition of something or someone higher than themselves—there comes a time when the bonds of the astral body are finally shaken off, while the soul sinks into brief unconsciousness of its surroundings, like the unconsciousness that follows the dropping off of the physical body, to be awakened by a sense of bliss, intense, immense, fathomless, undreamed of, the bliss of the heaven-world, of the world to which by its own nature it belongs. Low and vile may have been many of its passions, trivial and sordid many of its longings, but it had gleams of a higher nature, broken lights now and then from a purer region, and these must ripen as seeds to the time of their harvest, and, however poor and few, must yield their fair return. The man passes on to reap this harvest, and to eat and assimilate its fruit.[1]

---

[1] See Chapter V, on " Devachan ".

The astral corpse, as it is sometimes called, or the " shell " of the departed entity, consists of the fragments of the seven concentric shells before described, held together by the remaining magnetism of the soul. Each shell in turn has disintegrated, until the point is reached when mere scattered fragments of it remain; these cling by magnetic attraction to the remaining shells, and when one after another has been reduced to this condition, until the seventh or innermost is reached and itself disintegrates, the man himself escapes, leaving behind him these remains. The shell drifts vaguely about in the kāmalokic world, automatically and feebly repeating its accustomed vibrations, and as the remaining magnetism gradually disperses, it falls into a more and more decayed condition, and finally disintegrates completely, restoring its materials to the general mass of astral matter, exactly as does the physical body to the physical world. This shell drifts wherever the astral currents may carry it, and may be vitalized, if not too far gone, by the magnetism of embodied souls on earth, and so restored to some amount of activity. It will suck up magnetism as a sponge sucks up water, and will then take on an illusory appearance of vitality, repeating more vigorously any vibrations to which it was accustomed; these are often set up by the stimulus of thoughts common to the departed soul.

and friends and relations on earth, and such a vitalized shell may play quite respectably the part of a communicating intelligence; it is, however, distinguishable—apart from the use of astral vision —by its automatic repetitions of familiar thoughts, and by the total absence of all originality and of any traces of knowledge not possessed during physical life.

Just as souls may be delayed in their progress by foolish and inconsiderate friends, so may they be aided in it by wise and well-directed efforts. Hence all religions, which retain any traces of the occult wisdom of their Founders, enjoin the use of " prayers for the dead ". These prayers with their accompanying ceremonies are more or less useful according to the knowledge, the love, and the will-power by which they are ensouled. They rest on that universal truth of vibration by which the universe is built, modified, and maintained. Vibrations are set up by the uttered sounds, arranging astral matter into definite forms, ensouled by the thought enshrined in the words. These are directed towards the kāmalokic entity, and, striking against the astral body, hasten its disintegration. With the decay of occult knowledge these ceremonies have become less and less potent, until their usefulness has almost reached a vanishing-point. Nevertheless they are still sometimes performed by a man of knowledge,

and then exert their rightful influence. Moreover,
everyone can help his beloved departed by sending
to them thoughts of love and peace and longing for
their swift progress through the kāmalokic world
and their liberation from astral fetters. No one
should leave his " dead " to go on a lonely way,
unattended by loving hosts of these guardian angel
thought-forms, helping them forward to joy.

CHAPTER IV

THE MENTAL PLANE

THE mental plane, as its name implies, is that which belongs to consciousness working as thought; not of the mind as it works through the brain, but as it works in its own world, unencumbered with physical spirit-matter. This world is the world of the real man. The word "man" comes from the Sanskrit root "man", and this is the root of the Sanskrit verb "to think", so that *man* means *thinker*; he is named by his most characteristic attribute, intelligence. In English the word "mind" has to stand for the intellectual consciousness itself, and also for the effects produced on the physical brain by the vibrations of that consciousness; but we have now to conceive of the intellectual consciousness as an entity, an individual—a being, the vibrations of whose life are thoughts, thoughts which are images, not words. This individual is Manas, or the Thinker; [1] he is the Self, clothed in the matter,

[1] Derived from Manas is the technical name, the mānasic plane, Englished as "mental". We might call it the plane of the mind proper, to distinguish its activities from those of the mind working in the flesh.

and working within the conditions, of the higher subdivisions of the mental plane. He reveals his presence on the physical plane by the vibrations he sets up in the brain and nervous system; these respond to the thrills of his life by sympathetic vibrations, but in consequence of the coarseness of their materials they can reproduce only a small section of his vibrations, and even that very imperfectly. Just as science asserts the existence of a vast series of etheric vibrations, of which the eye can only see a small fragment, the solar light-spectrum, because it can vibrate only within certain limits, so can the physical thought-apparatus, the brain and nervous system, think only a small fragment of the vast series of mental vibrations set up by the Thinker in his own world. The most receptive brains respond up to the point of what we call great intellectual power; the exceptionally receptive brains respond up to the point of what we call genius; the exceptionally unreceptive brains respond only up to the point we call idiocy; but everyone sends beating against his brain millions of thought-waves to which it cannot respond, owing to the density of its materials, and just in proportion to its sensitiveness are the so-called mental powers of each. But before studying the Thinker, it will be well to consider his world, the mental plane itself.

9

The mental plane is that which is next to the astral, and is separated from it only by differences of materials, just as the astral is separated from the physical. In fact, we may repeat what was said as to the astral and the physical with regard to the mental and the astral. Life on the mental plane is more active than on the astral, and form is more plastic. The spirit-matter of that plane is more highly vitalized and finer than any grade of matter in the astral world. The ultimate atom of astral matter has innumerable aggregations of the coarsest mental matter for its encircling sphere-world, so that the disintegration of the astral atom yields a mass of mental matter of the coarsest kinds. Under these circumstances it will be understood that the play of the life-forces on this plane will be enormously increased in activity, there being so much less mass to be moved by them. The matter is in constant, ceaseless motion, taking form under every thrill of life, and adapting itself without hesitation to every changing motion. " Mind-stuff ", as it has been called, makes astral spirit-matter seem clumsy, heavy, and lustreless, although compared with the physical spirit-matter it is so fairy-light and luminous. But the law of analogy holds good, and gives us a clue to guide us through this super-astral region, the region that is our birthplace and our home, although, imprisoned in a foreign land, we know it not, and gaze at descriptions of it with the eye of aliens.

Once again here, as on the two lower planes, the subdivisions of the spirit-matter of the plane are seven in number. Once again, these varieties enter into countless combinations, of every variety of complexity, yielding the solids, liquids, gases, and ethers of the mental plane. The word " solid " seems indeed absurd, when speaking of even the most substantial forms of mind-stuff; yet as they are dense in comparison with other kinds of mental materials, and as we have no descriptive words save such as are based on physical conditions, we must even use it for lack of a better. Enough if we understand that this plane follows the general law and order of Nature, which is, for our globe, the septenary basis, and that the seven subdivisions of matter are of lessening densities, relatively to each other, as the physical solids, liquids, gases, and ethers; the seventh, or highest, subdivision being composed exclusively of the ultimate mental atoms.

These subdivisions are grouped under two headings, to which the somewhat inefficient and unintelligible epithets " formless " and " form " have been assigned.[1] The lower four—the first, second, third, and fourth subdivisions—are grouped together as " with form "; the higher three—the fifth, sixth,

[1] Arūpa, without form; rūpa, form. Rūpa is form, shape, body.

and seventh subdivisions—are grouped as "formless". The grouping is necessary, for the distinction is a real one, although one difficult to describe, and the regions are related in consciousness to the divisions in the mind itself—as will appear more plainly a little farther on. The distinction may perhaps be best expressed by saying that in the lower four subdivisions the vibrations of consciousness give rise to forms, to images or pictures, and every thought appears as a living shape; whereas in the higher three, consciousness, though still, of course, setting up vibrations, seems rather to send them out as a mighty stream of living energy, which does not body itself into distinct images while it remains in this higher region, but which steps up a variety of forms all linked by some common condition when it rushes into the lower worlds. The nearest analogy that I can find for the conception I am trying to express is that of abstract and concrete thoughts: an abstract idea of a triangle has no form, but connotes any plane figure contained within three right lines, the angles of which make two right angles; such an idea, with conditions but without shape, thrown into the lower world, may give birth to a vast variety of figures, right-angled, isosceles, scalene, of any colour and size, but all fulfilling the conditions—concrete triangles, each one with a definite shape of its own. The impossibility

of giving in words a lucid exposition of the difference in the action of consciousness in the two
regions is due to the fact that words are the symbols
of images and belong to the workings of the lower
mind in the brain, and are based wholly upon those
workings; while the " formless " region belongs to
the Pure Reason, which never works within the
narrow limits of language.

The mental plane is that which reflects the
Universal Mind in Nature, the plane which in our
little system corresponds with that of the Great
Mind in the Kosmos.[1] In its higher regions exist
all the archetypal ideas which are now in course of
concrete evolution, and in its lower the working
out of these into successive forms, to be duly reproduced in the astral and physical worlds. Its
materials are capable of combining under the
impulse of thought vibrations, and can give rise to
any combination which thought can construct; as
iron can be made into a spade for digging or into a
sword for slaying, so can mind-stuff be shaped into
thought-forms that help or that injure; the vibrating
life of the Thinker shapes the materials around him,
and according to his volitions so is his work. In
that region, thought and action, will and deed, are

[1] Mahat, the Third LOGOS, or Divine Creative Intelligence, the
Brahmā of the Hindus, the Mandjusri of the Northern Buddhists,
the Holy Spirit of the Christians.

one and the same thing—spirit-matter here becomes
the obedient servant of the life, adapting itself to
every creative motion.

These vibrations, which shape the matter of the
plane into thought-forms, give rise also—from their
swiftness and subtlety—to the most exquisite and
constantly changing colours, waves of varying shades
like the rainbow hues in mother-of-pearl, etherealized and brightened to an indescribable extent,
sweeping over and through every form, so that each
presents a harmony of rippling, living, luminous,
delicate colours, including many not ever known to
earth. Words can give no idea of the exquisite
beauty and radiance shown in combinations of this
subtle matter, instinct with life and motion. Every
seer who has witnessed it, Hindu, Buddhist, Christian, speaks in rapturous terms of its glorious
beauty, and ever confesses his utter inability to
describe it; words seem but to coarsen and deprive
it, however deftly woven in its praise.

Thought-forms naturally play a large part among
the living creatures that function on the mental
plane. They resemble those with which we are
already familiar in the astral world, save that they
are far more radiant and more brilliantly coloured,
are stronger, more lasting, and more fully vitalized.
As the higher intellectual qualities become more
clearly marked, these forms show very sharply

defined outlines, and there is a tendency to a
singular perfection of geometrical figures accompanied by an equally singular purity of luminous
colour. But, needless to say at the present stage
of humanity, there is a vast preponderance of cloudy
and irregularly shaped thoughts, the production of
the ill-trained minds of the majority. Rarely
beautiful artistic thoughts are also here encountered,
and it is little wonder that painters who have caught,
in dreamy vision, some glimpse of their ideal, oft
fret against their incapacity to reproduce its glowing
beauty in earth's dull pigments. These thought-
forms are built out of the elemental essence of the
plane, the vibrations of the thought throwing the
elemental essence into a corresponding shape, and
this shape having the thought as its informing life.
Thus again we have " artificial elementals " created
in a way identical with that by which they come
into being in the astral regions. All that is said in
Chapter II of their generation and of their importance may be repeated of those of the mental plane,
with here the additional responsibility on their
creators of the greater force and permanence belonging to those of this higher world. The elemental
essence of the mental plane is formed by the Monad
in the stage of its descent immediately preceding its
entrance into the astral world, and it constitutes the
Second Elemental Kingdom, existing on the four

lower subdivisions of the mental plane. The three higher subdivisions, the " formless ", are occupied by the First Elemental Kingdom, the elemental essence there being thrown by thought into brilliant coruscations, coloured streams, and flashes of living fire, instead of into definite shapes, taking as it were its first lessons in combined action, but not yet assuming definite limitations of forms.

On the mental plane, in both its great divisions, exist numberless Intelligences, whose lowest bodies are formed of the luminous matter and elemental essence of the plane—Shining Ones who guide the processes of natural order, overlooking the hosts of lower entities before spoken of, and yielding submission in their several hierarchies to their great Overlords of the seven Elements.[1] They are, as may readily be imagined, Beings of vast knowledge, of great power, and most splendid in appearance, radiant, flashing creatures, myriad-hued, like rainbows of changing supernal colours, of stateliest imperial mien, calm energy incarnate, embodiments of resistless strength. The description of the great Christian Seer leaps to the mind, when he wrote of a mighty angel: " A rainbow was upon his head, and his face was as it were the sun, and his feet as

[1] These are the Arūpa and Rūpa Devas of the Hindus and the Buddhists, the " Lords of the heavenly and the earthly " of the Zoroastrians, the Archangels and Angels of the Christians and Mahommedans.

pillars of fire." [1] "As the sound of many waters" are their voices, as echoes from the music of the spheres. They guide natural order, and rule the vast companies of the elements of the astral world, so that their cohorts carry on ceaselessly the processes of Nature with undeviating regularity and accuracy.

On the lower mental plane are seen many chelas at work in their mental bodies,[2] freed for the time from their physical vestures. When the body is wrapped in deep sleep the true man, the Thinker, may escape from it, and work untrammelled by its weight in these higher regions. From here he can aid and comfort his fellow-men by acting directly on their minds, suggesting helpful thoughts, putting before them noble ideas, more effectively and speedily than he can do when encased in the body. He can see their needs more clearly and therefore can supply them more perfectly, and it is his highest privilege and joy thus to minister to his struggling brothers, without their knowledge of his service or any idea of theirs as to the strong arm that lifts their burden, or the soft voice that whispers solace in their pain. Unseen, unrecognized, he works, serving his enemies as gladly and as freely as his

---

[1] *Revelation*, x, 1.

[2] Usually called the Māyāvi Rūpa, illusory body, when arranged for independent functioning in the mental world.

friends, dispensing to individuals the stream of beneficent forces that are poured down from the great Helpers in higher spheres. Here also are sometimes seen the glorious figures of the Masters, though for the most part They reside on the highest level of the " formless " division of the mental plane; and other Great Ones may also sometimes come hither on some mission of compassion requiring such lower manifestation.

Communication between intelligences functioning consciously on this plane, whether human or non-human, whether in or out of the body, is practically instantaneous, for it is with " the speed of thought ". Barriers of space have here no power to divide, and any soul can come into touch with anyone by merely directing his attention to him. Not only is communication thus swift, but it is also complete, if the souls are at about the same stage of evolution; no words fetter and obstruct the communion, but the whole thought flashes from the one to the other, or, perhaps more exactly, each sees the thought as conceived by the other. The real barriers between souls are the differences of evolution; the less evolved can know only as much of the more highly evolved as he is able to respond to; the limitation can obviously be felt only by the higher one, as the lesser has all that he can contain. The more evolved a soul, the more does he know of all around him, the nearer does he approach to realities; but the mental plane has also its veils of illusion, it must be remembered, though they be far fewer and thinner than those of the astral and the physical worlds. Each soul has its own mental atmosphere, and, as all impressions must come through this atmosphere, they are all distorted and coloured. The clearer and purer the atmosphere, and the less it is coloured by the personality, the fewer are the illusions that can befall it.

The three highest subdivisions of the mental plane are the habitat of the Thinker himself, and he dwells on one or other of these, according to the stage of his evolution. The vast majority live on the lowest level, in various stages of evolution; a comparatively few of the highly intellectual dwell on the second level, the Thinker ascending thither—to use a phrase more suitable to the physical than to the mental plane—when the subtler matter of that region preponderates in him, and thus necessitates the change; there is, of course, no " ascending ", no change of place, but he receives the vibrations of that subtler matter, being able to respond to them, and he himself is able to send out forces that throw its rare particles into vibration. The student should familiarize himself with the fact that rising in the scale of evolution does not move him from place to place, but renders him more and more able to receive impressions. *Every sphere is around us*, the astral, the mental, the buddhic, the nirvānic, and worlds higher yet, the life of the Supreme God; we need not stir to find them, for they are here; but our dull unreceptivity shuts them out more effectively than millions of miles of mere space. We are conscious only of that which affects us, which stirs us to responsive vibration, and as we become more and more receptive, as we draw into ourselves finer and finer matter, we come into contact with subtler and subtler worlds. Hence, rising from one level to another means that we are weaving our vestures of finer materials and can receive through them the contacts of finer worlds; and it means further that in the Self within these vestures diviner powers are waking from latency into activity, and are sending out their subtler thrills of life.

At the stage now reached by the Thinker, he is fully conscious of his surroundings and is in posses-sion of the memory of his past. He knows the bodies he is wearing, through which he is contacting the lower planes, and he is able to influence and guide them to a great extent. He sees the diffi-culties, the obstacles, they are approaching—the results of past careless living—and he sets himself to pour into them energies by which they may be better equipped for their task. His direction is sometimes felt in the lower consciousness as an imperiously compelling force that will have its way,. and that impels to a course of action for which all the reasons may not be clear to the dimmer vision caused by the mental and astral garments. Men who have done great deeds have occasionally left on record their consciousness of an inner uplifting and compelling power, which seemed to leave them no choice save to do as they had done. They were then acting as the real men; the Thinkers, that are the inner men, were doing the work consciously through the bodies that then were fulfilling their proper functions as vehicles of the individual. To these high powers all will come as evolution proceeds.

On the third level of the upper region of the mental plane dwell the Egos of the Masters, and of the Initiates who are Their chelas, the Thinkers having here a preponderance of the matter of this region in their bodies. From this world of subtlest mental forces the Masters carry on Their bene- ficent work for humanity, raining down noble ideals, inspiring thoughts, devotional aspirations, streams of spiritual and intellectual help for men. Every force there generated rays out in myriad directions, and the noblest, purest souls catch most readily these helpful influences. A discovery flashes into the mind of the patient searcher into Nature's secrets;. a new melody entrances the ear of a great musician;.

the answer to a long-studied problem illumines the intellect of a lofty philosopher; a new energy of hope and love suffuses the heart of an unwearied philanthropist. Yet men think that they are left uncared for, although the very phrases they use: " the thought occurred to me ", " the idea came to me ", " the discovery flashed on me ", unconsciously testify to the truth known to their inner selves, though the outer eyes be blind.

Let us now turn to the study of the Thinker and his vesture as they are found in men on earth. The body of the consciousness, conditioning it in the four lower subdivisions of the mental plane—the mental body, as we term it—is formed of combinations of the matter of these subdivisions. The Thinker, the individual, the Human Soul—formed in the way described in the latter part of this chapter—when he is coming into incarnation, first radiates forth some of his energy in vibrations that attract round him, and clothe him in matter drawn from the four lower subdivisions of his own plane. According to the nature of the vibrations are the kinds of matter they attract; the finer kinds answer the swifter vibrations and take form under their impulse, the coarser kinds similarly answer the slower ones; just as a wire will sympathetically sound out a note, i.e., a given number of vibrations, coming from a wire similar in weight and tension

to itself, but will remain dumb amid a chorus of
notes from wires dissimilar to itself in these respects,
so do the different kinds of matter assort themselves in answer to different kinds of vibrations.
Exactly according to the vibrations sent out by the
Thinker will be the nature of the mental body that
he thus draws around him, and this mental body is
what is called the lower mind, the lower Manas,
because it is the Thinker clothed in the matter of
the lower subdivisions of the mental plane and
conditioned by it in his further working. None of
his energies which are too subtle to move this
matter, too swift for its response, can express themselves through it; he is therefore limited by it,
conditioned by it, restricted by it in his expression
of himself. It is the first of his prison-houses during
his incarnate life, and while his energies are acting
within it he is largely shut off from his own higher
world, for his attention is with the outgoing energies
and his life is thrown with them into the mental
body, often spoken of as a vesture, or sheath, or
vehicle—any expression will serve which connotes
the idea that the Thinker is not the mental body,
but formed it and uses it in order to express as
much of himself as he can in the lower mental
region. It must not be forgotten that his energies,
still pulsing outwards, draw round him also the
coarser matter of the astral plane as his astral body;

and during his incarnate life the energies that express themselves through the lower kinds of mental matter are so readily changed by it into slower vibrations that are responded to by astral matter that the two bodies are continually vibrating together, and become very closely interwoven; the coarser the kinds of matter built into the mental body, the more intimate becomes this union, so that the two bodies are sometimes classed together and even taken as one.[1] When we come to study Reincarnation we shall find this fact assuming vital importance.

According to the stage of evolution reached by the man will be the type of mental body he forms on his way to become again incarnate, and we may study, as we did with the astral body, the respective mental bodies of three types of men—(a) an undeveloped man; (b) an average man; (c) a spiritually advanced man.

(a) In the undeveloped man the mental body is but little perceptible, a small amount of unorganized mental matter, chiefly from the lowest subdivisions of the plane, being all that represents it. This is

---

[1] Thus the Theosophist will speak of Kāma-Manas, meaning the mind as working in and with the desire-nature, affecting and affected by the animal nature. The Vedāntin classes the two together, and speaks of the Self as working in the manomayakosha, the sheath composed of the lower mind, emotions, and passions. The European psychologist makes "feelings" one section of his tripartite division of "mind", and includes under feelings both emotions and sensations.

played on almost entirely from the lower bodies, being set vibrating feebly by the astral storms raised by the contacts with material objects through the sense-organs. Except when stimulated by these astral vibrations it remains almost quiescent, and even under their impulses its responses are sluggish. No definite activity is generated from within, these blows from the outer world being necessary to arouse any distinct response. The more violent the blows, the better for the progress of the man, for each responsive vibration aids in the embryonic development of the mental body. Riotous pleasure, anger, rage, pain, terror, all these passions, causing whirlwinds in the astral body, awaken faint vibrations in the mental, and gradually these vibrations, stirring into commencing activity the mental consciousness, cause it to add something of its own to the impressions made on it from without. We have seen that the mental body is so closely mingled with the astral that they act as a single body, but the dawning mental faculties add to the astral passions a certain strength and quality not apparent in them when they work as purely animal qualities. The impressions made on the mental body are more permanent than those made on the astral, and they are consciously reproduced by it. Here memory and the organ of imagination begin, and the latter gradually moulds itself, the images from the outer

10

world working on the matter of the mental body and forming its materials into their own likeness. These images, born of the contacts of the senses, draw round themselves the coarsest mental matter; the dawning powers of consciousness reproduce these images, and thus accumulate a store of pictures that begin to stimulate action initiated from within, from the wish to experience again through the outer organs the vibrations that were found pleasant, and to avoid those productive of pain. The mental body then begins to stimulate the astral, and to arouse in it the desires that, in the animal, slumber until awakened by a physical stimulus; hence we see in the undeveloped man a persistent pursuit of sense-gratification never found in the lower animals, a lust, a cruelty, a calculation to which they are strangers. The dawning powers of the mind, yoked to the service of the senses, make of man a far more dangerous and savage brute than any animal, and the stronger and more subtle forces inherent in the mental spirit-matter lend to the passion-nature an energy and a keenness that we do not find in the animal-world. But these very excesses lead to their own correction by the sufferings which they cause, and these resultant experiences play upon the consciousness and set up new images on which the imagination works. These stimulate the consciousness to resist many of the vibrations that reach it by way of the astral body from the external world, and to exercise its volition in holding the passions back instead of giving them free rein. Such resistant vibrations are set up in, and attract towards, the mental body, finer combinations of mind-stuff, and tend also to expel from it the coarser combinations that vibrate responsively to the passional notes set up in the astral body; by this struggle between the vibrations set up by passion-images and the vibrations set up by the imaginative reproduction of past experiences, the mental body grows, begins to develop a definite organization, and to exercise more and more initiative as regards external activities. While the earth-life is spent in gathering experiences, the intermediate life is spent in assimilating them, as we shall see in detail in the following chapter, so that in each return to earth the Thinker has an increased stock of faculties to take shape as his mental body. Thus the undeveloped man, whose mind is the slave of his passions, grows into the average man, whose mind is a battleground in which passions and mental powers wage war with varying success, about balanced in their forces, but who is gradually gaining the mastery over his lower nature.

(b) In the average man, the mental body is much increased in size, shows a certain amount of organization, and contains a fair proportion of matter drawn from the second, third, and fourth subdivisions of the mental plane. The general law which regulates all the building up and modifying of the mental body may here be fitly studied, though it is the same principle already seen working in the lower realms of the astral and physical worlds. Exercise increases, disuse atrophies and finally destroys. Every vibration set up in the mental body causes a change in its constituents, throwing out of it, in the part affected, the matter that cannot vibrate sympathetically, and replacing it by suitable materials drawn from the practically illimitable store around. The more a series of vibrations is repeated, the more does the part affected by them increase in development; hence, it may be noted in passing, the injury done to the mental body by over-specialization of mental energies. Such mistaken direction of these powers causes a lopsided development of the mental body; it becomes proportionately over-developed in the region in which these forces are continually playing and proportionately undeveloped in other parts, perhaps equally important. A harmonious and proportionate all-round development is the object to be sought, and for this are needed a calm self-analysis and a definite direction of means to ends. A knowledge of this law further explains certain familiar experiences, and affords a sure hope of progress. When a new study is commenced, or a change in favour of high morality is initiated, the early stages are found to be fraught with difficulties; sometimes the effort is even abandoned because the obstacles in the way of its success appear to be insurmountable. At the beginning of any new mental undertaking, the whole automatism of the mental body opposes it; the materials, habituated to vibrate in a particular way, cannot accommodate themselves to the new impulses, and the early stage consists chiefly of sending out thrills of force which are frustrated, so far as setting up vibrations in the mental body are concerned, but which are the necessary preliminary to any such sympathetic vibrations, as they shake out of the body the old refractory materials and draw into it the sympathetic kinds. During this process, the man is not conscious of any progress; he is conscious only of the frustration of his efforts and of the dull resistance he encounters. Presently, if he persists, as the newly attracted materials begin to function, he succeeds better in his attempts, and at last, when all the old materials are expelled and the new are working, he finds himself succeeding without an effort, and his object is accomplished. The critical time is during the first stage; but if he trust in the law, as sure in its working as every other law in Nature, and persistently repeat his efforts, he *must* succeed; and a knowledge of this fact may cheer him when otherwise he would be sinking in despair. In this way, then, the average man may work on, finding with joy that as he steadily resists the promptings of the lower nature he is conscious they are losing their power over him, for he is expelling from his mental body all the materials that are capable of being thrown by them into sympathetic vibrations. Thus the mental body gradually comes to be composed of the finer constituents of the four lower subdivisions of the mental plane, until it has become the radiant and exquisitely beautiful form which is the mental body of the spiritually developed man.

(c) Spiritually developed man. From this body all the coarser combinations have been eliminated, so that the objects of the senses no longer find in it, or in the astral body connected with it, materials that respond sympathetically to their vibrations. It contains only the finer combinations belonging to each of the four subdivisions of the lower mental world, and of these again the materials of the third and fourth subplanes very much predominate in its composition over the materials of the second and first, making it responsive to all the higher workings of the intellect, to the delicate contacts of the higher arts, to all the pure thrills of the loftier emotions. Such a body enables the Thinker who is clothed in it to express himself much more fully in the lower mental region and in the astral and physical worlds; its materials are capable of a far wider range of responsive vibrations, and the impulses from a loftier realm mould it into nobler and subtler organization. Such a body is rapidly becoming ready to reproduce every impulse from the Thinker which is capable of expression on the lower subdivisions of the mental plane; it is growing into a perfect instrument for activities in this lower mental world.

A clear understanding of the nature of the mental body would much modify modern education, and would make it far more serviceable to the Thinker than it is at present. The general characteristics of this body depend on the past lives of the Thinker on earth, as will be thoroughly understood when we have studied Reincarnation and Karma. The body is constituted on the mental plane, and its materials depend on the qualities that the Thinker has garner-ed within himself as the results of his past experi-ences. All that education can do is to provide such external stimuli as shall arouse and encourage the growth of the useful faculties he already possesses, and help in the eradication of those that are undesirable. The drawing out of these inborn faculties, and not the cramming of the mind with facts, is the object of true education. Nor need memory be cultivated as a separate faculty, for memory depends on attention—that is on the steady

concentration of the mind on the subject studied—
and on the natural affinity between the subject and
the mind. If the subject be liked—that is, if the
mind has a capacity for it—memory will not fail,
provided due attention be paid. Therefore education should cultivate the habit of steady concentration, of sustained attention, and should be directed
according to the inborn faculties of the pupil.

Let us now pass into the " formless " divisions of
the mental plane, the region which is man's true
home during the cycle of his reincarnations, into
which he is born, a baby soul, an infant Ego, an
embryonic individuality, when he begins his purely
human evolution.[1]

The outline of this Ego, the Thinker, is oval in
shape, and hence H. P. Blavatsky speaks of this
body of Manas which endures throughout all his
incarnations as the Auric Egg. Formed of the
matter of the three highest subdivisions of the mental
plane, it is exquisitely fine, a film of rarest subtlety,
even at its first inception; and, as it develops, it
becomes a radiant object of supernal glory and
beauty, the shining One, as it has been aptly named.[2]
What is this Thinker? He is the divine Self, as
already said, limited, or individualized, by this subtle

[1] See Chapters VII and VIII, on " Reincarnation ".

[2] This is the Augoiedes of the Neo-Platonists, the " spiritual
body " of S. Paul.

body drawn from the materials of the "formless" region of the mental plane.[1] This matter—drawn around a ray of the Self, a living beam of the one Light and Life of the universe—shuts off this ray from its Source, so far as the external world is concerned, encloses it within a filmy shell of itself, and so makes it " an individual ". The life is the Life of the LOGOS, but all the powers of that Life are lying latent, concealed; everything is there potentially, germinally, as the tree is hidden within the tiny germ in the seed. This seed is dropped into the soil of human life that its latent forces may be quickened into activity by the sun of joy and the rain of tears, and be fed by the juices of the life-soil that we call experience, until the germ grows into a mighty tree, the image of its generating Sire. Human evolution is the evolution of the Thinker; he takes on bodies on the lower mental, the astral, and the physical planes, wears them through earthly, astral, lower mental life, dropping them successively at the regular stages of this life-cycle as he passes from world to world, but ever storing up within himself the fruits he has gathered by their use on each plane. At first, as little conscious as a baby's earthly body, he almost slept through life after life, till the experiences playing on him from without

[1] The Self, working in the Vignyānamayakosha, the sheath of discriminative knowledge, according to the Vedāntic classification.

awakened some of his latent forces into activity; but gradually he assumed more and more part in the direction of his life, until with manhood reached, he took his life into his own hands, and an ever-increasing control over his future destiny.

The growth of the permanent body which, with the divine consciousness, forms the Thinker, is extremely slow. Its technical name is the causal body, because he gathers up within it the results of all experiences, and these act as causes, moulding future lives. It is the only permanent one among the bodies used during incarnation, the mental, astral and physical bodies being reconstituted for each fresh life; as each perishes in turn, it hands on its harvest to the one above it, and thus all the harvests are finally stored in the permanent body; when the Thinker returns to incarnation, he sends out his energies, constituted of these harvests, on each successive plane, and thus draws round him new body after body suitable to his past. The growth of the causal body itself, as said, is very slow, for it can vibrate only in answer to impulses that can be expressed in the very subtle matter of which it is composed, thus weaving them into the texture of its being. Hence the passions, which play so large a part in the early stages of human evolution, cannot directly affect its growth. The Thinker can work into himself only the experiences that can be reproduced in the vibrations of the causal body, and these must belong to the mental region, and be highly intellectual or loftily moral in their character; otherwise its subtle matter can give no sympathetic vibration in answer. A very little reflection will convince any one how little material, suitable for the growth of this lofty body, he affords by his daily life; hence the slowness of evolution, the little progress made. The Thinker should have more of himself to put out in each successive life, and, when this is the case, evolution goes swiftly forward. Persistence in evil courses reacts in a kind of indirect way on the causal body, and does more harm than the mere retardation of growth; it seems after a long time to cause a certain incapacity to respond to the vibrations set up by the opposite good, and thus to delay growth for a considerable period after the evil has been renounced. Directly to injure the causal body, evil of a highly intellectual and refined kind is necessary, the " spiritual evil " mentioned in the various Scriptures of the world. This is fortunately rare, rare as spiritual good, and found only among the highly progressed, whether they be following the Right-hand or the Left-hand Path.[1]

---

[1] The Right-hand Path is that which leads to divine manhood, to Adeptship used in the service of the worlds. The Left-hand Path is that which also leads to Adeptship, but to Adeptship that

The habitat of the Thinker, of the Eternal Man, is on the fifth subplane, the lowest level of the "formless" region of the mental plane. The great masses of mankind are here, scarce yet awake, still in the infancy of their life. The Thinker develops consciousness slowly, as his energies, playing on the lower planes, there gather experience, which is indrawn with these energies as they return to him treasure-laden with the harvest of a life. This eternal Man, the individualized Self, is the actor in every body that he wears; it is his presence that gives the feeling of "I" alike to body and mind, the "I" being that which is self-conscious and which, by illusion, identifies itself with that vehicle in which it is most actively energizing. To the man of the senses the "I" is the physical body and the desire-nature; he draws from these his enjoyment, and he thinks of these as himself, for his life is in them. To the scholar the "I" is the mind, for in its exercise lies his joy and therein his life is concentrated. Few can rise to the abstract heights of spiritual philosophy, and feel this Eternal Man as "I", with memory ranging back over past lives and hopes ranging forward over future births. The physiologists tell us that if we cut the finger we do not really feel the pain there where the blood

is used to frustrate the progress of evolution and is turned to selfish individual ends. They are sometimes called the White and Black Paths respectively.

is flowing, but that the pain is felt in the brain, and is by imagination thrown outwards to the place of injury; the feeling of pain *in the finger* is, they say, an illusion; it is put by imagination at the point of contact with the object causing the injury; so also will a man feel pain in an amputated limb, or rather in the space the limb used to occupy. Similarly does the one " I," the Inner Man, feel suffering and joy in the sheaths which enwrap him, at the points of contact with the external world, and feels the sheath to be himself, knowing not that this feeling is an illusion, and that he is the sole actor and experiencer in every sheath.

Let us now consider, in this light, the relations between the higher and lower mind and their action on the brain. The mind, Manas, the Thinker, is one, and is the Self in the causal body; it is the source of innumerable energies, of vibrations of innumerable kinds. These it sends out, raying outwards from itself. The subtlest and finest of these are expressed in the matter of the causal body, which alone is fine enough to respond to them; they form what we call the Pure Reason, whose thoughts are abstract, whose method of gaining knowledge is intuition; its very " nature is knowledge ", and it recognizes truth at sight as congruous with itself. Less subtle vibrations pass outwards, attracting the matter of the lower mental region, and these are

the Lower Manas, or lower mind—the coarser
energies of the higher expressed in denser matter;
these we call the intellect, comprising reason, judgment, imagination, comparison, and the other
mental faculties; its thoughts are concrete, and its
method is logic; it argues, it reasons, it infers.
These vibrations, acting through astral matter on
the etheric brain, and by that on the dense physical
brain, set up vibrations therein, which are the
heavy and slow reproductions of themselves—heavy
and slow, because the energies lose much of their
swiftness in moving the heavier matter. This
feebleness of response when a vibration is initiated
in a rare medium and then passes into a dense one
is familiar to every student of physics. Strike a
bell in air and it sounds clearly; strike it in
hydrogen, and let the hydrogen vibrations have to
set up the atmospheric waves, and how faint the
result. Equally feeble are the workings of the brain
in response to the swift and subtle impacts of the
mind; yet that is all that the vast majority know
as their " consciousness ".

The immense importance of the mental workings
of this " consciousness " is due to the fact that it is
the only medium whereby the Thinker can gather
the harvest of experience by which he grows. While
it is dominated by the passions it runs riot, and he
is left unnourished and therefore unable to develop,

while it is occupied wholly in mental activities concerned with the outer world, it can arouse only his lower energies; only as he is able to impress on it the true object of its life, does it commence to fulfil its most valuable functions of gathering what will arouse and nourish his higher energies. As the Thinker develops he becomes more and more conscious of his inherent powers, and also of the workings of his energies on the lower planes, of the bodies which those energies have drawn around him. He at last begins to try to influence them, using his memory of the past to guide his will, and these impressions we call " conscience " when they deal with morals, and " flashes of intuition " when they enlighten the intellect. When these impressions are continuous enough to be normal, we speak of their aggregate as " genius ". The higher evolution of the Thinker is marked by his increasing control over his lower vehicles, by their increasing susceptibility to his influence, and their increasing contributions to his growth. Those who would deliberately aid in this evolution may do so by a careful training of the lower mind and of the moral character, by steady and well-directed effort. The habit of quiet, sustained, and sequential thought, directed to non-worldly subjects, of meditation, of study, develops the mind-body and renders it a better instrument; the effort to cultivate abstract thinking is also useful, as this raises the lower mind towards the higher, and draws into it the subtlest materials of the lower mental plane. In these and cognate ways all may actively co-operate in their own higher evolution, each step forward making the succeeding steps more rapid. No effort, not even the smallest, is lost, but is followed by its full effect, and every contribution gathered and handed inwards is stored in the trasure-house of the causal body for future use. Thus evolution, however slow and halting, is yet ever onwards, and the divine Life, ever unfolding in every soul, slowly subdues all things to itself.

CHAPTER V

DEVACHAN

THE word Devachan is the Theosophical name for heaven, and, literally translated, means the Shining Land, or the Land of the Gods.[1] It is a specially guarded part of the mental plane, whence all sorrow and all evil are excluded by the action of the great spiritual Intelligences who superintend human evolution; and it is inhabited by human beings who have cast off their physical and astral bodies, and who pass into it when their stay in Kāmaloka is completed. The devachanic life consists of two stages, of which the first is passed in the four lower subdivisions of the mental plane, in which the Thinker still wears the mental body and is conditioned by it, being employed in assimilating the materials gathered by it during the earth-life from which he has just emerged. The second stage is spent in the "formless" world, the Thinker escaping from the mental body, and living his own unencumbered life

---

[1] Devasthān, the place of the Gods, is the Sanskrit equivalent. It is the Svarga of the Hindus; the Sukhāvati of the Buddhists; the Heaven of the Zoroastrians and Christians, and of the less materialized among the Muhammadans.

11

in the full measure of the self-consciousness and knowledge to which he has attained.

The total length of time spent in Devachan depends upon the amount of material for the devachanic life which the soul has brought with it thither from its life on earth. The harvest of fruit for consumption and assimilation in Devachan consists of all the pure thoughts and emotions generated during earth-life, all the intellectual and moral efforts and aspirations, all the memories of useful work and plans for human service—everything which is capable of being worked into mental and moral faculty, thus assisting in the evolution of the soul. Not one is lost, however feeble, however fleeting; but selfish animal passions cannot enter, there being no material in which they can be expressed. Nor does all the evil in the past life, though it may largely preponderate over the good, prevent the full reaping of whatever scant harvest of good there may have been; the scantiness of the harvest may render the devachanic life very brief, but the most depraved, if he has had any faint longings after the right, any stirrings of tenderness, must have a period of devachanic life in which the seed of good may put forth its tender shoots, in which the spark of good may be gently fanned into a tiny flame.

In the past, when men lived with their hearts largely fixed on heaven and directed their lives with a view to enjoying its bliss, the period spent in Devachan was very long; lasting sometimes for many thousands of years; at the present time, men's minds being so much more centred on earth, and so few of their thoughts comparatively being directed towards the higher life, their devachanic periods are correspondingly shortened. Similarly, the time spent in the higher and lower regions of the mental plane [1] respectively is proportionate to the amount of thought generated severally in the mental and in the causal bodies; all the thoughts belonging to the personal self, to the life just closed—with all its ambitions, interests, loves, hopes and fears—all these have their fruition in the Devachan where forms are found; while those belonging to the higher mind, to the regions of abstract, impersonal thinking, have to be worked out in the " formless " devachanic region. The majority of people only just enter that lofty region to pass swiftly out again; some spend there a large portion of their devachanic existence; a few spend there almost the whole.

Ere entering into any details let us try to grasp some of the leading ideas which govern the devachanic life, for it is so different from physical life that any description of it is apt to mislead by its very strangeness. People realize so little of their

---

[1] Called technically the Arūpa and Rūpa Devachan—existing on the arūpa and rūpa levels of the mental plane.

mental life, even as led in the body, that when they are presented with a picture of mental life out of the body they lose all sense of reality, and feel as though they had passed into a world of dream.

The first thing to grasp is that mental life is far more intense, vivid, and nearer to reality than the life is of the senses. Everything we see and touch and hear and taste and handle down here is two removes farther from the reality than everything we contact in Devachan. We do not even there see things as they are, but the things that we see down here have two more veils of illusion enveloping them. Our sense of reality here is an entire delusion; we know nothing of things, of people, as they are; all that we know of them are the impressions they make on our senses, and the conclusions, often erroneous, which our reason deduces from the aggregate of these impressions. Get and put side by side the ideas of man held by his father, his closest friend, the girl who adores him, his rival in business, his deadliest enemy, and a casual acquaintance, and see how incongruous the pictures. Each can only give the impressions made on his own mind, and how far are they from the reality of what the man is, seen by eyes that pierce all veils and behold the whole man! We know of each of our friends, the impressions they make on us, and these are strictly limited by our capacity to receive; a child may have as his father a great statesman of lofty purpose and high aims, but that guide of a nation's destinies is to him only his merriest playfellow, his most enticing story-teller. We live in the midst of illusions, but have the feeling of reality, and this yields us content. In Devachan we shall also be surrounded by illusions—though, as said, two removes nearer to reality—and there also we shall have a similar feeling of reality which will yield us content.

The illusions of earth, though lessened, are not escaped from in the lower heavens, though contact is more real and more immediate. For it must never be forgotten that these heavens are part of a great evolutionary scheme, and, until man has found the real Self, his own unreality makes him subject to illusions. One thing, however, which produces the feeling of reality in earth-life and of unreality when we study Devachan, is that we look at earth-life from within, under the full sway of its illusions, while we contemplate Devachan from outside, free for the time from its veil of māyā.

In Devachan the process is reversed, and its inhabitants feel their own life to be the real one and look on the earth-life as full of the most patent illusions and misconceptions. On the whole, they are nearer the truth than the physical critics of their heaven-world.

Next, the Thinker—being clad only in the mental body and being in the untrammelled exercise of its powers—manifests the creative nature of these powers in a way and to an extent that down here we can hardly realize. On earth a painter, a sculptor, a musician, dream dreams of exquisite beauty, creating their visions by the powers of the mind; but when they seek to embody them in the coarse materials of earth they fall far short of the mental creation. The marble is too resistant for perfect form, the pigments too muddy for perfect colour. In heaven, all they think is at once reproduced in form, for the rare and subtle matter of the heaven-world is mind-stuff, the medium in which the mind normally works when free from passion, and it takes shape with every mental impulse. Each man, therefore, in a very real sense, makes his own heaven, and the beauty of his surroundings is indefinitely increased, according to the wealth and energy of his mind. As the soul develops his powers, his heaven grows more and more subtle and exquisite; all the limitations in heaven are self-created, and heaven expands and deepens with the expansion and deepening of the soul. While the soul is weak and selfish, narrow and ill-developed, his heaven shares these pettinesses; but it is always the best that is in the soul, however poor the best may be. As the man evolves, his devachanic lives become fuller, richer, more and more real, and advanced souls come into ever closer and closer contact with each other, enjoying wider and deeper intercourse. A life on earth, thin, feeble, vapid and narrow, mentally and morally, produces a comparatively thin, feeble, vapid and narrow life in Devachan, where only the mental and the moral survive. We cannot *have* more than we *are*, and our harvest is according to our sowing. " Be not deceived; God is not mocked; for whatsoever a man soweth, that," and neither more nor less, " shall he also reap." Our indolence and greediness would fain reap where we have not sown, but in this universe of law, the Good Law, mercifully just, brings to each the exact wages of his work.

The mental impressions, or mental pictures, we make of our friends will dominate us in Devachan. Round each soul throng those he loved in life, and every image of the loved ones that live in the heart becomes a living companion of the soul in heaven. And they are unchanged. They will be to us there as they were here, and not otherwise. The outer semblance of our friend as it affected our senses, we form out of mind-stuff in Devachan by the creative powers of the mind; what was here a mental picture is there—as in truth it was here, although we knew it not—an objective shape in living mind-stuff, abiding in our own mental atmosphere; only what is dull and dreamy here is forcibly living and vivid there. And with regard to the true communion, that of soul with soul! That is closer, nearer, dearer than anything we know here, for, as we have seen, there is no barrier on the mental plane between soul and soul; exactly in proportion to the reality of soul-life in us is the reality of soul-communion there; the mental image of our friend is our own creation; his form is as we knew and loved it; and his soul breathes through that form to ours just to the extent that his soul and ours can throb in sympathetic vibration. But we can have no touch with those we knew on earth if the ties were only of the physical or astral body, or if they and we were discordant in the inner life; therefore into our Devachan no enemy can enter, for sympathetic accord of minds and hearts can alone draw men together there. Separateness of heart and mind means separation in the heavenly life, for all that is lower than the heart and mind can find no means of expression there. With those who are far beyond us in evolution we come into contact just as far as we can respond to them; great ranges of their being will stretch beyond our ken, but all that we can touch is ours. Further, these greater ones can and do aid us in the heavenly life, under conditions we shall study presently, helping us to grow towards them, and thus to be able to receive more and more.

There is then no separation by space or time, but there is separation by absence of sympathy, by lack of accord between hearts and minds.

In heaven we are with all whom we love and with all whom we admire, and we commune with them to the limit of our capacity, or, if we are the more advanced, of theirs. We meet them in the forms we loved on earth, with perfect memory of our earthly relationships, for heaven is the flowering of all earth's buds, and the marred and feeble loves of earth expand into beauty and into power there. The communion being direct, no misunderstandings of words or thoughts can arise; each sees the thought his friend creates, or as much of it as he can respond to.

Devachan, the heaven-world, is a world of bliss, of joy unspeakable. But it is much more than this, much more than a rest for the weary. In Devachan all that was valuable in the mental and moral experiences of the Thinker during the life just ended is worked out, meditated over, and is gradually transmuted into definite mental and moral faculty, into powers which he will take with him to his next rebirth. He does not work into the mental body the actual memory of the past, for the mental body will, in due course, disintegrate; the memory of the past abides only in the Thinker himself, who has lived through it and who endures. But these facts of past experiences are worked into mental capacity, so that if a man has studied a subject deeply the effects of that study will be the creation of a special faculty to acquire and master that subject when it is first presented to him in another incarnation. He will be born with a special aptitude for that line of study, and will pick it up with great facility. Everything thought upon earth is thus utilized in Devachan; every aspiration is worked up into power; all frustrated efforts become faculties and abilities; struggles and defeats reappear as materials to be wrought into instruments of victory; sorrows and errors shine luminous as precious metals to be worked up into wise and well-directed volitions. Schemes of beneficence, for which power and skill to accomplish were lacking in the past, are in Devachan worked out in thought, acted out, as it were, stage by stage, and the necessary power and skill are developed as faculties of the mind to be put into use in a future life on earth, when the clever and earnest student shall be reborn as a genius, when the devotee shall be reborn as a saint. Life then, in Devachan, is no mere dream, no lotus-land of purposeless idling; it is the land in which the mind and heart develop, unhindered by gross matter and by trivial cares, where weapons are forged for earth's fierce battle-fields, and where the progress of the future is secured.

When the Thinker has consumed in the mental body all the fruits belonging to it of his earthly life, he shakes it off and dwells unencumbered in his own place. All the mental faculties which express themselves on the lower levels are drawn within the causal body—with the germs of the passional life that were drawn into the mental body when it left the astral shell to disintegrate in Kāmaloka—and these become latent for a time, lying within the causal body, forces which remain concealed for lack of material in which to manifest.[1] The mental body, the last of the temporary vestures of the true man, disintegrates, and its materials return to the general matter of the mental plane, whence they were drawn when the Thinker last descended into incarnation. Thus the causal body alone remains, the receptacle and treasure-house of all that has been assimilated from the life that is over. The Thinker has finished a round of his long pilgrimage and dwells for a while in his own native land.

His condition as to consciousness depends entirely on the point he has reached in evolution. In his early stages of life he will merely sleep, wrapped in

[1] The thoughtful student may here find a fruitful suggestion on the problem of continuing consciousness after the cycle of the universe is trodden. Let him place Īshvara in the place of the Thinker, and let the faculties that are the fruits of a life represent the human lives that are the fruits of a Universe. He may then catch some glimpses of what is necessary for consciousness, during the interval between universes.

unconsciousness, when he has lost his vehicles on
the lower planes. His life will pulse gently within
him, assimilating any little results from his closed
earth-existence that may be capable of entering into
his substance; but he will have no consciousness of
his surroundings. But as he develops, this period
of his life becomes more and more important, and
occupies a greater proportion of his devachanic
existence. He becomes self-conscious, and thereby
conscious of his surroundings—of the not-self—and
his memory spreads before him the panorama of his
life, stretching backwards into the ages of the past.
He sees the causes that worked out their effects in
the last of his life-experiences, and studies the causes
he has set going in this latest incarnation. He
assimilates and works into the texture of the causal
body all that was noblest and loftiest in the closed
chapter of his life, and by his inner activity he
develops and co-ordinates the materials in his causal
body. He comes into direct contact with great
souls, whether in or out of the body at the time,
enjoys communion with them, learns from their
riper wisdom and longer experience. Each succeeding devachanic life is richer and deeper; with
his expanding capacity to receive, knowledge flows
into him in fuller tides; more and more he learns to
understand the workings of the law, the conditions of
evolutionary progress; and thus returns to earth-life

each time with greater knowledge, more effective power, his vision of the goal of life becoming ever clearer and the way to it more plain before his feet.

To every Thinker, however unprogressed, there comes a moment of clear vision when the time arrives for his return to the life of the lower worlds. For a moment he sees his past and the causes working from it into the future, and the general map of his next incarnation is also unrolled before him. Then the clouds of lower matter surge round him and obscure his vision, and the cycle of another incarnation begins with the awakenings of the powers of the lower mind, and their drawing round them, by their vibrations, materials from the lower mental plane to form the new mental body for the opening chapter of his life-history. This part of our subject, however, belongs in its detail to the chapters on reincarnation.

We left the soul asleep,[1] having shaken off the last remains of his astral body, ready to pass out of Kāmaloka into Devachan, out of purgatory into heaven. The sleeper awakens to a sense of joy unspeakable, of bliss immeasurable, of peace that passeth understanding. Softest melodies are breathing round him, tenderest hues greet his opening eyes, the very air seems music and colour, the whole being is suffused with light and harmony.

[1] See Chapter III, on " Kāmaloka ".

Then through the golden haze dawn sweetly the faces loved on earth, etherealized into the beauty which expresses their noblest, loveliest emotions, unmarred by the troubles and the passions of the lower worlds. Who may tell the bliss of that awakening, the glory of that first dawning of the heaven-world?

We will now study the conditions in detail of the seven subdivisions of Devachan, remembering that in the four lower we are in a world of form, and a world, moreover, in which every thought presents itself at once as a form. This world of form belongs to the personality, and every soul is therefore surrounded by as much of his past life as has entered into his mind and can be expressed in pure mind-stuff.

The first, or lowest, region is a heaven of the least progressed souls, whose highest emotion on earth was a narrow, sincere, and sometimes unselfish love for family and friends. Or it may be that they felt some loving admiration for some one they met on earth who was purer and better than themselves, or felt some wish to lead a higher life, or some passing aspiration towards mental and moral expansion. There is not much material here out of which faculty can be moulded, and their life is but very slightly progressive; their family affections will be nourished and a little widened, and they will be reborn after a while with a somewhat improved

emotional nature, with more tendency to recognize
and respond to a higher ideal. Meanwhile they
are enjoying all the happiness they can receive;
their cup is but a small one, but it is filled to the
brim with bliss, and they enjoy all that they are
able to conceive of heaven. Its purity, its harmony,
play on their undeveloped faculties and woo them
to awaken into activity, and the inner stirrings begin
which must precede any manifested budding.

The next division of devachanic life comprises
men and women of every religious faith whose
hearts during their earthly lives had turned with
loving devotion to God, under any name, under
any form. The form may have been narrow, but
the heart rose up in aspiration, and it here finds the
object of its loving worship. The concept of the
Divine which was formed by their mind when on
earth here meets them in the radiant glory of
devachanic matter, fairer, diviner than their wildest
dreams. The Divine One limits Himself to meet
the intellectual limits of His worshipper, and in
whatever form the worshipper has loved and
worshipped Him, in that form He reveals Himself
to his longing eyes, and pours out on him the sweet-
ness of His answering love. The souls are steeped
in religious ecstasy, worshipping the One under the
forms their piety sought on earth, losing themselves
in the rapture of devotion, in communion with the

Object they adore. No one finds himself a stranger in the heavenly places, the Divine veiling Himself in the familiar form. Such souls grow in purity and in devotion under the sun of this communion, and return to earth with these qualities much intensified. Nor is all their devachanic life spent in this devotional ecstasy, for they have full opportunities of maturing other qualities they may possess of heart and mind.

Passing onwards to the third region, we come to those noble and earnest beings who were devoted servants of humanity while on earth, and largely poured out their love to God in the form of works for man. They are reaping the reward of their good deeds by developing larger powers of usefulness and increased wisdom in their direction. Plans of wider beneficence unroll themselves before the mind of the philanthropist, and like an architect, he designs the future edifice which he will build in a coming life on earth; he matures the schemes which he will then work out into actions and like a creative God plans his universe of benevolence, which shall be manifested in gross matter when the time is ripe. These souls will appear as the great philanthropists of yet unborn centuries, who will incarnate on earth with innate power of unselfish love and of power to achieve.

Most varied in character, perhaps, of all the heavens is the fourth, for here the powers of the most advanced souls find their exercise, so far as they can be expressed in the world of form. Here the kings of art and of literature are found, exercising all their powers of form, of colour, of harmony, and building greater faculties with which to be reborn when they return to earth. Noblest music, ravishing beyond description, peals forth from the mightiest monarchs of harmony that earth has known, as Beethoven, no longer deaf, pours out his imperial soul in strains of unexampled beauty, making even the heaven-world more melodious as he draws down harmonies from higher spheres, and sends them thrilling through the heavenly places. Here also we find the masters of painting and of sculpture, learning new hues of colour, new curves of undreamed beauty. And here also are others who failed, though greatly aspiring, and who are here transmuting longings into powers, and dreams into faculties, that shall be theirs in another life. Searchers into Nature are here, and they are learning her hidden secrets; before their eyes are unrolling systems of worlds with all their hidden mechanism, woven series of workings of unimaginable delicacy and complexity; they shall return to earth as great " discoverers ", with unerring intuitions of the mysterious ways of Nature. In this heaven also are found students of the deeper knowledge, the eager, reverent pupils who sought the

12

Teachers of the race, who longed to find a Teacher, and patiently worked at all that had been given out by some one of the great spiritual Masters who have taught humanity. Here their longing find their fruition, and Those they sought, apparently in vain, are now their instructors; the eager souls drink in the heavenly wisdom, and swift their growth and progress as they sit at their Master's feet. As teachers and as light-bringers shall they be born again on earth, born with the birthmark of the teacher's high office upon them.

Many a student on earth, all unknowing of these subtler workings, is preparing for himself a place in this fourth heaven, as he bends with a real devotion over the pages of some teacher or genius, over the teachings of some advanced soul. He is forming a link between himself and the teacher he loves and reverences, and in the heaven-world that soul-tie will assert itself, and draw together into communion the souls it links. As the sun pours down its rays into many rooms, and each room has all it can contain of the solar beams, so in the heaven-world do these great souls shine into hundreds of mental images of themselves created by their pupils, fill them with life, with their own essence, so that each student has his master to teach him and yet shuts out none other from his aid.

Thus, for periods long in proportion to the materials gathered for consumption upon earth, dwell men in these heaven-worlds of form, where all of good that the last personal life had garnered finds its full fruition, its full working out into minutest detail. Then as we have seen, when everything is exhausted, when the last drop has been drained from the cup of joy, the last crumb eaten of the heavenly feast, all that has been worked up into faculty, that is of permanent value, is drawn within the causal body, and the Thinker shakes off him the then disintegrating body through which he has found expression on the lower levels of the devachanic world. Rid of this mental body, he is in his own world, to work up whatever of his harvest can find material suitable for it in that high realm.

A vast number of souls touch the lowest level of the formless world as it were but for a moment, taking brief refuge there, since all lower vehicles have fallen away. But so embryonic are they that they have as yet no active powers that they can function independently; and they become unconscious as the mental body slips away into disintegration. Then, for a moment, they are aroused to consciousness, and a flash of memory illumines their past and they see its pregnant causes; and a flash of foreknowledge illumines their future, and they see such effects as will work out in the coming life.

This is all that very many are as yet able to experience of the formless world. For here again, as ever, the harvest is according to the sowing, and how should they who sowed nothing for that lofty region expect to reap any harvest therein?

But many souls have during their earth-life, by deep thinking and noble living, sown much seed, the harvest of which belongs to this fifth devachanic region, the lowest of the three heavens of the formless world. Great is now their reward for having so risen above the bondage of the flesh and of passion, and they begin to experience the real life of man, the lofty existence of the soul itself, unfettered by vestures belonging to the lower worlds. They learn truths by direct vision, and see the fundamental causes of which all concrete objects are the results; they study the underlying unities, whose presence is masked in the lower worlds by the variety of irrelevant details. Thus they gain a deep knowledge of law, and learn to recognize in its changeless workings below results apparently the most incongruous, thus building into the body that endures firm unshakable convictions, that will reveal themselves in earth-life as deep intuitive certainties of the soul, above and beyond all reasoning. Here also the man studies his own past, and carefully disentangles the causes he has set going; he marks their interacting, the resultants accuring from them,

and sees something of their working out in lives yet
in the future.

In the sixth heaven are more advanced souls,
who during earth-life had felt but little attraction
for its passing shows, and who had devoted all
their energies to the higher intellectual and moral
life. For them there is no veil upon the past, their
memory is perfect and unbroken, and they plan
the infusion into their next life of energies that will
neutralize many of the forces that are working for
hindrance, and strengthen many of those that are
working for good. This clear memory enables them
to form definite and strong determinations as to
actions which are to be done and actions which are
to be avoided, and these volitions they will be able
to impress on their lower vehicles in their next birth,
making certain classes of evils impossible, contrary
to what is felt to be the deepest nature, and certain
kinds of good inevitable, the irresistible demands of
a voice that will not be denied. These souls are
born into the world with high and noble qualities
which render a base life impossible, and stamp the
babe from its cradle as one of the pioneers of
humanity. The man who has attained to this sixth
heaven sees unrolled before him the vast treasures
of the Divine Mind in creative activity, and can
study the archetypes of all the forms that are being
gradually evolved in the lower worlds. There he

may bathe himself in the fathomless ocean of the Divine Wisdom, and unravel the problems connected with the working out of those archetypes, the partial good that seems as evil to the limited vision of men encased in flesh. In this wider outlook, phenomena assume their due relative proportions, and he sees the justification of the divine ways, no longer to him " past finding out " so far as they are concerned with the evolution of the lower worlds. The questions over which on earth he pondered, and whose answers ever eluded his eager intellect, are here solved by an insight that pierces through phenomenal veils and sees the connecting links which make the chain complete. Here also the soul is in the immediate presence of, and in full communion with, the greater souls that have evolved in our humanity, and, escaped from the bonds which make " the past " of earth, he enjoys " the ever-present " of an endless and unbroken life. Those we speak of here as " the mighty dead " are there the glorious living, and the soul enjoys the high rapture of their presence, and grows more like them as their strong harmony attunes his vibrant nature to their key.

Yet higher, lovelier, gleams the seventh heaven, where the Masters and Initiates have their intellectual home. No soul can dwell there ere yet it has passed while on earth through the narrow gateway of Initiation, the strait gate that " leadeth unto life " unending.[1] That world is the source of the strongest intellectual and moral impulses that flow down to earth; thence are poured forth the invigorating streams of the loftiest energy. The intellectual life of the world has there its root; thence genius receives its purest inspirations. To the souls that dwell there it matters little whether, at the time, they be or be not connected with the lower vehicles; they ever enjoy their lofty self-consciousness and their communion with those around them; whether, when " embodied ", they suffuse their lower vehicles with as much of this consciousness as they can contain is a matter for their own choice—they can give or withhold as they will. And more and more their volitions are guided by the will of the Great Ones, whose will is one with the will of the Logos, the will which seeks ever the good of the worlds. For here are being eliminated the last vestiges of separateness [2] in all who have not yet reached final emancipation—all, that is, who are not yet Masters—and, as these perish, the will becomes more and more harmonized with the will that guides the worlds.

[1] See Chapter XI, on " Man's Ascent ". The Initiate has stepped out of the ordinary line of evolution, and is treading a shorter and steeper road to human perfection.

[2] Ahamkāra, the " I "-making principle, necessary in order that self-consciousness may be evolved, but transcended when its work is over.

Such is an outline of the " seven heavens " into one or other of which men pass in due time after the " change that men call death ". For death is only a change that gives the soul a partial liberation, releasing him from the heaviest of his chains. It is but a birth into a wider life, a return after brief exile on earth to the soul's true home, a passing from a prison into the freedom of the upper air. Death is the greatest of earth's illusions; there is no death, but only changes in life conditions. Life is continuous, unbroken, unbreakable; " unborn, eternal, ancient, constant "; it perishes not with the perishing of the bodies that clothe it. We might as well think that the sky is falling when a pot is broken, as imagine that the soul perishes when the body falls to pieces.[1]

The physical, astral, and mental planes are " the three worlds " through which lies the pilgrimage of the soul, again and again repeated. In these three worlds revolves the wheel of human life, and souls are bound to that wheel throughout their evolution, and are carried by it to each of these worlds in turn. We are now in a position to trace a complete life-period of the soul, the aggregate of these periods making up its life, and we can also distinguish

[1] A simile used in the *Bhagavad Purāna*.

clearly the difference between personality and individuality.

A soul when its stay in the formless world of Devachan is over, begins a new life-period by putting forth the energies which function in the form-world of the mental plane, these energies being the resultant of the preceding life-periods. These passing outwards, gather round themselves, from the matter of the four lower mental levels, such materials as are suitable for their expression, and thus the new mental body for the coming birth is formed. The vibration of these mental energies arouses the energies which belong to the desire-nature, and these begin to vibrate; as they awake and throb, they attract to themselves suitable materials for their expression from the matter of the astral world, and these form the new astral body for the approaching incarnation. Thus the Thinker becomes clothed with his mental and astral vestures, exactly expressing the faculties evolved during the past stages of his life. He is drawn, by forces which will be explained later,[1] to the family which is to provide him with a suitable physical encasement, and becomes connected with this encasement through his astral body. During pre-natal life the mental body becomes involved with the lower vehicles, and this connection becomes closer and

[1] See Chapter VII, on " Reincarnation ".

closer through the early years of childhood, until at the seventh year they are as completely in touch with the Thinker himself as the stage of evolution permits. He then begins to slightly control his vehicles, if sufficiently advanced, and what we call conscience is his monitory voice. In any case, he gathers experience through these vehicles, and during the continuance of earth-life, stores the gathered experience in its own proper vehicle, in the body connected with the plane to which the experience belongs. When the earth-life is over the physical body drops away, and with it his power of contacting the physical world, and his energies are therefore confined to the astral and mental planes. In due course, the astral body decays, and the outgoings of his life are confined to the mental plane, the astral faculties being gathered up and laid by within himself as latent energies. Once again, in due course, its assimilative work completed, the mental body disintegrates, its energies in turn becoming latent in the Thinker, and he withdraws his life entirely into the formless devachanic world, his own native habitat. Thence, all the experiences of his life-period in the three worlds being transmuted into faculties and powers for future use, and contained within himself, he anew commences his pilgrimage and treads the cycle of another life-period with increased power and knowledge.

The personality consists of the transitory vehicles through which the Thinker energizes in the physical, astral, and lower mental worlds, and of all the activities connected with these. These are bound together by the links of memory caused by impressions made on the three lower bodies; and, by the self-identification of the Thinker with his vehicles, the personal " I " is set up. In the lower stages of evolution this " I " is in the physical and passional vehicles, in which the greatest activity is shown, later it is in the mental vehicle, which then assumes predominance. The personality, with its transient feelings, desires, passions, thus forms a quasi-independent entity, though drawing all its energies from the Thinker it enwraps, and as its qualifications, belonging to the lower worlds, are often in direct antagonism to the permanent interests of the " Dweller in the body ", conflict is set up in which victory inclines sometimes to the temporary pleasure, sometimes to the permanent gain. The life of a personality begins when the Thinker forms his new mental body, and it endures until that mental body disintegrates at the close of its life in the form-world of Devachan.

The individuality consists of the Thinker himself, the immortal tree that put out all these personalities as leaves, to last through the spring, summer, and autumn of human life. All that the leaves take in and assimilate enriches the sap that courses through their veins, and in the autumn this is withdrawn into the parent trunk, and the dry leaf falls and perishes. The Thinker alone lives forever; he is the man for whom " the hour never strikes ", the eternal youth who, as the *Bhagavad Gītā* has it, puts on and casts off bodies as a man puts on new garments and throws off the old. Each personality is a new part for the immortal Actor, and he treads the stage of life over and over again, only in the life-drama each character he assumes is the child of the preceding ones and the father of those to come, so that the life-drama is a continuous history, the history of the Actor who plays the successive parts.

To the three worlds that we have studied is confined the life of the Thinker, while he is treading the earlier stages of human evolution. A time will come in the evolution of humanity when its feet will enter loftier realms, and reincarnation will be of the past. But while the wheel of birth and death is turning and man is bound thereon by desires that pertain to the three worlds, his life is led in these three regions.

To the realms that lie beyond we now may turn, albeit but little can be said of them that can be either useful or intelligible. Such little as may be said, however, is necessary for the outlining of the Ancient Wisdom.

CHAPTER VI

THE BUDDHIC AND NIRVĀNIC PLANES

WE have seen that man is an intelligent self-conscious entity, the Thinker, clad in bodies belonging to the lower mental, astral, and physical planes; we have now to study the Spirit which is his innermost Self, the source whence he proceeds.

The Divine Spirit, a ray from the LOGOS, partaking of His own essential Being, has the triple nature of the LOGOS Himself, and the evolution of man as man consists in the gradual manifestation of these three aspects, their development from latency into activity, man thus repeating in miniature the evolution of the universe. Hence he is spoken of as the microcosm, the universe being the macrocosm; he is called the mirror of the universe, the image, or reflection, of God; [1] and hence also the ancient axiom, " As above, so below ". It is this infolded Deity that is the guarantee of man's final triumph; this is the hidden motive power that makes evolution at once possible and inevitable, the upward-lifting

[1] " Let us make man in our image, after our likeness."—*Gen.* i, 26.

force that slowly overcomes every obstacle and every difficulty. It was this Presence that Matthew Arnold dimly sensed when he wrote of the " Power, not ourselves, that makes for righteousness ", but he erred in thinking " not ourselves ", for it is the very innermost Self of all—truly not our separated selves but our Self.[1]

This Self is the One, and hence is spoken of as the Monad,[2] and we shall need to remember that this Monad is the outbreathed life of the Logos, containing within itself germinally, or in a state of latency, all the divine powers and attributes. These powers are brought into manifestation by the impacts arising from contact with the objects of the universe into which the Monad is thrown; the friction caused by these gives rise to responsive thrills from the life subjected to their stimuli, and one by one the energies of the life pass from latency into activity. The human Monad—as it is called for the sake of distinction—shows, as we have already said, the three aspects of the Deity, being the perfect image of God, and in the human cycle these three aspects are developed one after the other. These aspects are the three great attributes of the

[1] Ātmā, the reflection of Paramātmā.

[2] It is called the Monad, whether it be the Monad of spirit-matter, Ātmā; or the Monad of form, Ātmā-Buddhi; or the human Monad, Ātmā-Buddhi-Manas. In each case it is a unit and acts as a unit, whether the unit be one-faced, two-faced or three-faced.

Divine Life as manifested in the universe, existence, bliss, and intelligence,[1] the three LOGOI severally showing these forth with all the perfection possible within the limits of manifestation. In man, these aspects are developed in the reversed order—intelligence, bliss, existence—" existence " implying the manifestation of the divine powers. In the evolution of man that we have so far studied we have been watching the development of the third aspect of the hidden Deity—the development of consciousness as intelligence. Manas, the Thinker, the human Soul, is the image of the Universal Mind, of the Third LOGOS, and all his long pilgrimage on the three lower planes is devoted to the evolution of this third aspect, the intellectual side of the divine nature in man. While this is proceeding, we may consider the other divine energies as rather brooding over the man, the hidden source of his life, than as actively developing their forces within him. They play within themselves, unmanifest. Still the preparation of these forces for manifestation is slowly proceeding; they are being roused from that unmanifested life that we speak of as latency by the ever-increasing energy of the vibrations of the intelligence, and the bliss-aspect begins to send outwards its first vibrations—faint pulsings of its

[1] Satchitānanda is often used in the Hindu Scriptures as the abstract name of Brahman, the Trimūrti being the concrete manifestations of these.

manifested life thrill forth. This bliss-aspect is named in the Theosophical terminology Buddhi, a name derived from the Sanskrit word for wisdom, and it belongs to the fourth, or buddhic, plane of our universe, the plane in which there is still duality, but where there is no separation. Words fail me to convey the idea, for words belong to the lower planes where duality and separation are ever connected, yet some approach to the idea may be gained. It is a state in which each is himself, with a clearness and vivid intensity which cannot be approached on lower planes, and yet in which each feels himself to include all others, to be one with them, inseparate and inseparable.[1] Its nearest analogy on earth is the condition between two persons who are united by a pure, intense love, which makes them feel as one person, causing them to think, feel, act, live as one, recognizing no barrier, no difference, no mine and thine, no separation.[2] It is a faint echo from this plane which makes men seek happiness by union between

[1] The reader should refer back to the Introduction, p. 40, and re-read the description given by Plotinus of this state, commencing: " They likewise see all things ". And he should note the phrases, " Each thing likewise is everything ", and " In each, however, a different quality predominates ".

[2] It is for this reason that the bliss of divine love has in many Scriptures been imaged by the profound love of husband and wife, as in the *Bhagavad Purāna* of the Hindus, the *Song of Solomon* of the Hebrews and Christians. This also is the love of the Sufi mystics, and indeed of all mystics.

themselves and the object of their desire, no matter what that object may be. Perfect isolation is perfect misery; to be stripped naked of everything, to be hanging in the void of space, in utter solitude, nothing anywhere save the lone individual, shut out from all, shut into the separated self—imagination can conceive no horror more intense. The antithesis to this is union, and perfect union is perfect bliss.

As this bliss-aspect of the Self begins to send outwards its vibrations, these vibrations, as on the planes below, draw round themselves the matter of the plane on which they are functioning, and thus is formed gradually the buddhic body, or bliss-body, as it is appropriately termed.[1] The only way in which the man can contribute to the building of this glorious form is by cultivating pure, unselfish, all-embracing, beneficient love, love that " seeketh not its own "—that is, love that is neither partial, nor seeks any return for its outflowing. This spontaneous outpouring of love is the most marked of the divine attributes, the love that gives everything, that asks nothing. Pure love brought the universe into being, pure love maintains it, pure love draws it upwards towards perfection, towards bliss. And wherever man pours out love on all

[1] The Ānandamayakosha, or bliss-sheath, of the Vedāntins. It is also the body of the sun, the solar body, of which a little is said in the Upanishads and elsewhere.

13

who need it, making no difference, seeking no return, from pure spontaneous joy in the outpouring, there that man is developing the bliss-aspect of the Deity within him, and is preparing that body of beauty and joy ineffable into which the Thinker will rise, casting away the limits of separateness, to find himself, and yet one with all that lives. This is " the house not made with hands, eternal in the heavens ", whereof wrote St. Paul, the great Christian Initiate; and he raised charity, pure love, above all other virtues, because by that alone can man on earth contribute to that glorious dwelling. For a similar reason is separateness called " the great heresy " by the Buddhist, and " union " is the goal of the Hindu; liberation is the escape from the limitations that keep us apart, and selfishness is the root-evil, the destruction whereof is the destruction of all pain.

The fifth plane, the nirvānic, is the plane of the highest human aspect of the God within us, and this aspect is named by Theosophists Ātmā, or the Self. It is the plane of pure existence, of divine powers in their fullest manifestation in our fivefold universe—what lies beyond on the sixth and seventh planes is hidden in the unimaginable light of God. This ātmic, or nirvānic, consciousness, the consciousness belonging to life on the fifth plane, is the consciousness attained by those lofty Ones, the first fruits of humanity, who have already completed the cycle of human evolution, and who are called Masters.[1] They have solved in Themselves the problem of uniting the essence of individuality with non-separateness, and live, immortal Intelligences, perfect in wisdom, in bliss, in power.

When the human Monad comes forth from the Logos, it is as though from the luminous ocean of Ātmā a tiny thread of light was separated off from the rest by a film of buddhic matter, and from this hung a spark which becomes enclosed in an egg-like casing of matter belonging to the formless levels of the mental plane. " The spark hangs from the flame by the finest thread of Fohat." [2] As evolution proceeds, this luminous egg grows larger and more opalescent, and the tiny thread becomes a wider and wider channel through which more and more of the ātmic life pours down. Finally, they merge —the third with the second, and the twain with the first, as flame merges with flame and no separation can be seen.

The evolution of the fourth and fifth planes belongs to a future period of our race, but those who

[1] Known also as Mahātmās, great Spirits and Jīvanmuktas, liberated souls, who remain connected with physical bodies for the helping forward of humanity. Many other great Beings also live on the nirvānic plane.

[2] Book of Dzyan, Stanza vii, 5; The Secret Doctrine, vol. i, p. 66, 1893 Edn.; vol. i, p. 98, Adyar Edn.

choose the harder path of swifter progress may tread it even now, as will be explained later.[1] On that path the bliss-body is quickly evolved, and a man begins to enjoy the consciousness of that loftier region, and knows the bliss which comes from the absence of separative barriers, the wisdom which flows in when the limits of the intellect are transcended. Then is the wheel escaped from, which binds the soul in the lower worlds, and then is the first foretaste of the liberty which is found perfected on the nirvānic plane.

The nirvānic consciousness is the antithesis of annihilation; it is existence raised to a vividness and intensity inconceivable to those who know only the life of the senses and the mind. As the farthing rushlight to the splendour of the sun at noon, so is the nirvānic to the earth-bound consciousness, and to regard it as annihilation because the limits of the earthly consciousness have vanished, is as though a man, knowing only the rushlight, should say that light could not exist without a wick immersed in tallow. That Nirvāna *is* has been borne witness to in the past in the Scriptures of the world by Those who enjoy it and live its glorious life, and is still borne witness to by others of our race who have climbed that lofty ladder of perfected humanity, and who remain in touch with earth that the feet of

[1] See Chapter XI, on " Man's Ascent ".

our ascending race may mount its rungs unfal-
teringly.

In Nirvāna dwell the mighty Beings who accomplished Their own human evolution in past universes, and who came forth with the LOGOS when
He manifested Himself to bring this universe into
existence. They are His Ministers in the administration of the worlds, the perfect agents of His will.
The Lords of all the hierarchies of the Gods, and
lower ministrants that we have seen working on the
lower planes have here Their abiding-place, for
Nirvāna is the heart of the universe, whence all its
life-currents proceed. Hence the Great Breath
comes forth, the life of all, and thither it is indrawn
when the universe has reached its term. There is
the Beatific Vision for which mystics long, there the
unveiled Glory, the Supreme Goal.

The Brotherhood of Humanity—nay, the Brotherhood of all things—has its sure foundation on the
spiritual planes, the ātmic and buddhic, for here
alone is unity, and here alone perfect sympathy is
found. The intellect is the separative principle in
man, that marks off the " I " from the " not-I ",
that is conscious of itself, and sees all else as outside
itself and alien. It is the combative, struggling,
self-assertive principle, and from the plane of the

intellect downwards the world presents a scene of conflict, bitter in proportion as the intellect mingles in it. Even the passion-nature is only spontaneously combative, when it is stirred by the feeling of desire and finds anything standing between itself and the object of its desire; it becomes more and more aggressive as the mind inspires its activity, for then it seeks to provide for the gratification of future desires, and tries to appropriate more and more from the stores of Nature. But the intellect is spontaneously combative, its very nature being to assert itself as different from others, and here we find the root of separateness, the ever-springing source of divisions among men.

But unity is at once felt when the buddhic plane is reached, as though we stepped from a separate ray, diverging from all other rays, into the sun itself, from which radiate all the rays alike. A being standing in the sun, suffused with its light, and pouring it forth, would feel no difference between ray and ray, but would pour forth along one as readily and easily as along another. And so with the man who has once consciously attained the buddhic plane; he *feels* the brotherhood that others speak of as an ideal, and pours himself out into any one who wants assistance, giving mental, moral, astral, physical help exactly as it is needed. He sees all beings as himself, and feels that all he has is theirs as much as his; nay, in many cases, as more theirs than his, because their need is greater, their strength being less. So do the elder brothers in a family bear the family burdens, and shield the little ones from suffering and privation; to the spirit of brotherhood weakness is a claim for help and loving protection, not an opportunity for oppression. Because They had reached this level and mounted even higher, the great Founders of religions have ever been marked by Their everwelling compassion and tenderness, ministering to the physical as well as to the inner wants of men, to every man according to his need. The consciousness of this inner unity, the recognition of the One Self dwelling equally in all, is the one sure foundation of Brotherhood; all else save this is frangible.

This recognition, moreover, is accompanied by the knowledge that the stage in evolution reached by different human and non-human beings depends chiefly on what we may call their age. Some began their journey in time very much later than others, and, though the powers in each be the same, some have unfolded far more of those powers than others, simply because they have had a longer time for the process than their younger brethren. As well blame and despise the seed because it is not yet the flower, the bud because it is not yet the fruit, the babe because it is not yet the man, as blame and despise the germinal or baby souls around us because they have not yet developed to the stage we ourselves occupy. We do not blame ourselves because we are not yet as Gods; in time we shall stand where our Elder Brothers are standing. Why should we blame the still younger souls who are not yet as we? The very word brotherhood connotes identity of blood and inequality of development; and it therefore represents exactly the link between all creatures in the universe—identity of essential life, and differences in the stages reached in the manifestation of that life. We are one in our origin, one in the method of our evolution, one in our goal, and the differences of our age and stature but give opportunity for the growth of the tenderest and closest ties. All that a man would do for his brother of the flesh, dearer to him than himself, is the measure of what he owes to each who shares with him the one Life. Men are shut out from their brothers' hearts by differences of race, of class, of country; the man who is wise by love rises above all these petty differences, and sees all drawing their life from the one source, all as part of his family.

The recognition of this Brotherhood intellectually, and the endeavour to live it practically, are so stimulative of the higher nature of man, that it was made the one obligatory object of the Theosophical

Society, the single "article of belief" that all who would enter its fellowship must accept. To live it, even to a small extent, cleanses the heart and purifies the vision; to live it perfectly would be to eradicate all stain of separateness and to let the pure shining of the Self irradiate us, as a light through flawless glass.

Never let it be forgotten that this Brotherhood *is*, whether men ignore it or deny it. Man's ignorance does not change the laws of Nature, nor vary by one hair's breadth her changeless, irresistible march. Her laws crush those who oppose them, and break into pieces everything which is not in harmony with them. Therefore can no nation endure that outrages Brotherhood, no civilization can last that is built on its antithesis. We have not to make Brotherhood; it exists. We have to attune our lives into harmony with it, if we desire that we and our works shall not perish.

It may seem strange to some that the buddhic plane—a thing to them misty and unreal—should thus influence all planes below it, and that its forces should ever break into pieces all that cannot harmonize itself with them in the lower worlds. Yet so it is, for this universe is an expression of spiritual forces, and they are the guiding, moulding energies pervading all things, and slowly, surely subduing all things to themselves. Hence this Brotherhood, which is a spiritual unity, is a far more real thing than any outward organization; it is a life and not a form, " wisely and sweetly ordering all things ". It may take innumerable forms, suitable to the times, but the life is one; happy they who see its presence, and make themselves the channels of its living force.

———

The student has now before him the constituents of the human constitution, and the regions to which these constituents respectively belong; so a brief summary should enable him to have a clear idea of this complicated whole.

The human Monad is Ātmā-Buddhi-Manas, or, as sometimes translated, the Spirit, Spiritual Soul, and Soul, of man. The fact that these three are but aspects of the Self makes possible man's immortal existence, and though these three aspects are manifested separately and successively, their substantial unity renders it possible for the Soul to merge itself in the Spiritual Soul, giving to the latter the precious essence of individuality, and for this individualized Spiritual Soul to merge itself in the Spirit, colouring it—if the phrase may be permitted—with the hues due to individuality while leaving uninjured its essential unity with all other rays of Logos and

with the Logos Himself. These three form the
seventh, sixth, and fifth principles of man, and the
materials which limit or encase them, *i.e.*, which
make their manifestation and activity possible, are
drawn respectively from the fifth (nirvānic), the
fourth (buddhic), and the third (mental) planes of
our universe. The fifth principle further takes to
itself a lower body on the mental plane, in order to
come into contact with the phenomenal worlds, and
thus intertwines itself with the fourth principle, the
desire-nature, or Kāma, belonging to the second or
astral plane. Descending to the first, the physical,
plane, we have the third, second and first principles
—the specialized life, or Prāna, the etheric double,
its vehicle; the dense body, which contacts the
coarser materials of the physical world. We have
already seen that sometimes Prāna is not regarded
as a " principle ", and then the interwoven desire
and mental bodies take rank together as Kāma-
Manas; the pure intellect is called the Higher
Manas, and the mind apart from desire, Lower
Manas. The most convenient conception of man is
perhaps that which most closely represents the facts
as to the one permanent life and the various forms
in which it works and which condition its energies,
causing the variety in manifestation. Then we
see the Self as the one Life, the source of all
energies, and the forms as the buddhic, causal

mental, astral, and physical (etheric and dense) bodies.[1]

Putting together the two ways of looking at the same thing, we may construct a table:

PRINCIPLES	LIFE	FORMS
Ātmā. Spirit	Ātmā	Bliss-Body
Buddhi. Spiritual Soul		Causal Body
Higher Manas ⎱ Human Soul Lower Manas ⎰		Mental Body
Kāma. Animal Soul		Astral Body
Linga Sharīra [2]		Etheric Double
Sthūla Sharīra		Dense Body

It will be seen that the difference is merely a question of names, and that the sixth, fifth, fourth, and third " principles " are merely Ātmā working in the buddhic, causal, mental, and astral bodies, while the second and first " principles " are the two lowest bodies themselves.   This sudden change in

---

[1] Those of our readers who are more familiar with the Vedāntic classification may find the following table of the form-side useful:

Buddhic body	Ānandamayakosha.
Causal body	Vijnyānamayakosha.
Mental body ⎱ Astral body ⎰	Manomayakosha.
Physical body ⎰ etheric	Prānamayakosha.
⎱ dense	Annamayakosha.

[2] Linga Sharīra was the name originally given to the etheric body and must not be confused with the Linga Sharīra of Hindu philosophy. Sthūla Sharīra is the Sanskrit name for the dense body.

the method of naming is apt to cause confusion in the mind of the student, and as H. P. Blavatsky, our revered teacher, expressed much dissatisfaction with the then current nomenclature as confused and misleading, and desired others and myself to try and improve it, the above names, as descriptive, simple, and representing the facts, are here adopted.

The various subtle bodies of man that we have now studied form in their aggregate what is usually called the " aura " of the human being. This aura has the appearance of an egg-shaped luminous cloud, in the midst of which is the dense physical body, and from its appearance it has often been spoken of as though it were nothing more than such a cloud. What is usually called the aura is merely such parts of the subtle bodies as extend beyond the periphery of the dense physical body; each body is complete in itself, and interpenetrates those that are coarser than itself; it is larger or smaller according to its development, and all that part of it that over-laps the surface of the dense physical body is termed the aura. The aura is thus composed of the over-lapping portions of the etheric double, the desire body, the mental body, the causal body, and in rare cases the buddhic body, illuminated by the ātmic radiance. It is sometimes dull, coarse, and dingy; sometimes magnificently radiant in size, light, and colour; it depends entirely on the stage of evolution

reached by the man, on the development of his
different bodies, on the moral and mental character
he has evolved.   All his varying passions, desires,
and thoughts are herein written in form, in colour,
in light, so that " he that runs may read " if he
have eyes for such script.   Character is stamped
thereon as well as fleeting changes, and no decep-
tion is there possible as in the mask we call the
physical body.   The increase in size and beauty of
the aura is the unmistakable mark of the man's
progress, and tells of the growth and purification of
the Thinker and his vehicles.

CHAPTER VII

REINCARNATION

WE are now in a position to study one of the pivotal doctrines of the Ancient Wisdom, the doctrine of reincarnation. Our view of it will be clearer and more in congruity with natural order, if we look at it as universal in principle, and then consider the special case of the reincarnation of the human soul. In studying it, this special case is generally wrenched from its place in natural order, and is considered as a dislocated fragment, greatly to its detriment. For all evolution consists of an evolving life, passing from form to form as it evolves, and storing up in itself the experience gained through the forms; the reincarnation of the human soul is not the introduction of a new principle into evolution, but the adaptation of the universal principle to meet the conditions rendered necessary by the individualization of the continuously evolving life.

Mr. Lafcadio Hearn [1] has put this point well in considering the bearing of the idea of

[1] Mr. Hearn has lost his way in expression—but not, I think, in his inner view—in part of his exposition of the Buddhist statement of this doctrine, and his use of the word " Ego " will mislead the reader of his very interesting chapter on this subject, if the

pre-existence on the scientific thought of the West.

He says:

With the acceptance of the doctrine of evolution, old forms of thought crumbled; new ideas everywhere arose to take the place of worn-out dogmas; and we now have the spectacle of a general intellectual movement in directions strangely parallel with Oriental philosophy. The unprecedented rapidity and multiformity of scientific progress during the last fifty years could not have failed to provoke an equally unprecedented intellectual quickening among the non-scientific. That the highest and most complex organisms have been developed from the lowest and simplest; that a single physical basis of life is the substance of the whole living world; that no line of separation can be drawn between the animal and vegetable; that the difference between life and non-life is only a difference of degree, not of kind; that matter is not less incomprehensible than mind, while both are but varying manifestations of one and the same unknown reality— these have already become the commonplaces of the new philosophy. After the first recognition even by theology of physical evolution, it was easy to predict that the recognition of physical evolution could not be indefinitely delayed; for the barrier erected by old dogma to keep men from looking backward had been broken down. And to-day for the student of scientific psychology the idea of pre-existence passes out of the realm of theory into the realm of fact, proving the Buddhist explanation of the universal mystery quite as plausible as any other. "None but very hasty thinkers," wrote the late Professor Huxley, "will reject it on the ground of inherent absurdity. Like the doctrine of evolution itself, that of transmigration has its roots in the world of reality; and it may claim distinction between the real and the illusory ego is not steadily kept in mind.

such support as the great argument from analogy is capable of supplying." (*Evolution of Ethics*, p. 61, ed., 1894) [1]

Let us consider the Monad of form, Ātma-Buddhi. In this Monad, the outbreathed life of the Logos, lie hidden all the divine powers, but, as we have seen, they are latent, not manifest and functioning. They are to be gradually aroused by external impacts, it being of the very nature of life to vibrate in answer to vibrations that play upon it. As all possibilities of vibrations exist in the Monad, any vibrations touching it will arouse its corresponding vibratory power, and in this way one force after another will pass from the latent to the active [2] state. Herein lies the secret of evolution; the environment acts on the form of the living creature —and all things, be it remembered, live—and this action, transmitted through the enveloping form to the life, the Monad, within it, arouses responsive vibrations which thrill outwards from the Monad through the form, throwing its particles, in turn, into vibrations, and rearranging them into a shape corresponding, or adapted, to the initial impact. This is the action and reaction between the environment and the organism, which have been recognized by all biologists, and which are considered by some

---

[1] *Kokoro, Hints and Echoes of Japanese Inner Life*. By Lafcadio Hearn, pp. 237-239 (London, 1896).

[2] From the static to the kinetic condition, the physicist would say.

14

as giving a sufficient mechanical explanation of evolution. Their patient and careful observation of these actions and reactions yields, however, no explanation as to why the organism should thus react to stimuli, and the Ancient Wisdom is needed to unveil the secret of evolution, by pointing to the Self in the heart of all forms, the hidden mainspring of all the movements in Nature.

Having grasped this fundamental idea of a life containing the possibility of responding to every vibration that can reach it from the external universe, the actual response being gradually drawn forth by the play upon it of external forces, the next fundamental idea to be grasped is that of the continuity of life and forms. Forms transmit their peculiarities to other forms that proceed from them, these other forms being part of their own substance, separated off to lead an independent existence. By fission, by budding, by extrusion of germs, by development of the offspring within the maternal womb, a physical continuity is preserved, every new form being derived from a preceding form and reproducing its characteristics.[1] Science groups these facts under the name of the law of heredity, and its observations on the transmission of form are worthy of attention, and are illuminative of the workings of

[1] The student might wisely familiarize himself with the researches of Weissman on the continuity of germ-plasm.

Nature in the phenomenal world. But it must be remembered that it applies only to the building of the physical body, into which enter the materials provided by the parents.

Her more hidden workings, those workings of life without which form could not be, have received no attention, not being susceptible of physical observation, and this gap can only be filled by the teachings of the Ancient Wisdom, given by Those who of old used superphysical powers of observation, and verifiable gradually by every pupil who studies patiently in Their schools.

There is continuity of life as well as continuity of form, and it is the continuing life—with ever more and more of its latent energies rendered active by the stimuli received through successive forms—which resumes into itself the experiences obtained by its incasings in form; for when the form perishes, the life has the record of those experiences in the increased energies aroused by them, and is ready to pour itself into the new forms derived from the old, carrying with it this accumulated store. While it was in the previous form, it played through it adapting it to express each newly awakened energy; the form hands on these adaptations, inwrought into its substance, to the separated part of itself that we speak of as its offspring, which, being of its substance, must needs have the peculiarities of that substance; the life pours itself into that offspring with all its awakened powers, and moulds it yet further; and so on and on. Modern science is proving more and more clearly that heredity plays an ever-decreasing part in the evolution of the higher creatures, that mental and moral qualities are not transmitted from parents to offspring, and that the higher the qualities the more patent is this fact; the child of a genius is ofttimes a dolt; commonplace parents give birth to a genius. A continuing substratum there must be, in which mental and moral qualities inhere, in order that they may increase, else would Nature, in this most important department of her work, show erratic uncaused production instead of orderly continuity. On this science is dumb, but the Ancient Wisdom teaches that this continuing substratum is the Monad, which is the receptacle of all results, the storehouse in which all experiences are garnered as increasingly active powers.

These two principles firmly grasped—of the Monad with potentialities becoming powers, and of the continuity of life and form—we can proceed to study their working out in detail, and we shall find that they solve many of the perplexing problems of modern science, as well as the yet more heart-searching problems confronted by the philanthropist and the sage.

Let us start by considering the Monad as it is first subjected to the impacts from the formless levels of the mental plane, the very beginning of the evolution of form. Its first faint responsive thrillings draw round it some of the matter of that plane, and we have the gradual evolution of the First Elemental Kingdom, already mentioned.[1] The great fundamental types of the Monad are seven in number, sometimes imaged as like the seven colours of the solar spectrum, derived from the three primary.[2] Each of these types has its own colouring of characteristics, and this colouring persists throughout the æonian cycle of its evolution, affecting all the series of living things that are animated by it. Now begins the process of subdivision in each of these types, that will be carried on, subdividing and ever subdividing, until the individual is reached. The current set up by the commencing outward-going energies of the Monad—to follow one line of evolution will suffice; the other six are like unto it in principle—have but brief form-life, yet whatever experience can be gained through them is represented by an increasedly responsive life in the Monad who is their source and cause; and as this

[1] See Chapter IV, on " The Mental Plane ".

[2] " As above, so below." We instinctively remember three LOGOI and the seven primeval Sons of the Fire; in Christian Symbolism, the Trinity and the " Seven Spirits that are before the throne "; or in Zoroastrian, Ahuramazda and the seven Ameshaspentas.

responsive life consists of vibrations that are often incongruous with each other, a tendency towards separation is set up within the Monad, the harmoniously vibrating forces grouping themselves together for, as it were, concerted action, until various sub-Monads, if the epithet may for a moment be allowed, are formed, alike in their main characteristics, but differing in details, like shades of the same colour. These become, by impacts from the lower levels of the mental plane, the Monads of the Second Elemental Kingdom, belonging to the form-region of that plane, and the process continues, the Monad ever adding to its power to respond, each Monad being the inspiring life of countless forms, through which it receives vibrations, and, as the forms disintegrate, constantly vivifying new forms; the process of subdivision also continues from the cause already described. Each Monad thus continually incarnates itself in forms, and garners within itself as awakened powers all the results obtained through the forms it animates. We may well regard these Monads as the souls of groups of forms; and as evolution proceeds, these forms show more and more attributes, the attributes being the powers of the monadic group-soul manifested through the forms in which it is incarnated. The innumerable sub-Monads of this Second Elemental Kingdom presently reach a stage of evolution at which they begin to respond to the vibrations of astral matter, and they begin to act on the astral plane, becoming the Monads of the Third Elemental Kingdom, and repeating in this grosser world all the processes already accomplished on the mental plane. They become more and more numerous as monadic group-souls, showing more and more diversity in detail, the number of forms animated by each becoming less as the specialized characteristics become more and more marked. Meanwhile, it may be said in passing, the everflowing stream of life from the Logos supplies new Monads of form on the higher levels, so that the evolution proceeds continuously, and as the more-evolved Monads incarnate in the lower worlds their place is taken by the newly emerged Monads in the higher.

By this ever-repeated process of the reincarnation of the Monads, or monadic group-souls, in the astral worlds, their evolution proceeds, until they are ready to respond to the impacts upon them from physical matter. When we remember that the ultimate atoms of each plane have their sphere-walls composed of the coarsest matter of the plane immediately above it, it is easy to see how the Monads become responsive to the impacts from one plane after another. When, in the First Elemental Kingdom, the Monad had become accustomed to

thrill responsively to the impacts of the matter of
that plane, it would soon begin to answer to vibrations received *through the coarsest forms of that matter*
from the matter of the plane next below. So, in
its coatings of matter that were the forms composed
of the coarsest materials of the mental plane, it
would become susceptible to vibrations of astral
atomic matter; and, when incarnated in forms of
the coarsest astral matter, it would similarly become
responsive to the impacts of atomic physical ether,
the sphere-walls of which are constituted of the
grossest astral materials. Thus the Monad may be
regarded as reaching the physical plane; and there
it begins, or, more accurately, all these monadic
group-souls begin to incarnate themselves in filmy
physical forms, the etheric doubles of the future
dense minerals of the physical world. Into these
filmy forms the nature-spirits build the denser
physical materials, and thus minerals of all kinds
are formed, the most rigid vehicles in which the
evolving life incloses itself, and through which the
least of its powers can express themselves. Each
monadic group-soul has its own mineral expressions,
the mineral forms in which it is incarnated, and the
specialization has now reached a high degree. These
monadic group-souls are sometimes called in their
totality the mineral Monad, or the Monad incarnating in the mineral kingdom.

From this time forward the awakened energies of the Monad play a less passive part in evolution. They begin to seek expression actively to some extent when once aroused into functioning, and to exercise a distinctly moulding influence over the forms in which they are imprisoned. As they become too active for their mineral embodiment, the beginnings of the more plastic forms of the vegetable kingdom manifest themselves, the nature-spirits aiding this evolution throughout the physical kingdoms. In the mineral kingdom there had already been shown a tendency towards the definite organization of form, the laying down of certain lines [1] along which the growth proceeded. This tendency governs henceforth all the building of forms, and is the cause of the exquisite symmetry of natural objects, with which every observer is familiar. The monadic group-souls in the vegetable kingdom undergo division and subdivision with increasing rapidity, in consequence of the still greater variety of impacts to which they are subjected, the evolution of families, genera, and species being due to this invisible subdivision. When any genus, with its generic monadic group-soul, is subjected to very varying conditions, *i.e.*, when the forms connected with it receive very different

[1] The axes of growth, which determine form. They appear definitely in crystals.

impacts, a fresh tendency to subdivide is set up in the Monad, and various species are evolved, each having its own specific monadic group-soul. When Nature is left to her own working the process is slow, although the nature-spirits do much towards the differentiation of species; but when man has been evolved, and when he begins his artificial systems of cultivation, encouraging the play of one set of forces, warding off another, then this differentiation can be brought about with considerable rapidity, and specific differences are readily evolved. So long as actual division has not taken place in the monadic group-soul, the subjection of the forms to similar influences may again eradicate the separative tendency but when that division is completed the new species are definitely and firmly established, and are ready to send out offshoots of their own.

In some of the longer-lived members of the vegetable kingdom the element of personality begins to manifest itself, the stability of the organism rendering possible this foreshadowing of individuality. With a tree, living for scores of years, the recurrence of similar conditions causing similar impacts, the seasons ever returning year after year, the consecutive internal motions caused by them, the rising of the sap, the putting forth of leaves, the touches of the wind, of the sunbeams, of the rain—all these outer influences with their rhythmical progression

—set up responsive thrillings in the monadic group-soul, and as the sequence impresses itself by continual repetition, the recurrence of one leads to the dim expectation of its oft-repeated successor. Nature evolves no quality suddenly, and these are the first faint adumbrations of what will later be memory and anticipation.

In the vegetable kingdom also appear the fore-shadowings of sensation, evolving in its higher members to what the Western psychologist would term " massive " sensations of pleasure and discomfort.[1] It must be remembered that the Monad has drawn round itself materials of the planes through which it has descended, and hence is able to contact impacts from those planes, the strongest and those most nearly allied to the grossest forms of matter being the first to make themselves felt. Sunshine and the chill of its absence at last impress themselves on the monadic consciousness; and its astral coating, thrown into faint vibrations, gives rise to the slight massive kind of sensation spoken of. Rain and drought affecting the mechanical constitution of the form, and its power to convey vibrations to the ensouling Monad are another of the " pairs of opposites ", the play of which arouses the recognition of difference, which is the root alike of all sensation,

---

[1] The " massive " sensation is one that pervades the organism and is not felt especially in any one part more than in others. It is the antithesis of the " acute ".

and later of all thought. Thus by their repeated plant-reincarnations the monadic group-souls in the vegetable kingdom evolve, until those that ensoul the highest members of the kingdom are ready for the next step.

This step carries them into the animal kingdom, and here they slowly evolve in their physical and astral vehicles a very distinct personality. The animal, being free to move about, subjects itself to a greater variety of conditions than can be experienced by the plant, rooted to a single spot, and this variety, as ever, promotes differentiation. The monadic group-soul, however, which animates a number of wild animals of the same species or sub-species, while it receives a great variety of impacts, since they are for the most part repeated continually and are shared by all the members of the group, differentiates but slowly.

These impacts aid in the development of the physical and astral bodies, and through them the monadic group-soul gathers much experience. When the form of a member of the group perishes, the experience gathered through that form is accumulated in the monadic group-soul, and may be said to colour it; the slightly increased life of the monadic group-soul, poured into all the forms which compose its group, shares among all the experience of the perished form, and in this way continually repeated experiences, stored up in the monadic group-soul, appear as instincts, " accumulated hereditary experiences " in the new forms. Countless birds having fallen a prey to hawks, chicks just out of the egg will cower at the approach of one of the hereditary enemies, for the life that is incarnated in them knows the danger, and the innate instinct is the expression of its knowledge. In this way are formed the wonderful instincts that guard animals from innumerable habitual perils, while a new danger finds them unprepared and only bewilders them.

As animals come under the influence of man, the monadic group-soul evolves with greatly increased rapidity, and, from causes similar to those which affect plants under domestication, subdivision of the incarnating life is more readily brought about. Personality evolves and becomes more and more strongly marked; in the earlier stages it may almost be said to be compound—a whole flock of wild creatures will act as though moved by a single personality, so completely are the forms dominated by the common soul, it, in turn, being affected by the impulses from the external world. Domesticated animals of the higher types, the elephant, the horse, the cat, the dog, show a more individualized personality—two dogs, for instance, may act very differently under the impact of the same circumstances.

The monadic group-soul incarnates in a decreasing number of forms as it gradually approaches the point at which complete individualization will be reached. The desire-body, or kāmic vehicle, becomes considerably developed, and persists for some time after the death of the physical body, leading an independent existence in kāma-loka. At last the decreasing number of forms animated by a monadic group-soul comes down to unity, and it animates a succession of single forms —a condition differing from human reincarnation only by the absence of Manas, with its causal and mental bodies. The mental matter brought down by the monadic group-soul begins to be susceptible to impacts from the mental plane, and the animal is then ready to receive the third great outpouring of the life of the Logos—the tabernacle is ready for the reception of the human Monad.

The human Monad is, as we have seen, triple in its nature, its three aspects being denominated, respectively, the Spirit, the spiritual Soul, and the human Soul: Ātmā, Buddhi, Manas. Doubtless, in the course of aeons of evolution, the upwardly evolving Monad of form might have unfolded Manas by progressive growth, but both in the human race in the past, and in the animals of the present, such has not been the course of Nature. When the house was ready the tenant was sent down: from the higher planes of being the ātmic life descended, veiling itself in Buddhi, as a golden thread; and its third aspect, Manas, showing itself in the higher levels of the formless world of the mental plane, germinal Manas within the form was fructified, and the embryonic causal body was formed by the union. This is the individualization of the spirit, the incasing of it in form, and this spirit incased in the causal body is the soul, the individual, the real man. This is his birth-hour; for though his essence be eternal, unborn and undying, his birth in time as an individual is definite.

Further, this outpoured life reaches the evolving forms not directly but by intermediaries. The human race having attained the point of receptivity, certain great Ones, called Sons of Mind,[1] cast into men the monadic spark of Ātmā-Buddhi-Manas, needed for the formation of the embryonic soul. And some of these great Ones actually incarnated in human forms, in order to become the guides and teachers of the infant humanity. These Sons of Mind had completed Their own intellectual evolution in other worlds, and came to this younger world, our earth, for the purpose of thus aiding in the evolution of the human race. They are, in truth, the spiritual fathers of the bulk of our humanity.

---

[1] Mānasa-putra is the technical name, being merely the Sanskrit for Sons of Mind.

Other intelligences of much lower grace, men who had evolved in preceding cycles in another world, incarnated among the descendants of the race that received its infant souls in the way just described. As this race evolved, the human taber-nacles improved, and myriads of souls that were awaiting the opportunity of incarnation, that they might continue their evolution, took birth among its children. These partially evolved souls are also spoken of in the ancient records as Sons of Mind, for they were possessed of mind, although compar-atively it was but little developed—childish souls we may call them, in distinguishment from the embryonic souls of the bulk of humanity, and the mature souls of the great Teachers. These child-souls, by reason of their more evolved intelligence, formed the leading types of the ancient world, the classes higher in mentality, and therefore in the power of acquiring knowledge, that dominated the masses of less developed men in antiquity. And thus arose, in our world, the enormous differences in mental and moral capacity which separate the most highly evolved from the least evolved races, and which, even within the limits of a single race, separate the lofty philosophic thinker from the well-nigh animal type of the most depraved of his own nation. These differences are but differences of the stage of evolution, of the age of the soul, and they

have been found to exist throughout the whole
history of humanity on this globe. Go back as far
as we may in historic records, and we may find lofty
intelligence and debased ignorance side by side,
and the occult records, carrying us backwards, tell
a similar story of the early millennia of humanity.
Nor should this distress us, as though some had
been unduly favoured and others unduly burdened
for the struggle of life. The loftiest soul had its
childhood and its infancy, albeit in previous worlds,
where other souls were as high above it as others
are below it now; the lowest soul shall climb to
where our highest are standing, and souls yet
unborn shall occupy its present place in evolution.
Things seem unjust because we wrench our world
out of its place in evolution, and set it apart in
isolation, with no forerunners and no successors.
It is our ignorance that sees the injustice; the ways
of Nature are equal, and she brings to all her
children infancy, childhood, and manhood. Nor
hers the fault if our folly demands that all souls
shall occupy the same stage of evolution at the same
time, and cries " Unjust! " if the demand be not
fulfilled.

We shall best understand the evolution of the
soul, if we take it up at the point where we left it,
when animal-man was ready to receive, and did
receive, the embryonic soul. To avoid a possible

15

misapprehension, it may be well to say that there were not henceforth two Monads in man—the one that had built the human tabernacle, and the one that descended into that tabernacle, and whose lowest aspect was the human soul. To borrow a simile again from H. P. Blavatsky, as two rays of the sun may pass through a hole in a shutter, and mingling together form but one ray though they had been twain, so is it with these rays from the Supreme Sun, the divine Lord of our universe. The second ray, as it entered into the human tabernacle, blended with the first, merely adding to it fresh energy and brilliance, and the human Monad, *as a unit*, began its mighty task of unfolding the higher powers in man of that divine Life whence it came.

The embryonic soul, the Thinker, had at the beginning for its embryonic mental body the mind-stuff envelope that the Monad of form had brought with it, but had not yet organized into any possibility of functioning. It was the mere germ of a mental body, attached to a mere germ of a causal body, and for many a life the strong desire-nature had its will with the soul, whirling it along the road of its own passions and appetites and dashing up against it all the furious waves of its own uncontrolled animality. Repulsive as this early life of the soul may at first seem to some when looked at from the higher stage that we have now attained, it was a necessary one for the germination of the seeds of mind. Recognition of difference, the perception that one thing is different from another, is a preliminary essential to thinking at all. And, in order to awaken this perception in the as yet unthinking soul, strong and violent contrasts had to strike upon it, so as to force their differences upon it—blow after blow of riotous pleasure, blow after blow of crushing pain. The external world hammered on the soul through the desire nature, till perceptions began to be slowly made, and, after countless repetitions, to be registered. The little gains made in each life were stored up by the Thinker, as we have already seen, and thus slow progress was made.

Slow progress, indeed, for scarcely anything was *thought*, and hence scarcely anything was done in the way of organizing the mental body. Not until many perceptions had been registered in it as mental images was there any material on which mental action, initiated from within, could be based; this would begin when two or more of these mental images were drawn together, and some inference, however elementary, was made from them. That inference was the beginning of reasoning, the germ of all the systems of logic which the intellect of man has since evolved or assimilated. These inferences would at first all be made in the service of the desire-nature, for the increasing of pleasure, the lessening of pain; but each one would increase the activity of the mental body, and would stimulate it into more ready functioning.

It will readily be seen that at this period of his infancy man had no knowledge of good or of evil; right and wrong had for him no existence. The right is that which is in accordance with the divine will, which helps forward the progress of the soul, which tends to the strengthening of the higher nature of man and to the training and subjugation of the lower; the wrong is that which retards evolution, which retains the soul in the lower stages after he has learned the lessons they have to teach, which tends to the mastery of the lower nature over the higher, and assimilates man to the brute he should be outgrowing instead of to the God he should be evolving. Ere man could know what was right he had to learn the existence of law, and this he could only learn by following all that attracted him in the outer world, by grasping at every desirable object, and then by learning from experience, sweet or bitter, whether his delight was in harmony or in conflict with the law. Let us take an obvious example, the taking of pleasant food, and see how infant man might learn therefrom the presence of a natural law. At the first taking, his hunger was appeased, his taste was gratified, and only pleasure resulted from the experience, for his action was in harmony with law. On another occasion, desiring to increase pleasure, he ate overmuch and suffered in consequence, for he transgressed against the law. A confusing experience to the dawning intelligence, how the pleasurable became painful by excess. Over and over again he would be led by desire into excess, and each time he would experience the painful consequences, until at last he learned moderation, *i.e.*, he learned to conform his bodily acts in this respect to physical law; for he found that there were conditions which affected him and which he could not control, and that only by observing them could physical happiness be insured. Similar experiences flowed in upon him through all the bodily organs, with undeviating regularity; his outrushing desires brought him pleasure or pain just as they worked with the laws of Nature or against them, and, as experience increased, it began to guide his steps, to influence his choice. It was not as though he had to begin his experience anew with every life, for on each new birth he brought with him mental faculties a little increased, an ever-accumulating store.

I have said that the growth in these early days was very slow, for there was but the dawning of mental action, and when the man left his physical body at death he passed most of his time in Kāma-loka, sleeping through a brief devachanic period of unconscious assimilation of any minute mental experiences not yet sufficiently developed for the active heavenly life that lay before him after many days. Still, the enduring causal body was there, to be the receptacle of his qualities, and to carry them on for further development into his next life on earth. The part played by the monadic group-soul in the earlier stages of evolution is played in man by the causal body, and it is this continuing entity who, in all cases, makes evolution possible. Without him, the accumulation of mental and moral experiences, shown as faculties, would be as impossible as would be the accumulation of physical experiences, shown as racial and family characteristics without the continuity of physical plasm. Souls without a past behind them, springing suddenly into existence, out of nothing, with marked mental and moral peculiarities, are a conception as monstrous as would be the corresponding conception of babies suddenly appearing from nowhere, unrelated to anybody, but showing marked racial and family types. Neither the man nor his physical vehicle is uncaused, or caused by the direct creative power of the Logos; here, as in so many other cases, the invisible things are clearly seen by their analogy with the visible, the visible being, in very truth, nothing more than the images, the reflections, of things unseen. Without a continuity in the physical plasm, there would be no means for the evolution of physical peculiarities; without the continuity of the intelligence, there would be no means for the evolution of mental and moral qualities. In both cases, without continuity, evolution would be stopped at its first stage, and the world would be a chaos of infinite and isolated beginnings instead of a cosmos continually becoming.

We must not omit to notice that in these early days much variety is caused in the type and in the nature of individual progress by the environment which surrounds the individual. Ultimately all the souls have to develop all their powers, but the order in which these powers are developed depends on the circumstances amid which the soul is placed. Climate, the fertility or sterility of Nature, the life of the mountain or of the plain, of the inland forest or the ocean shore—these things and countless others will call into activity one set or another of the awakening mental energies. A life of extreme hardship, of ceaseless struggle with Nature, will develop very different powers from those evolved amid the luxuriant plenty of a tropical island; both sets of powers are needed, for the soul is to conquer every region of Nature, but striking differences may thus be evolved even in souls of the same age, and one may appear to be more advanced than the other, according as the observer estimates most highly the more " practical " or the more " contemplative " powers of the soul, the active outward-going energies, or the quiet inward-turned musing faculties. The perfected soul possesses all, but the soul in the making must develop them successively, and thus arises another cause of the immense variety found among human beings.

For again, it must be remembered that human evolution is individual. In a group informed by a single monadic group-soul the same instincts will be found in all, for the receptacle of the experiences is that monadic group-soul, and it pours its life into all the forms dependent upon it. But each man has his own physical vehicle and one only at a time, and the receptacle of all experiences is the causal body, which pours its life into its one physical vehicle, and can affect no other physical vehicle, being connected with none other. Hence we find differences separating individual men greater than ever separated closely allied animals, and hence also the evolution of qualities cannot be studied in men in the mass, but only in the continuing individual. The lack of power to make such a study leaves science unable to explain why some men tower above their fellows, intellectual and moral giants, unable to trace the intellectual evolution of a Shankarāchārya or a Pythagoras, the moral evolution of a Buddha or of a Christ.

Let us now consider the factors in reincarnation, as a clear understanding of these is necessary for the explanation of some of the difficulties—such as the alleged loss of memory—which are felt by those unfamiliar with the idea. We have seen that man, during his passage through physical death, Kāma-loka and Devachan, loses, one after the other, his various bodies, the physical, the astral, and the mental. These are all disintegrated, and their particles re-mix with the materials of their several planes. The connection of the man with the phys-ical vehicle is entirely broken off and done with; but the astral and mental bodies hand on to the man himself, to the Thinker, the germs of the faculties and qualities resulting from the activities of the earth-life, and these are stored within the causal body, the seeds of his next astral and mental bodies. At this stage, then, only the man himself is left, the labourer who has brought his harvest home, and has lived upon it till it is all worked up into himself. The dawn of a new life begins, and he must go forth again to his labour until the even.

The new life begins by the vivifying of the mental germs, and they draw upon the materials of the lower mental levels, till a mental body has grown up from them that represents exactly the mental stage of the man, expressing all his mental faculties as organs; the experiences of the past do not exist as mental images in this new body; as mental images they perished when the old mind-body perished, and only their essence, their effects on faculty, remain; they were the food of the mind, the materials which it wove into powers; and in the new body they reappear as powers, they determine its materials, and they form its organs. When the man, the Thinker, has thus clothed himself with a new body for his coming life on the lower mental levels, he proceeds, by vivifying the astral germs, to provide himself with an astral body for his life on the astral plane. This, again, exactly represents his desire-nature, faithfully reproducing the qualities he evolved in the past, as the seed reproduces its parent tree. Thus the man stands, fully equipped for his next incarnation, the only memory of the events of his past being in the causal body, in his own enduring form, the one body that passes on from life to life.

Meanwhile, action external to himself is being taken to provide him with a physical body suitable for the expression of his qualities. In past lives he had made ties with, contracted liabilities towards, other human beings, and some of these will partly determine his place of birth and his family.[1] He

[1] This and the following causes determining the outward circumstances of the new life will be fully explained in Chapter IX, on "Karma".

has been a source of happiness or of unhappiness to others; this is a factor in determining the conditions of his coming life. His desire-nature is well disciplined, or unregulated and riotous; this will be taken into account in the physical heredity of the new body. He has cultivated certain mental powers, such as the artistic; this must be considered, as here again physical heredity is an important factor where delicacy of nervous organization and tactile sensibility are required. And so on, in endless variety. The man may, certainly will, have in him many incongruous characteristics, so that only some can find expression in any one body that could be provided, and a group of his powers suitable for simultaneous expression must be selected. All this is done by certain mighty spiritual Intelligences,[1] often spoken of as the Lords of Karma, because it is their function to superintend the working out of causes continually set going by thoughts, desires, and actions. They hold the threads of destiny which each man has woven, and guide the reincarnating man to the environment determined by his past, unconsciously self-chosen through his past life.

The race, the nation, the family, being thus determined, what may be called the mould of the

---

[1] Spoken of by H .P. Blavatsky in *The Secret Doctrine*. They are the Lipika, the Keepers of the kārmic Records, and the Mahārājas, who direct the practical working out of the decrees of the Lipika.

physical body—suitable for the expression of the man's qualities, and for the working out of the causes he has set going—is given by these great Ones, and the new etheric double, a copy of this, is built within the mother's womb by the agency of an elemental, the thought of the Kārmic Lords being its motive power. The dense body is built into the etheric double molecule by molecule, following it exactly, and here physical heredity has full sway in the materials provided. Further, the thoughts and passions of surrounding people, especially of the continually present father and mother, influence the building elemental in its work, the individual with whom the incarnating man had formed ties in the past thus affecting the physical conditions growing up for his new life on earth. At a very early stage the new astral body comes into connection with the new etheric double, and exercises considerable influence over its formation, and through it the mental body works upon the nervous organization, preparing it to become a suitable instrument for its own expression in the future. This influence, commenced in antenatal life—so that when a child is born its brain-formation reveals the extent and balance of its mental and moral qualities—is continued after birth, and this building of brain and nerves, and their correlation to the astral and mental bodies, go on till the seventh year of childhood, at which age the connection between the man and his physical vehicle is complete, and he may be said to work through it henceforth more than upon it. Up to this age, the consciousness of the Thinker is more upon the astral plane than upon the physical, and this is often evidenced by the play of psychic faculties in young children. They see invisible comrades and fairy landscapes, hear voices inaudible to their elders, catch charming and delicate fancies from the astral world. These phenomena generally vanish as the Thinker begins to work effectively through the physical vehicle, and the dreamy child becomes the commonplace boy or girl, oftentimes much to the relief of bewildered parents, ignorant of the cause of their child's " queerness ". Most children have at least a touch of this " queerness ", but they quickly learn to hide away their fancies and visions from their unsympathetic elders, fearful of blame for " telling stories ", or of what the child dreads far more—ridicule. If parents could see their children's brains, vibrating under an inextricable mingling of physical and astral impacts, which the children themselves are quite incapable of separating, and receiving sometimes a thrill—so plastic are they—even from the higher regions, giving a vision of ethereal beauty, of heroic achievement, they would be more patient with, more responsive to, the confused prattlings of the little ones, trying to translate into the difficult medium of unaccustomed words the elusive touches of which they are conscious, and which they try to catch and retain. Reincarnation, believed in and understood, would relieve child-life of its most pathetic aspect, the unaided struggle of the soul to gain control over its new vehicles, and to connect itself fully with its densest body without losing the power to impress the rarer ones in a way that would enable them to convey to the denser their own more subtle vibrations.

CHAPTER VIII

REINCARNATION (*Continued*)

THE ascending stages of consciousness through which the Thinker passes as he reincarnates during his long cycle of lives in three lower worlds are clearly marked out, and the obvious necessity for many lives in which to experience them, if he is to evolve at all, may carry to the more thoughtful minds the clearest conviction of the truth of reincarnation.

The first of the stages is that in which all the experiences are sensational, the only contribution made by the mind consisting of the recognition that contact with some object is followed by a sensation of pleasure, while contact with others is followed by a sensation of pain. These objects form mental pictures, and the pictures soon begin to act as a stimulus to seek the objects associated with pleasure, when those objects are not present, the germs of memory and of mental initiative thus making their appearance. The first rough division of the external world is followed by the more complex idea of the bearing of quantity on pleasure and pain, already referred to.

At this stage of evolution memory is very short-lived, or, in other words, mental images are very transitory. The idea of forecasting the future from the past, even to the most rudimentary extent, has not dawned on the infant Thinker, and his actions are guided from outside, by the impacts that reach him from the external world, or at furthest by the promptings of his appetites and passions, craving gratification. He will throw away anything for an immediate satisfaction, however necessary the thing may be for his future well-being; the need of the moment overpowers every other consideration. Of human souls in this embryonic condition, numerous examples can be found in books of travel, and the necessity for many lives will be impressed on the mind of anyone who studies the mental condition of the least evolved savages, and compares it with the mental condition of even average humanity among ourselves.

Needless to say that the moral capacity is no more evolved than the mental; the idea of good and evil has not yet been conceived. Nor is it possible to convey to the quite undeveloped mind even elementary notions of either good or bad. Good and pleasant are to it interchangeable terms, as in the well-known case of the Australian savage mentioned by Charles Darwin. Pressed by hunger, the man speared the nearest living creature that could serve as food, and this happened to be his wife; a European remonstrated with him on the wickedness of his deed, but failed to make any impression; for from the reproach that to eat his wife was very bad he only deduced the inference that the stranger thought she had proved nasty or indigestible, and he put him right by smiling peacefully as he patted himself after his meal, and declaring in a satisfied way, " She is very good ". Measure in thought the moral distance between that man and S. Francis of Assisi, and it will be seen that there must either be evolution of souls as there is evolution of bodies, or else in the realm of the soul there must be constant miracle, dislocated creations.

There are two paths along either of which man may gradually emerge from this embryonic mental condition. He may be directly ruled and controlled by men far more evolved than himself, or he may be left slowly to grow unaided. The latter case would imply the passage of uncounted millennia, for without example and without discipline, left to the changing impacts of external objects, and to friction with other men as undeveloped as himself, the inner energies could be but very slowly aroused. As a matter of fact, man has evolved by the road of direct

16

precept and example and of enforced discipline. We have already seen that when the bulk of average humanity received the spark which brought the Thinker into being, there were some of the greater Sons of Mind who incarnated as Teachers, and that there was also a long succession of lesser Sons of Mind, at various stages of evolution, who came into incarnation as the crest-wave of the advancing tide of humanity. These ruled the less evolved, under the beneficent sway of the great Teachers, and the compelled obedience to elementary rules of right living—very elementary at first, in truth—much hastened the development of mental and moral faculties in the embryonic souls. Apart from all other records the gigantic remains of civilizations that have long since disappeared—evidencing great engineering skill, and intellectual conceptions far beyond anything possible by the mass of the then infant humanity—suffice to prove that there were present on earth men with minds that were capable of greatly planning and greatly executing.

Let us continue the early stage of the evolution of consciousness. Sensation was wholly lord of the mind and the earliest mental efforts were stimulated by desire. This led the man, slowly and clumsily, to forecast, to plan. He began to recognize a definite association of certain mental images, and, when one appeared, to expect the appearance of the other that had invariably followed in its wake. He began to draw inferences, and even to initiate action on the faith of these inferences—a great advance. And he began also to hesitate now and again to follow the vehement promptings of desire, when he found, over and over again, that the gratification demanded was associated in his mind with the subsequent happening of suffering. This action was much quickened by the pressure upon him of verbally expressed laws; he was forbidden to seize certain gratifications, and was told that suffering would follow disobedience. When he had seized the delight-giving object and found the suffering follow upon the pleasure, the fulfilled declaration made a far stronger impression on his mind than would have been made by the unexpected—and therefore to him fortuitous—happening of the same thing unforetold. Thus conflict continually arose between memory and desire, and the mind grew more active by the conflict, and was stirred into livelier functioning. The conflict, in fact, marked the transition to the second great stage.

Here began to show itself the germ of will. Desire and will guide a man's actions, and will has even been defined as the desire which emerges triumphant from the contest of desires. But this is a crude and superficial view, explaining nothing. Desire is the outgoing energy of the Thinker, determined in its direction by the attraction of external objects. Will is the outgoing energy of the Thinker, determined in its direction by the conclusions drawn by the reason from past experiences, or by the direct intuition of the Thinker himself. Otherwise put: desire is guided from without, will from within. At the beginning of man's evolution, desire has complete sovereignty, and hurries him hither and thither; in the middle of his evolution, desire and will are in continual conflict, and victory lies sometimes with the one, sometimes with other; at the end of his evolution desire has died, and will rules with unopposed, unchallenged sway. Until the Thinker is sufficiently developed to see directly, will is guided by him through the reason; and as the reason can draw its conclusions only from its stock of mental images—its experience—and that stock is limited, the will constantly commands mistaken actions. The suffering which flows from these mistaken actions increases the stock of mental images, and thus gives the reason an increased store from which to draw its conclusions. Thus progress is made and wisdom is born.

Desire often mixes itself up with will, so that what appears to be determined from within is really largely prompted by the cravings of the lower nature for objects which afford it gratification. Instead of an open conflict between the two, the lower subtly insinuates itself into the current of the higher and turns its course aside. Defeated in the open field, the desires of the personality thus conspire against their conqueror, and often win by guile what they failed to win by force. During the whole of this second great stage, in which the faculties of the lower mind are in full course of evolution, conflict is the normal condition, conflict between the rule of sensations and the rule of reason.

The problem to be solved in humanity is the putting an end to conflict while preserving the freedom of the will; to determine the will inevitably to the best, while yet leaving that best as a matter of choice. The best is to be chosen, but by a self-initiated volition, that shall come with all the certainty of a foreordained necessity. The certainty of a compelling law is to be obtained from countless wills, each one left free to determine its own course. The solution of that problem is simple when it is known, though the contradiction looks irreconcilable when first presented. Let man be left free to choose his own actions, but let every action bring about an inevitable result; let him run loose amid all objects of desire and seize whatever he will, but let him have all the results of his choice, be they delightful or grievous. Presently he will freely reject the objects whose possession ultimately causes him pain; he will no longer desire them when he has experienced to the full that their possession ends in sorrow. Let him struggle to hold the pleasure and avoid the pain, he will none the less be ground between the stones of law, and the lesson will be repeated any number of times found necessary; reincarnation offers as many lives as are needed by the most sluggish learner. Slowly desire for an object that brings suffering in its train will die, and when the thing offers itself in all its attractive glamour it will be rejected, not by compulsion but by free choice. It is no longer desirable, it has lost its power. Thus with thing after thing; choice more and more runs in harmony with law. " There are many roads of error; the road of truth is one; " when all the paths of error have been trodden, when all have been found to end in suffering, the choice to walk in the way of truth is unswerving, because based on knowledge. The lower kingdoms work harmoniously, compelled by law; man's kingdom is a chaos of conflicting wills, fighting against, rebelling against law; presently there evolves from it a nobler unity, a harmonious choice of voluntary obedience, an obedience that, being voluntary, based on knowledge and on memory of the results of disobedience, is stable and can be drawn aside by no temptation. Ignorant, inexperienced, man would always have been in danger of falling; as a God, knowing good and evil by experience, his choice of the good is raised forever beyond possibility of change.

Will in the domain of morality is generally entitled conscience, and it is subject to the same difficulties in this domain as in its other activities. So long as actions are in question which have been done over and over again, of which the consequences are familiar either to reason or to the Thinker himself, the conscience speaks quickly and firmly. But when unfamiliar problems arise, as to the working out of which experience is silent, conscience cannot speak with certainty; it has but a hesitating answer from the reason, which can draw only a doubtful inference, and the Thinker cannot speak if his experience does not include the circumstances that have now arisen. Hence conscience often decides wrongly; that is, the will, failing clear direction from either the reason or the intuition, guides action amiss. Nor can we leave out of consideration the influences which play upon the mind from without, from the thought-forms of others, of friends, of the family, of the community, of the nation.[1] These all surround and penetrate the mind with their own atmosphere, distorting the appearance of everything, and throwing all things out of proportion. Thus influenced, the reason often does not even judge calmly from its own

[1] Chapter II, on " The Astral Plane ".

experiences, but draws false conclusions as it studies its materials through a distorting medium.

The evolution of moral faculties is very largely stimulated by the affections, animal and selfish as these are during the infancy of the Thinker. The laws of morality are laid down by the enlightened reason, discerning the laws by which Nature moves, and bringing human conduct into consonance with the Divine Will. But the impulse to obey these laws, when no outer force compels, has its roots in love, in that hidden divinity in man which seeks to pour itself out, to give itself to others. Morality begins in the infant Thinker when he is first moved by love to wife, to child, to friend, to do some action that serves the loved one without any thought of gain to himself thereby. It is the first conquest over the lower nature, the complete subjugation of which is the achievement of moral perfection. Hence the importance of never killing out, or strivings to weaken, the affection, as is done in many of the lower kinds of occultism. However impure and gross the affections may be, they offer possibilities of moral evolution from which the cold-hearted and self-isolated have shut themselves out. It is an easier task to purify than to create love, and this is why " the sinners " have been said by great Teachers to be nearer the kingdom of heaven than the Pharisees and scribes.

The third great stage of consciousness sees the development of the higher intellectual powers; the mind no longer dwells entirely on mental images obtained from sensations, no longer reasons on purely concrete objects, nor is concerned with the attributes which differentiate one from another. The Thinker, having learned clearly to discriminate between objects by dwelling upon their unlikenesses, now begins to group them together by some attribute which appears in a number of objects otherwise dissimilar and makes a link between them. He draws out, abstracts, his common attributes, and sets all objects that possess it apart from the rest which are without it; and in this way he evolves the power of recognizing identity amid diversity, a step toward the much later recognition of the One underlying the many. He thus classifies all that is around him, developing the synthetic faculty, and learning to construct as well as to analyse. Presently he takes another step, and conceives of the common property as an idea, apart from all the objects in which it appears, and thus constructs a higher kind of mental image than the image of a concrete object —the image of an idea that has no phenomenal existence in the worlds of form, but which exists on the higher levels of the mental plane, and affords material on which the Thinker himself can work. The lower mind reaches the abstract idea by reason, and in thus doing accomplishes its loftiest flight, touching the threshold of the formless world, and dimly seeing that which lies beyond. The Thinker sees these ideas, and lives among them habitually, and when the power of abstract reasoning is developed and exercised the Thinker is becoming effective in his own world, and is beginning his life of active functioning in his own sphere. Such men care little for the life of the senses, care little for external observation, or for mental application to images of external objects; their powers are indrawn, and no longer rush outwards in the search for satisfaction. They dwell calmly within themselves, engrossed with the problems of philosophy, with the deeper aspects of life and thought, seeking to understand causes rather than troubling themselves with effects, and approaching nearer and nearer to the recognition of the One that underlies all the diversities of external nature.

In the fourth stage of consciousness that One is seen, and with the transcending of the barrier set up by the intellect the consciousness spreads out to embrace the world, seeing all things in itself and as parts of itself, and seeing itself as a ray of the Logos, and therefore as one with Him. Where is then the Thinker? He has become Consciousness, and, while the spiritual Soul can at will use any of his lower vehicles, he is no longer limited to their use, nor needs them for this full and conscious life. Then is compulsory reincarnation over and the man has destroyed death; he has verily achieved immortality. Then has he become "a pillar in the temple of my God and shall go out no more ".

To complete this part of our study, we need to understand the successive quickenings of the vehicles of consciousness, the bringing them one by one into activity as the harmonious instruments of the human Soul.

We have seen that from the very beginning of his separate life the Thinker has possessed coatings of mental, astral, etheric, and dense physical matter. These form the media by which his life vibrates outwards, the bridge of consciousness, as we may call it, along which all impulses from the Thinker may reach the dense physical body, all impacts from the outer world may reach him. But this general use of the successive bodies as parts of a connected whole is a very different thing from the quickening of each in turn to serve as a distinct vehicle of consciousness, independently of those below it, and it is this quickening of the vehicles that we have now to consider.

The lowest vehicle, the dense physical body, is the first one to be brought into harmonious working order; the brain and the nervous system have to be elaborated and to be rendered delicately responsive to every thrill which is within their gamut of vibratory power. In the early stages, while the physical dense body is composed of the grosser kinds of matter, this gamut is extremely limited, and the physical organ of mind can respond only to the slowest vibrations sent down. It answers far more promptly, as is natural, to the impacts from the external world caused by objects similar in materials to itself. Its quickening as a vehicle of consciousness consists in its being made responsive to the vibrations that are initiated within, and the rapidity of this quickening depends on the co-operation of the lower nature with the higher, its loyal subordination of itself in the service of its inner ruler. When, after many, many life-periods, it dawns upon the lower nature that it exists for the sake of the soul, that all its value depends on the help it can bring to the soul, that it can win immortality only by merging itself in the soul, then its evolution proceeds with giant strides. Before this, the evolution has been unconscious; at first, the gratification of the lower nature was the object of life, and, while this was a necessary preliminary for calling out the energies of the Thinker, it did nothing directly to render the body a vehicle of consciousness; the direct working upon it begins when the life of the man establishes its centre in the mental body, and when thought commences to dominate sensation. The exercise of the mental powers works on the brain and the nervous system, and the coarser materials are gradually expelled to make room for the finer, which can vibrate in unison with the thought-vibrations sent to them. The brain becomes finer in constitution, and increases by ever more complicated convolutions the amount of surface available for the coating of nervous matter adapted to respond to thought-vibrations. The nervous system becomes more delicately balanced, more sensitive, more alive to every thrill of mental activity. And when the recognition of its function as an instrument of the soul, spoken of above, has come, then active co-operation in performing this function sets in. The personality begins deliberately to discipline itself, and to set the permanent interests of the immortal individual above its own transient gratifications. It yields up the time that might be spent in the pursuit of lower pleasures to the evolution of mental powers; day by day time is set apart for serious study; the brain is gladly surrendered to receive impacts from within instead of from without, is trained to answer to consecutive thinking, and is taught to refrain from throwing up its own useless disjointed images, made by past impressions. It is taught to remain at rest when it is not wanted by its master; to answer, not to initiate vibrations.[1] Further, some discretion and discrimination will be used as to the food-stuffs which supply physical materials to the brain. The use of the coarser kinds will be discontinued, such as animal flesh and blood and alcohol, and pure food will build up a pure body. Gradually the lower vibrations will find no materials capable of responding to them, and the physical body thus becomes more and more entirely a vehicle of consciousness, delicately responsive to all the thrills of thought and keenly sensitive to the vibrations sent outwards by the Thinker. The etheric double so closely follows the constitution of the dense body that it is not necessary to study separately its purification and quickening; it does not normally serve as a separate vehicle of consciousness, but works synchronously with its dense partner, and when separated from it either by accident or by death, it responds very feebly to the vibrations initiated within. Its function in truth is not to serve as a vehicle of mental consciousness, but as a vehicle of Prāna, of specialized life-force, and its dislocation from the denser particles to which it conveys the life-currents is therefore disturbing and mischievous.

---

[1] One of the signs that it is being accomplished is the cessation of the confused jumble of fragmentary images which are set up during sleep by the independent activity of the physical brain.

The astral body is the second vehicle of consciousness to be vivified, and we have already seen the changes through which it passes as it becomes organized for its work.[1] When it is thoroughly organized, the consciousness, which has hitherto worked within it, imprisoned by it, when in sleep it has left the physical body and is drifting about in the astral world, begins not only to receive the impressions through it of astral objects that form the so-called dream-consciousness, but also to perceive astral objects by its senses—that is, it begins to relate the impressions received to the objects which give rise to those impressions. These perceptions are at first confused, just as are the perceptions at first made by the mind through a new physical baby-body, and they have to be corrected by experience in the one case as in the other. The Thinker has gradually to discover the new powers which he can use through this subtler vehicle, and by which he can control the astral elements and defend himself against astral dangers. He is not left alone to face this new world unaided, but is taught and helped and—until he can guard himself—protected by those who are more experienced than himself in the ways of the astral world.

When the brain is coming under control this kind of dream is very seldom experienced.

[1] See Chapter II, on " The Astral Plane ".

Gradually the new vehicle of consciousness comes completely under his control, and life on the astral plane is as natural and as familiar as life on the physical.

The third vehicle of consciousness, the mental body, is rarely, if ever, vivified for independent action without the direct instruction of a teacher, and its functioning belongs to the life of the disciple at the present stage of human evolution.[1]   As we have already seen, it is rearranged for separate functioning [2] on the mental plane, and here again experience and training are needed ere it comes fully under its owner's control. A fact—common to all these three vehicles of consciousness, but more apt to mislead perhaps in the subtler than in the denser, because it is generally forgotten in their case, while it is so obvious that it is remembered in the denser—is that they are subject to evolution, and that with their higher evolution their powers to receive and to respond to vibrations increase. How many more shades of colour are seen by a trained eye than by an untrained! How many overtones are heard by a trained ear, where the untrained hears only the single fundamental note! As the physical senses grow more keen the world becomes fuller and fuller, and where the peasant is conscious

---

[1] See Chapter XI, on " Man's Ascent ".

[2] See Chapter IV, on " The Mental Plane ".

only of his furrow and his plough, the cultured mind is conscious of hedgerow flower and quivering aspen, of rapturous melody down-dropping from the skylark and the whirring of tiny wings through the adjoining wood, of the scudding of rabbits under the curled fronds of the bracken, and the squirrels playing with each other through the branches of the beeches, of all the gracious movements of wild things, of all the fragrant odours of field and woodland, of all the changing glories of the cloud-flecked sky, and of all the chasing lights and shadows on the hills. Both the peasant and the cultured have eyes, both have brains, but of what differing powers of observation, of what differing powers to receive impressions! Thus also in other worlds. As the astral and mental bodies begin to function as separate vehicles of consciousness, they are in, as it were, the peasant stage of receptivity, and only fragments of the astral and mental worlds with their strange and elusive phenomena, make their way into consciousness; but they evolve rapidly, embracing more and more, and conveying to consciousness a more and more accurate reflection of its environment. Here, as everywhere else, we have to remember that our knowledge is not the limit of Nature's powers, and that in the astral and mental worlds, as in the physical, we are still children, picking up a few shells cast up

17

by the waves, while the treasures hid in the ocean are still unexplored.

The quickening of the causal body as a vehicle of consciousness follows in due course the quickening of the mental body, and opens up to man a yet more marvellous state of consciousness, stretching backwards into an illimitable past, onwards into the reaches of the future. Then the Thinker not only possesses the memory of his own past and can trace his growth through the long succession of his incarnate and excarnate lives, but he can also roam at will through the storied past of the earth, and learn the weighty lessons of world-experience, studying the hidden laws which guide evolution and the deep secrets of life hidden in the bosom of Nature. In that lofty vehicle of consciousness he can reach the veiled Isis, and lift a corner of her down-dropped veil; for there he can face her eyes without being blinded by her lightning glances and he can see in the radiance that flows from her the causes of the world's sorrow and its ending, with heart pitiful and compassionate, but no longer wrung with helpless pain. Strength and calm and wisdom come to those who are using the causal body as a vehicle of consciousness, and who behold with opened eyes the glory of the Good Law.

When the buddhic body is quickened as a vehicle of consciousness the man enters into the bliss of non-separateness, and knows in full and vivid realization his unity with all that is. As the predominant element of consciousness in the causal body is knowledge, and ultimately wisdom, so the predominant element of consciousness in the buddhic body is bliss and love. The serenity of wisdom chiefly marks the one, while tenderest compassion streams forth inexhaustibly from the other; when to these is added the godlike and unruffled strength that marks the functioning of Ātmā, then humanity is crowned with divinity, and the God-man is manifest in all the plenitude of his power, of his wisdom, of his love.

The handing down to the lower vehicles of such part of the consciousness belonging to the higher as they are able to receive does not immediately follow on the successive quickening of the vehicles. In this matter individuals differ very widely, according to their circumstances and their work, for this quickening of the vehicles above the physical rarely occurs till probationary discipleship [1] is reached, and then the duties to be discharged depend on the needs of the time. The disciple, and even the aspirant for discipleship, is taught to hold all his powers entirely for the service of the world, and the sharing of the lower consciousness in the knowledge of the higher is for the most part determined by the needs of the

[1] See Chapter XI, on " Man's Ascent ".

works in which the disciple is engaged. It is necessary that the disciple should have the full use of his
vehicles of consciousness on the higher planes, as
much of his work can be accomplished only in them;
but the conveying of a knowledge of that work to
the physical vehicle, which is in no way concerned
in it, is a matter of no importance and the convey-
ance or non-conveyance is generally determined by
the effect that the one course or the other would
have on the efficiency of his work on the physical
plane. The strain on the physical body when the
higher consciousness compels it to vibrate responsively is very great at the present stage of evolution,
and unless the external circumstances are very
favourable this strain is apt to cause nervous
disturbance, hypersensitiveness with its attendant
evils. Hence most of those who are in full possession of the quickened higher vehicles of consciousness, and whose most important work is done out
of the body, remain apart from the busy haunts of
men, if they desire to throw down into the physical
consciousness the knowledge they use on the higher
planes, thus preserving the sensitive physical vehicle
from the rough usage and clamour of ordinary
life.

The main preparations to be made for receiving
in the physical vehicle the vibrations of the higher
consciousness are: its purification from grosser

materials by pure food and pure life; the entire
subjugation of the passions, and the cultivation of an
even, balanced temper and mind, unaffected by the
turmoil and vicissitudes of external life; the habit of
quiet meditation on lofty topics, turning the mind
away from the objects of the senses, and from the
mental images arising from them, and fixing it on
higher things; the cessation of hurry, especially of
that restless, excitable hurry of the mind, which
keeps the brain continually at work and flying from
one subject to another; the genuine love for the
things of the higher world, that makes them more
attractive than the objects of the lower, so that the
mind rests contentedly in their companionship as in
that of a well-loved friend. In fact, the preparations are much the same as those necessary for the
conscious separation of " soul " from " body " and
those were elsewhere stated by me as follows. The
student

   " must begin by practising extreme temperance
in all things, cultivating an equable and a serene state
of mind; his life must be clean and his thoughts pure,
his body held in strict subjection to the soul, and
his mind trained to occupy itself with noble and lofty
themes; he must habitually practise compassion, sympathy, helpfulness to others, with indifference to
troubles and pleasures affecting himself, and he must
cultivate courage, steadfastness, and devotion. In
fact, he must live the religion and ethics that other
people for the most part only talk. Having by per-
severing practice learned to control his mind to some

extent so that he is able to keep it fixed on one line of thought for some little time, he must begin its more rigid training, by a daily practice of concentration on some difficult or abstract subject, or on some lofty object of devotion; this concentration means the firm fixing of the mind on one single point, without wandering, and without yielding to any distractions caused by external objects, by the activity of the senses, or by that of the mind itself. It must be braced up to an unswerving steadiness and fixity, until gradually it will learn so to withdraw its attention from the outer world and from the body that the senses will remain quiet and still, while the mind is intensely alive with all its energies drawn inwards to be launched at a single point of thought, the highest to which it can attain. When it is able to hold itself thus with comparative ease it is ready for a further step, and by a strong but calm effort of the will it can throw itself beyond the highest thought it can reach *while working in the physical brain*, and in that effort will rise to and unite itself with the higher consciousness and find itself free of the body. When this is done there is no sense of sleep or dream nor any loss of consciousness; the man finds himself outside his body, but as though he had merely slipped off a weighty encumbrance, not as though he had lost any part of himself; he is not really 'disembodied', but has risen out of his gross body 'in a body of light', which obeys his slightest thought and serves as a beautiful and perfect instrument for carrying out his will. In this he is free of the subtle worlds, but will need to train his faculties long and carefully for reliable work under the new conditions.

" Freedom from the body may be obtained in other ways: by the rapt intensity of devotion or by special methods that may be imparted by a great teacher to his disciple. Whatever the way, the end is the same—the setting free of the soul in full consciousness, able to examine its new surroundings in regions beyond the treading of the man of flesh. At will it can return to the body and re-enter it, and under these circumstances it can impress on the brain-mind, and thus retain while in the body, the memory of the experiences it has undergone." [1]

Those who have grasped the main ideas sketched in the foregoing pages will feel that these ideas are in themselves the strongest proof that reincarnation is a fact in Nature. It is necessary, in order that the vast evolution implied in the phrase, " the evolution of the soul ", may be accomplished. The only alternative—putting aside for the moment the materialistic idea that the soul is only the aggregate of the vibrations of a particular kind of physical matter—is that each soul is a new creation, made when a babe is born, and stamped with virtuous or with vicious tendencies, endowed with ability or with stupidity, by the arbitrary whim of the creative power. As the Muhammadan would say, his fate is hung round his neck at birth, for a man's fate depends on his character and his surroundings, and a newly created soul flung into the world must be doomed to happiness or misery according to the circumstances environing him and the character stamped upon him. Predestination in its most

[1] " Conditions of Life after Death ", *Nineteenth Century*, November 1896.

offensive form is the alternative of reincarnation. Instead of looking on men as slowly evolving, so that the brutal savage of to-day will in time evolve the noblest qualities of saint and hero, and thus, seeing in the world a wisely planned and wisely directed process of growth, we shall be obliged to see in it a chaos of most unjustly treated sentient beings, awarded happiness or misery, knowledge or ignorance, virtue or vice, wealth or poverty, genius or idiocy, by an arbitrary external will, unguided by either justice or mercy—a veritable pandemonium, irrational and unmeaning. And this chaos is supposed to be the higher part of a cosmos, in the lower regions of which are manifested all the orderly and beautiful workings of a law that ever evolves higher and more complex forms from the lower and the simpler, that obviously " makes for righteousness ", for harmony, and for beauty.

If it be admitted that the soul of the savage is destined to live and to evolve, and that he is not doomed for eternity to his present infant state, but that his evolution will take place after death and in other worlds, then the principle of soul-evolution is conceded, and the question of the place of evolution alone remains. Were all souls on earth at the same stage of evolution, much might be said for the contention that further worlds are needed for the evolution of souls beyond the infant stage. But we have around us souls that are far advanced, and that were born with noble mental and moral qualities. By parity of reasoning, we must suppose them to have been evolved in other worlds ere their one birth in this, and we cannot but wonder why an earth that offers varied conditions, fit for little-developed and also for advanced souls, should be paid only one flying visit by souls at every stage of development, all the rest of their evolution being carried on in worlds similar to this, equally able to afford all the conditions needed to evolve the souls at different stages of evolution, as we find them to be when they are born here. The Ancient Wisdom teaches, indeed, that the soul progresses through many worlds, but it also teaches that he is born in each of these worlds over and over again, until he has completed the evolution possible in that world. The worlds themselves, according to its teaching, form an evolutionary chain, and each plays its own part as a field for certain stages of evolution. Our own world offers a field suitable for the evolution of the mineral, vegetable, animal and human kingdoms, and therefore collective or individual reincarnation goes on upon it in all these kingdoms. Truly, further evolution lies before us in other worlds, but in the divine order they are not open to us until we have learned and mastered the lessons our own world has to teach.

There are many lines of thought that lead us to the same goal of reincarnation, as we study the world around us. The immense differences that separate man from man have been already noticed as implying an evolutionary past behind each soul; and attention has been drawn to these as differentiating the individual reincarnation of men—all of whom belong to a single species—from the reincarnation of monadic group-souls in the lower kingdoms. The comparatively small differences that separate the physical bodies of men, all being externally recognizable as men, should be contrasted with the immense differences that separate the primitive man and the noblest human type in mental and moral capacities. Primitive men are often splendid in physical development and with large cranial contents, but how different their minds from that of a philosopher or of a saint!

If high mental and moral qualities are regarded as the accumulated results of civilized living, then we are confronted by the fact that the ablest men of the present are overtopped by the intellectual giants of the past, and that none of our own day reaches the moral altitude of some historical saints. Further, we have to consider that genius has neither parent nor child; that it appears suddenly and not as the apex of a gradually improving family, and is itself generally sterile, or, if a child be born to it,.

it is a child of the body, not of the mind. Still more significantly, a musical genius is for the most part born in a musical family, because that form of genius needs for its manifestation a nervous organization of a peculiar kind, and nervous organization falls under the law of heredity. But how often in such a family its object seems over when it has provided a body for a genius, and it then flickers out and vanishes in a few generations into the obscurity of average humanity! Where are the descendants of Bach, of Beethoven, of Mozart, of Mendelssohn, equal to their sires? Truly genius does not descend from father to son, like the family physical types of the Stuart and the Bourbon.

On what ground, save that of reincarnation, can the "infant prodigy" be accounted for? Take as an instance the case of the child who became Dr. Young, the discoverer of the undulatory theory of light, a man whose greatness is scarcely yet sufficiently widely recognized. As a child of two he could read "with considerable fluence", and before he was four he had read through the Bible twice; at seven he began arithmetic, and mastered Walkingham's *Tutor's Assistant* before he had reached the middle of it under his tutor, and a few years later we find him mastering, while at school, Latin, Greek, Hebrew, mathematics, book-keeping, French, Italian, turning and telescope-making, and delighting in Oriental literature. At fourteen he was to be placed under private tuition with a boy a year and a half younger, but, the tutor first engaged failing to arrive, Young taught the other boy.[1] Sir William Rowan Hamilton showed power even more precocious. He began to learn Hebrew when he was barely three, and " at the age of seven he was pronounced by one of the Fellows of Trinity College, Dublin, to have shown a greater knowledge of the language than many candidates for a fellowship. At the age of thirteen he had acquired considerable knowledge of at least thirteen languages. Among these, besides the classical and the modern European languages, were included Persian, Arabic, Sanskrit, Hindustani, and even Malay. . . . He wrote, at the age of fourteen, a complimentary letter to the Persian Ambassador, who happened to visit Dublin; and the latter said he had not thought there was a man in Britain who could have written such a document in the Persian language." A relative of his says: " I remember him a little boy of six, when he would answer a difficult mathematical question, and run off gaily to his little cart. At twelve he engaged Colburn, the American ' calculating boy,' who was then being exhibited as a curiosity in Dublin, and he had not always the worst of the encounter." When he was eighteen,

[1] *Life of Dr. Thomas Young*, by G. Peacock, D. D.

Dr. Brinkley (Royal Astronomer of Ireland) said of him in 1823: " This young man, I do not say *will* be, but *is*, the first mathematician of his age." " At college his career was perhaps unexampled. Among a number of competitors of more than ordinary merit, he was first in every subject, and at every examination." [1]

Let the thoughtful student compare these boys with a semi-idiot, or even with an average lad, note how, starting with these advantages, they become leaders of thought, and then ask himself whether such souls have no past behind them.

Family likenesses are generally explained as being due to the " law of heredity ", but differences in mental and in moral character are continually found within a family circle, and these are left unexplained. Reincarnation explains the likenesses by the fact that a soul in taking birth is directed to a family which provides by its physical heredity a body suitable to express his characteristics; and it explains the unlikenesses by attaching the mental and moral character to the individual himself, while showing that ties set up in the past have led him to take birth in connection with some other individual of that family.[2] A " matter of significance in connection with twins is that during infancy they will

---

[1] *North British Review*, September 1866.
[2] See Chapter IX, on " Karma ".

often be indistinguishable from each other, even to the keen eye of mother and of nurse; whereas, later in life, when Manas has been working on his physical encasement, he will have so modified it that the physical likeness lessens and the differences of character stamp themselves on the mobile features." [1] Physical likeness with mental and moral unlikeness seems to imply the meeting of two different lines of causation.

The striking dissimilarity found to exist between people of about equal intellectual power in assimilating particular kinds of knowledge is another " pointer " to reincarnation. A truth is recognized at once by one, while the other fails to grasp it even after long and careful observation. Yet the very opposite may be the case when another truth is presented to them, and it may be seen by the second and missed by the first. " Two students are attracted to Theosophy and begin to study it; at a year's end one is familiar with its main conceptions and can apply them, while the other is struggling in a maze. To the one each principle seemed familiar on presentation; to the other new, unintelligible, strange. The believer in reincarnation understands that the teaching is old to the one and new to the other; one learns quickly *because he remembers*, he is but recovering past knowledge; the other learns

[1] *Reincarnation*, by Annie Besant, p. 64.

slowly because his experience has not included these truths of Nature, and he is acquiring them toilfully for the first time." [1] So also ordinary intuition is " merely recognition of a fact familiar in a past life, though met with for the first time in the present ", [2] another sign of the road along which the individual has travelled in the past.

The main difficulty with many people in the reception of the doctrine of reincarnation is their own absence of memory of their past. Yet they are every day familiar with the fact that they have forgotten very much even of their lives in their present bodies, and that the early years of childhood are blurred and those of infancy a blank. They must also know that events of the past which have entirely slipped out of their normal consciousness are yet hidden away in dark caves of memory and can be brought out again vividly in some forms of disease or under the influence of mesmerism. A dying man has been known to speak a language heard only in infancy, and unknown to him during a long life; in delirium, events long forgotten have presented themselves vividly to the consciousness. Nothing is really forgotten; but much is hidden out of sight of the limited vision of our waking consciousness,

---

[1] *Reincarnation*, p. 67.

[2] *Ibid.*

the most limited form of our consciousness, although the only consciousness recognized by the vast majority. Just as the memory of some of the present life is indrawn beyond the reach of this waking consciousness, and makes itself known again only when the brain is hypersensitive and thus able to respond to vibrations that usually beat against it unheeded, so is the memory of the past lives stored up out of reach of the physical consciousness. It is all with the Thinker, who alone persists from life to life; he has the whole book of memory within his reach, for he is the only " I " that has passed through all the experiences recorded therein. Moreover, he can impress his own memories of the past on his physical vehicle, as soon as it has been sufficiently purified to answer to his swift and subtle vibrations and then the man of flesh can share his knowledge of the storied past. The difficulty of memory does not lie in forgetfulness, for the lower vehicle, the physical body, has never passed through the previous lives of its owner; it lies in the absorption of the present body in its present environment, in its coarse irresponsiveness to the delicate thrills in which alone the soul can speak. Those who would remember the past must not have their interests centered in the present, and they must purify and refine the body till it is able to receive impressions from the subtler spheres.

Memory of their own past lives, however, is possessed by a considerable number of people who have achieved the necessary sensitiveness of the physical organism, and to these, of course, reincarnation is no longer a theory, but has become a matter of personal knowledge. They have learned how much richer life becomes when memories of past lives pour into it, when the friends of this brief day are found to be the friends of the long-ago, and old remembrances strengthen the ties of the fleeting present. Life gains security and dignity when it is seen with a long vista behind it, and when the loves of old reappear in the loves of to-day. Death fades into its proper place as a mere incident in life, a change from one scene to another, like a journey that separates bodies but cannot sunder friend from friend. The links of the present are found to be part of a golden chain that stretches backwards, and the future can be faced with a glad security in the thought that these links will endure through days to come, and form part of that unbroken chain.

Now and then we find children who have brought over a memory of their immediate past, for the most part when they have died in childhood and are reborn almost immediately. In the West such cases are rarer than in the East, because in the West the first words of such a child would be met

18

with disbelief, and he would quickly lose faith in his own memories. In the East, where belief in reincarnation is almost universal, the child's remembrances are listened to, and where the opportunity serves they have been verified.

There is another important point with respect to memory that will repay consideration. The memory of past *events* remains, as we have seen, with the Thinker only, but the results of those events embodied in *faculties* are at the service of the lower man. If the whole of these past events were thrown down into the physical brain, a vast mass of experiences in no classified order, without arrangement, the man could not be guided by the outcome of the past, nor utilize it for present help. Compelled to make a choice between two lines of action, he would have to pick, out of the unarranged facts of his past, events similar in character, trace out their results, and after long and weary study arrive at some conclusion—a conclusion very likely to be vitiated by the overlooking of some important factor, and reached long after the need for decision had passed. All the events, trivial and important, of some hundreds of lives would form a rather unwieldy and chaotic mass for reference in an emergency that demanded a swift decision. The far more effective plan of Nature leaves to the Thinker the memory of the events, provides a long period of excarnate existence for the mental body, during which all the events are tabulated and compared and their results are classified; then these results are embodied as faculties, and these faculties form the next mental body of the Thinker. In this way, the enlarged and improved faculties are available for immediate use, and, the results of the past being in them, a decision can be come to in accordance with those results and without any delay. The clear quick insight and prompt judgment are nothing else than the outcome of past experiences, moulded into an effective form for use; they are surely more useful instruments than would be a mass of unassimilated experiences, out of which the relevant ones would have to be selected and compared, and from which inferences would have to be drawn, on each separate occasion on which a choice arises.

From all these lines of thought, however, the mind turns back to rest on the fundamental necessity for reincarnation if life is to be made intelligible, and if injustice and cruelty are not to mock the helplessness of man. With reincarnation man is a dignified, immortal being, evolving towards a divinely glorious end; without it, he is a tossing straw on the stream of chance circumstances, irresponsible for his character, for his actions, for his destiny. With it, he may look forward with fearless hope, however low in the scale

of evolution he may be to-day, for he is on the
ladder to divinity, and the climbing to its summit is
only a question of time; without it, he has no
reasonable ground of assurance as to progress in the
future, nor indeed any reasonable ground of assurance in a future at all. Why should a creature
without a past look forward to a future? He may
be a mere bubble on the ocean of time. Flung
into the world from nonentity, with qualities, good
or evil, attached to him without reason or desert,
why should he strive to make the best of them?
Will not his future, if he have one, be as isolated,
as uncaused, as unrelated as his present? In dropping reincarnation from its beliefs, the modern
world has deprived God of His justice and has
bereft man of his security; he may be " lucky " or
" unlucky ", but the strength and dignity conferred
by reliance on a changeless law are rent away from
him, and he is left tossing helplessly on an un-
navigable ocean of life.

CHAPTER IX

KARMA

HAVING traced the evolution of the soul by the way
of reincarnation, we are now in a position to study
the great law of causation under which rebirths are
carried on, the law which is named Karma. Karma
is a Sanskrit word, literally meaning "action"; as
all actions are effects flowing from preceding causes,
and as each effect becomes a cause of future effects,
this idea of cause and effect is an essential part of
the idea of action, and the word action, or karma,
is therefore used for causation, or for the unbroken
linked series of causes and effects that make up all
human activity. Hence the phrase is sometimes
used of an event: " This is my karma," *i.e.*, " This
event is the effect of a cause set going by me in the
past." No one life is isolated; it is the child of all
the lives before it, the parent of all the lives that
follow it, in the total aggregate of the lives that
make up the continuing existence of the individual.
There is no such thing as " chance " or as
" accident "; every event is linked to a preceding

cause, to a following effect; all thoughts, deeds, circumstances are causally related to the past and will causally influence the future; as our ignorance shrouds from our vision alike the past and the future, events often appear to us to come suddenly from the void, to be "accidental", but this appearance is illusory and is due entirely to our lack of knowledge. Just as the savage, ignorant of the laws of the physical universe, regards physical events as uncaused, and the results of unknown physical laws as "miracles", so do many, ignorant of moral and mental laws, regard moral and mental events as uncaused, and the results of unknown moral and mental laws as good and bad "luck".

When at first this idea of inviolable, immutable law in a realm hitherto vaguely ascribed to chance dawns upon the mind, it is apt to result in a sense of helplessness, almost of moral and mental paralysis. Man seems to be held in the grip of an iron destiny, and the resigned "kismet" of the Moslem appears to be the only philosophical utterance. Just so might the primitive man feel when the idea of physical law first dawns on his intelligence, and he learns that every movement of his body, every movement in external Nature, is carried on under immutable laws. Gradually he learns that natural laws only lay down conditions under which all workings must be carried on, but do not prescribe the workings; so that man remains ever free at the centre, while limited in his external activities by the conditions of the plane on which those activities are carried on. He learns further that while the conditions master him, constantly frustrating his strenuous efforts, so long as he is ignorant of them, or, knowing them, fights against them, he masters them and they become his servants and helpers when he understands them, knows their directions and calculates their forces.

In truth science is possible only on the physical plane because its laws *are* inviolable, immutable. Were there no such things as natural laws, there could be no sciences. An investigator makes a number of experiments, and from the results of these he learns how Nature works; knowing this, he can calculate how to bring about a certain desired result, and if he fails in achieving that result he knows that he has omitted some necessary condition—either his knowledge is imperfect, or he has made a miscalculation. He reviews his knowledge, revises his methods, recasts his calculations, with a serene and complete certainty that if he asks his question rightly Nature will answer him with unvarying precision. Hydrogen and oxygen will not give him water to-day and prussic acid tomorrow; fire will not burn him to-day and freeze him tomorrow. If water be a fluid to-day and a solid tomorrow, it is because the conditions surrounding it have been altered, and the reinstatement of the original conditions will bring about the original result. Every new piece of information about the laws of Nature is not a fresh restriction but a fresh power, for all these energies of Nature become forces which he can use in proportion as he understands them. Hence the saying that " knowledge is power", for exactly in proportion to his knowledge can he utilize these forces; by selecting those with which he will work, by balancing one against another, by neutralizing opposing energies that would interfere with his object, he can calculate beforehand the result, and bring about what he predetermines. Understanding and manipulating causes, he can predict effects, and thus the very rigidity of Nature which seemed at first to paralyze human action can be used to produce an infinite variety of results. Perfect rigidity in each separate force makes possible perfect flexibility in their combinations. For the forces being of every kind, moving in every direction, and each being calculable, a selection can be made and the selected forces so combined as to yield any desired result. The object to be gained being determined, it can be infallibly obtained by a careful balancing of forces in the combination put together as a cause. But, be it remembered, knowledge is requisite thus to guide events, to bring about desired results. The ignorant man stumbles helplessly along, striking himself against the immutable laws and seeing his efforts fail, while the man of knowledge walks steadily forward, foreseeing, causing, preventing, adjusting, and bringing about that at which he aims, not because he is lucky but because he understands. The one is the toy, the slave of Nature, whirled along by her forces; the other is her master, using her energies to carry him onwards in the direction chosen by his will.

That which is true of the physical realm of law is true also of the moral and mental worlds, equally realms of law. Here also the ignorant is a slave, the sage is a monarch; here also the inviolability, the immutability, that were regarded as paralyzing, are found to be the necessary conditions of sure progress and of clear-sighted direction of the future. Man can become the master of his destiny only because that destiny lies in a realm of law, where knowledge can build up the science of the soul and place in the hands of man the power of controlling his future—of choosing alike his future character and his future circumstances. The knowledge of karma, that threatened to paralyze, becomes an inspiring, a supporting, an uplifting force.

Karma is, then, the law of causation, the law of cause and effect. It was put pointedly by the

Christian Initiate, S. Paul: " Be not deceived: God is not mocked: for whatsoever a man soweth that shall he also reap." [1] Man is continually sending out forces on all the plans on which he functions; these forces—themselves in quantity and quality the effects of his past activities—are causes which he sets going in each world he inhabits; they bring about certain definite effects both on himself and on others, and as these causes radiate forth from himself as centre over the whole field of his activity, he is responsible for the results they bring about. As a magnet has its " magnetic field ", an area within which all its forces play, larger or smaller according to its strength, so has every man a field of influence within which play the forces he emits, and these forces work in curves that return to their forthsender, that re-enter the centre whence they emerged.

As the subject is a very complicated one, we will subdivide it, and then study the subdivisions one by one.

Three classes of energies are sent forth by man in his ordinary life, belonging respectively to the three worlds that he inhabits: mental energies on the mental plane, giving rise to the causes we call thoughts; desire energies on the astral plane, giving rise to those we call desires; physical energies

[1] *Galatians*, vi, 7.

aroused by these, and working on the physical plane, giving rise to the causes we call actions. We have to study each of these in its workings, and to understand the class of effects to which each gives rise, if we wish to trace intelligently the part that each plays in the perplexed and complicated combinations we set up, called in their totality " our karma ". When a man, advancing more swiftly than his fellows, gains the ability to function on higher planes, he then becomes the centre of higher forces, but for the present we may leave these out of account and confine ourselves to ordinary humanity, treading the cycle of reincarnation in the three worlds.

In studying these three classes of energies we shall have to distinguish between their effect on the man who generates them and their effect on others who come within the field of his influence; for a lack of understanding on this point often leaves the student in a slough of hopeless bewilderment.

Then we must remember that every force works on its own plane and reacts on the planes below it in proportion to its intensity; the plane on which it is generated gives it its special characteristics, and in its reactions on lower planes it sets up vibrations in their finer or coarser materials according to its own original nature. The motive which generates the activity determines the plane to which the force belongs.

Next, it will be necessary to distinguish between the ripe karma, ready to show itself as inevitable events in the present life; the karma of character, showing itself in tendencies that are the outcome of accumulated experiences, and that are capable of being modified in the present life by the same power (the Ego) that created them in the past; the karma that is now making, and will give rise to future events and future character.[1]

Further, we have to realize that while a man makes his own individual karma he also connects himself thereby with others, thus becoming a member of various groups—family, national, racial—and as a member he shares in the collective karma of each of these groups.

It will be seen that the study of karma is one of much complexity; however, by grasping the main principles of its working as set out above, a coherent idea of its general bearing may be obtained without much difficulty, and its details can be studied at leisure as opportunity offers. Above all, let it never be forgotten, whether details are understood or not, that each man makes his own karma, creating alike his own capacities and his own limitations; and that working at any time with these self-created

[1] These divisions are familiar to the student as Prārabdha (commenced, to be worked out in the life); Sanchita (accumulated), a part of which is seen in the tendencies; Kriyamāna, in course of making.

capacities, and within these self-created limitations, he is still himself, the living soul, and can strengthen or weaken his capacities, enlarge or contract his limitations.

The chains that bind him are of his own forging, and he can file them away or rivet them more strongly; the house he lives in is of his own building, and he can improve it, let it deteriorate, or rebuild it, as he will. We are ever working in plastic clay and can shape it to our fancy, but the clay hardens and becomes as iron, retaining the shape we gave it. A proverb from the *Hitopadesha* runs, as translated by Sir Edwin Arnold:

> Look! the clay dries into iron, but the potter moulds the clay:
> Destiny to-day is master—Man was master yesterday.

Thus we are all masters of our tomorrows, however much we are hampered to-day by the results of our yesterdays.

Let us now take in order the divisions already set out under which karma may be studied.

Three classes of causes, with their effects on their creator and on those he influences. The first of these classes is composed of our thoughts. Thought is the most potent factor in the creation of human karma, for in thought the energies of the SELF are working in mental matter, the matter which, in its finer kinds, forms the individual vehicle, and even in its coarser kinds responds swiftly to every vibration of self-consciousness. The vibrations which we call thought, the immediate activity of the Thinker, give rise to forms of mind-stuff, or mental images, which shape and mould his mental body, as we have already seen; every thought modifies this mental body, and the mental faculties in each successive life are made by the thinkings of the previous lives. A man can have no thought-power, no mental ability, that he has not himself created by patiently repeated thinkings; on the other hand, no mental image that he has thus created is lost, but remains as material for faculty, and the aggregate of any group of mental images is built into a faculty which grows stronger with every additional thinking, or creation of a mental image, of the same kind. Knowing this law, the man can gradually make for himself the mental character he desires to possess and he can do it as definitely and as certainly as a bricklayer can build a wall. Death does not stop his work, but by setting him free from the encumbrance of the body facilitates the process of working up his mental images into definite organ we call a faculty, and he brings this back with him to his next birth on the physical plane, part of the brain of the new body being moulded so as to serve as the organ of this faculty, in a way to be explained presently. All these faculties together form the mental body for his opening life on earth, and his brain and nervous system are shaped to give this mental body expression on the physical plane. Thus the mental images created in one life appear as mental characteristics and tendencies in another, and for this reason it is written in one of the Upanishads: "Man is a creature of reflection; that which he reflects on in this life he becomes the same hereafter." [1] Such is the law, and it places the building of our mental character entirely in our own hands; if we build well, ours the advantage and the credit; if we build badly; ours the loss and the blame. Mental character, then, is a case of individual karma in its action on the individual who generates it.

This same man that we are considering, however, affects others by his thoughts. For these mental images that form his own mental body set up vibrations, thus reproducing themselves in secondary forms. These generally, being mingled with desire, take up some astral matter, and I have therefore elsewhere [2] called these secondary thought-forms astro-mental images. Such forms leave their creator and lead a quasi-independent life—still keeping up a magnetic tie with their progenitor. They come into contact with and affect others, in

---

[1] *Chhāndogyopanishad*, IV, xiv, 1.

[2] *Karma*, p. 25. (Theosophical Manual, No. IV.)

this way setting up kārmic links between these others and himself; thus they largely influence his future environment. In such fashion are made the ties which draw people together for good or evil in later lives; which surround us with relatives, friends, and enemies; which bring across our path helpers and hinderers, people who benefit and who injure us, people who love us without our winning in this life, and who hate us though in this life we have done nothing to deserve their hatred. Studying these results, we grasp a great principle—that while our thoughts produce our mental and moral character in their action on ourselves, they help to determine our human associates in the future by their effects on others.

The second great class of energies is composed of our desires—our outgoings after objects that attract us in the external world; as a mental element always enters into these in man, we may extend the term "mental images" to include them, although they express themselves chiefly in astral matter. These in their action on their progenitor mould and form his body of desire, or astral body, shape his fate when he passes into Kāmaloka after death, and determine the nature of his astral body in his next rebirth. When the desires are bestial, drunken, cruel, unclean, they are the fruitful causes of con-genital diseases, of weak and diseased brains, giving rise to epilepsy, catalepsy, and nervous diseases of all kinds, of physical malformations and deformities, and, in extreme cases, of monstrosities. Bestial appetites of an abnormal kind or intensity may set up links in the astral world which for a time chain the Egos, clothed in astral bodies shaped by these appetites, to the astral bodies of animals to which these appetites properly belong, thus delaying their reincarnation; where this fate is escaped, the bestially shaped astral body will sometimes impress its characteristics on the forming physical body of the babe during antenatal life, and produce the semihuman horrors that are occasionally born.

Desires—because they are outgoing energies that attach themselves to objects—always attract the man towards an environment in which they may be gratified. Desires for earthly things, linking the soul to the outer world, draw him towards the place where the objects of desire are most readily obtainable, and therefore it is said that a man is born according to his desires.[1] They are one of the cases that determine the place of rebirth.

The astro-mental images caused by desires affect others as do those generated by thoughts. They, therefore, also link us with other souls, and often by the strongest ties of love and hatred, for at the present stage of human evolution an ordinary man's

[1] See *Brihadāranyakopanishad*, IV, iv, 5-7, and context.

19

desires are generally stronger and more sustained than his thoughts. They thus play a great part in determining his human surroundings in future lives and may bring into those lives persons and influences of whose connection with himself he is totally unconscious. Suppose a man by sending out a thought of bitter hatred and revenge has helped to form in another the impulse which results in a murder; the creator of that thought is linked by his karma to the committer of the crime, although they have never met on the physical plane, and the wrong he has done to him, by helping to impel him to a crime, will come back as an injury in the infliction of which the whilom criminal will play his part. Many a " bolt from the blue " that is felt as utterly undeserved is the effect of such a cause, and the soul thereby learns and registers a lesson while the lower consciousness is writhing under a sense of injustice. Nothing can strike a man that he has not deserved, but his absence of memory does not cause a failure in the working of the law. We thus learn that our desires in their action on ourselves produce our desire-nature, and through it largely affect our physical bodies in our next birth; that they play a great part in determining the place of rebirth; and by their effect on others they help to draw around us our human associates in future lives.

The third great class of energies, appearing on the physical plane as actions, generate much karma by their effects on others, but only slightly affect directly the Inner Man. They are effects of his past thinkings and desires, and the karma they represent is for the most part exhausted in their happening. Indirectly they affect him in proportion as he is moved by them to fresh thoughts and desires or emotions, but the generating force lies in these and not in the actions themselves. Again, if actions are often repeated, they set up a habit of the body which acts as a limitation to the expression of the Ego in the outer world; this, however, perishes with the body, thus limiting the karma of the action to a single life so far as its effect on the soul is concerned. But it is far otherwise when we come to study the effects of actions on others, the happiness or unhappiness caused by these, and the influence exercised by these as examples. They link us to others by this influence and are thus a third factor in determining our future human associates, while they are the chief factor in determining what may be called our non-human environment. Broadly speaking, the favourable or unfavourable nature of the physical surroundings into which we are born depends on the effect of our previous actions in spreading happiness or unhappiness among other people. The physical results on others of actions on the physical plane work out karmically in repaying to the actor physical good or bad surroundings in a future life. If he has made people physically happy by sacrificing wealth or time or trouble, this action kārmically brings him favourable physical circumstances conducive to physical happiness. If he has caused people widespread physical misery, he will reap kārmically from his action wretched physical circumstances conducive to physical suffering. And this is so, whatever may have been his motive in either case—a fact which leads us to consider the law that:

Every force works on its own plane. If a man sows happiness for others on the physical plane, he will reap conditions favourable to happiness for himself on that plane, and his motive in sowing it does not affect the result. A man might sow wheat with the object of speculating with it to ruin his neighbour, but his bad motive would not make the wheat-grains grow up as dandelions. Motive is a mental or astral force, according as it arises from will or desire, and it reacts on moral and mental character or on the desire-nature severally. The causing of physical happiness by an action is a physical force and works on the physical plane. " By his actions man affects his neighbours on the physical plane; he spreads happiness around him or he causes distress, increasing or diminishing the sum of human welfare. This increase or diminution of happiness may be due to very different motives—good, bad, or mixed. A man may do an act that gives widespread enjoyment from sheer benevolence, from a longing to give happiness to his fellow-creatures. Let us say that from such a motive he presents a park to a town for the free use of its inhabitants; another may do a similar act from mere ostentation, from desire to attract attention from those who can bestow social honours (say, he might give it as purchase-money for a title); a third may give a park from mixed motives, partly unselfish, partly selfish. The motives will severally affect these three men's characters in their future incarnations, for improvement, for degradation, for small results. But the effect of the action in causing happiness to a large number of people does not depend on the motive of the giver; the people enjoy the park equally, no matter what may have prompted its gift, and this enjoyment, due to the action of the giver, establishes for him a kārmic claim on Nature, a debt due to him that will be scrupulously paid. He will receive a physically comfortable or luxurious environment, as he has given widespread physical enjoyment, and his sacrifice of physical wealth will bring him his due reward, the kārmic fruit of his action. This is his right. But the use he makes of his position, the happiness he derives from his wealth and his surroundings, will depend chiefly on his character, and here again the just reward accures to him, *each* seed bearing its appropriate harvest." [1] Truly, the ways of karma are equal. It does not withhold from the bad man the result which justly follows from an action which spreads happiness, and it also deals out to him the deteriorated character earned by his bad motive, so that in the midst of wealth he will remain discontented and unhappy. Nor can the good man escape physical suffering if he causes physical misery by mistaken actions done from a good motive; the misery he caused will bring him misery in his physical surroundings, but his good motive, improving his character, will give him a source of perennial happiness within himself, and he will be patient and contented amid his troubles. Many a puzzle may be answered by applying these principles to the facts we see around us.

These respective effects of motive and of the results (or fruits) of actions are due to the fact that each force has the characteristics of the plane on which it was generated, and the higher the plane the more potent and the more persistent the force. Hence motive is far more important than action, and a mistaken action done with a good motive is productive of more good to the doer than a well-chosen

[1] *Karma*, pp. 50, 51.

action done with a bad motive. The motive, reacting on the character, gives rise to a long series of effects, for the future actions guided by that character will all be influenced by its improvement or its deterioration; whereas the action, bringing on its doer physical happiness or unhappiness, according to its results on others, has in it no generating force, but is exhausted in its results. If bewildered as to the path of right action by a conflict of apparent duties, the knower of karma diligently tries to choose the best path, using his reason and his judgment to the utmost; he is scrupulously careful about his motive, eliminating selfish considerations and purifying his heart; then he acts fearlessly, and if his action turns out to be a blunder he willingly accepts the suffering which results from his mistake as a lesson which will be useful in the future. Meanwhile, his high motive has ennobled his character for all time to come.

This general principle that the force belongs to the plane on which it is generated is one of far-reaching import. If it be liberated with the motive of gaining physical objects, it works on the physical plane and attaches the actor to that plane. If it aims at devachanic objects, it works on the deva-chanic plane and attaches the actor thereto. If it has no motive save the divine service, it is set free on the spiritual plane, and therefore cannot attach the individual, since the *individual* is asking for nothing.

The three kinds of karma. Ripe karma is that which is ready for reaping and which is therefore inevitable. Out of all the karma of the past there is a certain amount which can be exhausted within the limits of a single life; there are some kinds of karma that are so incongruous that they could not be worked out in a single physical body, but would require very different types of body for their expression; there are liabilities contracted towards other souls, and all these souls will not be in incarnation at the same time; there is karma that must be worked out in some particular nation or particular social position, while the same man has other karma that needs an entirely different environment. Part only, therefore, of his total karma can be worked out in a given life, and this part is selected by the great Lords of Karma—of whom something will presently be said—and the soul is guided to incarnate in a family, a nation, a place, a body, suitable for the exhaustion of that aggregate of causes which can be worked out together. This aggregate of causes fixes the length of that particular life; gives to the body its characteristics, its powers, and its limitations; brings into contact with the man the souls incarnated within that life-period to whom he has contracted obligations, surrounding him with relatives, friends, and enemies; marks out the social conditions into which he is born, with their accompanying advantages and disadvantages; selects the mental energies he can show forth by moulding the organization of the brain and nervous system with which he has to work; puts together the causes that result in troubles and joys in his outer career and that can be brought into a single life. All this is the " ripe karma ", and this can be sketched out in a horoscope cast by a competent astrologer. In all this the man has no power of choice; all is fixed by the choices he has made in the past, and he must discharge to the uttermost farthing the liabilities he has contracted.

The physical, astral, and mental bodies which the soul takes on for a new life-period are, as we have seen, the direct result of his past, and they form a most important part of this ripe karma. They limit the soul on every side, and his past rises up in judgment against him, marking out the limitations which he has made for himself. Cheerfully to accept these, and diligently to work at their improvement, is the part of the wise man, for he cannot escape from them.

There is another kind of ripe karma that is of very serious importance—that of inevitable actions. Every action is the final expression of a series of thoughts; to borrow an illustration from chemistry, we obtain a saturated solution of thought by adding thought after thought of the same kind, until another thought—or even an impulse, a vibration, from without—will produce the solidification of the whole, the action which expresses the thoughts. If we persistently reiterate thoughts of the same kind, say of revenge, we at last reach the point of saturation, and any impulse will solidify these into action and a crime results. Or we may have persistently reiterated thoughts of help to another to the point of saturation, and when the stimulus of opportunity touches us they crystallize out as an act of heroism. A man may bring over with him some ripe karma of this kind, and the first vibration that touches such a mass of thoughts ready to solidify into action will hurry him without his renewed volition, unconsciously, unto the commission of the act. He cannot stop to think; he is in the condition in which the first vibration of the mind causes action; poised on the very point of balancing, the slightest impulse sends him over. Under these circumstances a man will marvel at his own commission of some crime, or at his own performance of some sublime act of self-devotion. He says: " I did it without thinking ", unknowing that he had thought so often that he had made that action inevitable. When a man has willed to do an act many times, he at last fixes his will irrevocably, and it is only a question of opportunity when he will act. So long as he can think, his freedom of choice remains, for he can set the new thought against the old and gradually wear it out by the reiteration of opposing thoughts; but when the next thrill of the soul in response to a stimulus means action, the power of choice is exhausted.

Herein lies the solution of the old problem of necessity and free will; man by the exercise of free will gradually creates necessities for himself, and between the two extremes lie all the combinations of free will and necessity which make the struggles within ourselves of which we are conscious. We are continually making habits by the repetitions of purposive actions guided by the will; then the habit becomes a limitation, and we perform the action automatically. Perhaps we are then driven to the conclusion that the habit is a bad one, and we begin laboriously to unmake it by thoughts of the opposite kind, and, after many an inevitable lapse into it, the new thought-current turns the stream, and we regain our full freedom, often again gradually to make another fetter. So old thought-forms persist and limit our thinking capacity, showing as individual and as national prejudices. The majority do not know that they are thus limited and go on serenely in their chains, ignorant of their bondage; those who learn the truth about their own nature become free. The constitution of our brain and nervous system is one of the most marked necessities in life; these we have made inevitable by our past thinkings, and they now limit us and we often chafe against them. They can be improved slowly and gradually; the limits can be expanded, but they cannot be suddenly transcended.

Another form of this ripe karma is where some past evil-thinking has made a crust of evil habits around a man which imprisons him and makes an evil life; the actions are the inevitable outcome of his past, as just explained, and they have been held over, even through several lives, in consequence of those lives not offering opportunities for their manifestation. Meanwhile the soul has been growing and has been developing noble qualities. In one life this crust of past evil is thrown out by opportunity, and because of this the soul cannot show his later development; like a chicken, ready to be hatched, he is hidden within the imprisoning shell, and only the shell is visible to the external eye. After a time that karma is exhausted, and some apparently fortuitous event—a word from a great Teacher, a book, a lecture—breaks the shell and the soul comes forth free. These are the rare, sudden, but permanent " conversions ", the " miracles of divine grace ", of which we hear; all perfectly intelligible to the knower of karma, and falling within the realm of law.

The accumulated karma that shows itself as character is, unlike the ripe, always subject to modifications. It may be said to consist of tendencies, strong or weak, according to the thought-force that has gone to their making, and these can be further strengthened or weakened by fresh streams of thought-force sent to work with or against them. If we find in ourselves tendencies of which we disapprove, we can set ourselves to work to eliminate them; often we fail to withstand a temptation, overborne by the strong outrushing stream of desire, but the longer we can hold out against it, even though we fail in the end, the nearer are we to overcoming it. Every such failure is a step towards success, for the resistance wears away part of the energy, and there is less of it available for the future.

The karma which is in the course of making has been already studied.

Collective karma. When a group of people is considered kārmically, the play of kārmic forces upon each as a member of the group introduces a new factor into the karma of the individual. We know that when a number of forces play on a point, the motion of the point is not in the direction of any one of these forces, but in the direction which is the result of their combination. So the karma of a group is the resultant of the interacting forces of the individuals composing it, and all the individuals are carried along in the direction of that resultant. An Ego is drawn by his individual karma into a family, having set up in previous lives ties which closely connect him with some of the other Egos composing it; the family has inherited property from a grandfather and is wealthy; an heir turns up, descended from the grandfather's elder brother, who had been supposed to have died childless, and the wealth passes to him and leaves the father of the family heavily indebted; it is quite possible that our Ego has had no connection in the past with this heir, to whom in past lives the father had contracted some obligation which has resulted in this catastrophe, and yet he is threatened with suffering by his action, being involved in the family karma. If, in his own individual past, there was a wrong-doing which can be exhausted by suffering caused by the family karma, he is left involved in it; if not, he is by some " unforeseen circumstances " lifted out of it, perchance by some benevolent stranger who feels an impulse to adopt and educate him, the stranger being one who in the past was his debtor.

Yet more clearly does this come out, in the working of such things as railway accidents, shipwrecks, floods, cyclones, etc. A train is wrecked, the catastrophe being immediately due to the action of the drivers, the guards, the railway directors, the makers or employees of that line, who, thinking themselves wronged, send clustering thoughts of discontent and anger against it as a whole. Those who have in their accumulated karma—but not necessarily in their ripe karma—the debt of a life suddenly cut short, may be allowed to drift into this accident and pay their debt; another, intending to go by the train, but with no such debt in his past, is " providentially " saved by being late for it.

Collective karma may throw a man into the troubles consequent on his nation going to war, and here again he may discharge debts of his past not necessarily within the ripe karma of his then life. In no case can a man suffer that which he has not deserved, but, if an unforeseen opportunity should arise to discharge a past obligation, it is well to pay it and be rid of it for evermore.

The " Lords of Karma " are the great spiritual Intelligences who keep the kārmic records and adjust the complicated workings of kārmic law. They are described by H. P. Blavatsky in *The Secret Doctrine* as the Lipika, the Recorders of Karma, and the Mahārājas [1] and Their hosts, who are " the agents of Karma upon earth ".[2] The Lipika are They who know the kārmic record of every man, and who with omniscient wisdom select and combine portions of that record to form the plan of a single

[1] The Mahādevas, or Chaturdevas of the Hindus.
[2] *Op. cit.*, Vol. I, pp. 153 to 157, 1893 Edn.; Vol. I, pp. 187 to 190, Adyar Edn.

life; They give the "idea" of the physical body
which is to be the garment of the reincarnating soul,
expressing his capacities and his limitations; this is
taken by the Mahārājas and worked into a detailed
model, which is committed to one of Their inferior
agents to be copied; this copy is the etheric double,
the matrix of the dense body, the materials for these
being drawn from the mother and subject to physical heredity. The race, the country, the parents,
are chosen for their capacity to provide suitable
materials for the physical body of the incoming
Ego, and suitable surroundings for his early life.
The physical heredity of the family affords certain
types and has evolved certain peculiarities of material combinations; hereditary diseases, hereditary
finenesses of nervous organization, imply definite
combinations of physical matter, capable of transmission. An Ego who has evolved peculiarities in
his mental and astral bodies, needing special physical peculiarities for their expression, is guided to
parents whose physical heredity enables them to
meet these requirements. Thus an Ego with high
artistic faculties devoted to music would be guided
to take his physical body in a musical family, in
which the materials supplied for building the etheric
double and the dense body would have been made
ready to adapt themselves to his needs, and the
hereditary type of nervous system would furnish the

delicate apparatus necessary for the expression of his faculties. An Ego of very evil type would be guided to a coarse and vicious family, whose bodies were built of the coarsest combinations, such as would make a body able to respond to the impulses from his mental and astral bodies. An Ego who had allowed his astral body and lower mind to lead him into excesses, and had yielded to drunkenness, for instance, would be led to incarnate in a family whose nervous systems were weakened by excess, and would be born from drunken parents, who would supply diseased materials for his physical envelope. The guidance of the Lords of Karma thus adjusts means to ends, and insures the doing of justice; the Ego brings with him his kārmic possessions of faculties and desires, and he receives a physical body suited to be their vehicle.

As the soul must return to earth until he has discharged all his liabilities, thus exhausting all his individual karma, and as in each life thoughts and desires generate fresh karma, the question may arise in the mind: " How can this constantly renewing bond be put an end to? How can the soul attain his liberation? " Thus we come to the " ending of karma", and have to investigate how this may be.

The binding element in karma is the first thing to be clearly grasped. The outward-going energy of the soul attaches itself to some object, and the

20

soul is drawn back by this tie to the place where that attachment may be realized by union with the object of desire; so long as the soul attaches himself to any object, he must be drawn to the place where that object can be enjoyed. Good karma binds the soul as much as does bad, for any desire, whether for objects here or in Devachan, must draw the soul to the place of its gratification.

Action is prompted by desire, an act is done not for the sake of doing the act, but for the sake of obtaining by the act something that is desired, of acquiring its results, or, as it is technically called, of enjoying its fruit. Men work, not because they want to dig, or build, or weave, but because they want the fruits of digging, building, and weaving, in the shape of money or of goods. A barrister pleads, not because he wants to set forth the dry details of a case, but because he wants wealth, fame, and rank. Men around us on every side are labouring for something, and the spur to their activity lies in the fruit it brings them and not in the labour. Desire for the fruit of action moves them to activity, and enjoyment of that fruit rewards their exertions.

Desire is, then, the binding element in karma, and when the soul no longer desires any object in earth or in heaven, his tie to the wheel of reincarnation that turns in the three worlds is broken. Action itself has no power to hold the soul, for with

the completion of the action it slips into the past.
But the ever-renewed desire for fruit constantly
spurs the soul into fresh activities, and thus new
chains are continually being forged.

Nor should we feel any regret when we see men
constantly driven to action by the whip of desire,
for desire overcomes sloth, laziness, inertia,[1] and
prompts men to the activity that yields them experience. Note the savage, idly dozing on the
grass; he is moved to activity by hunger, the desire
for food, and is driven to exert patience, skill, and
endurance to gratify his desire. Thus he develops
mental qualities, but when his hunger is satisfied he
sinks again into a dozing animal. How entirely
have mental qualities been evolved by the promptings of desire, and how useful have proved desires
for fame, for posthumous renown! Until man is
approaching divinity he needs the urgings of desires,
and the desires simply grow purer and less selfish
as he climbs upwards. But none the less desires
bind him to rebirth, and if he would be free he
must destroy them.

When a man begins to long for liberation, he is
taught to practise " renunciation of the fruits of
action "; that is, he gradually eradicates in himself
the wish to possess any object; he at first voluntarily

---

[1] The student will remember that these show the dominance
of the tāmasic guna, and while it is dominant men do not emerge
from the lowest of the three stages of their evolution.

and deliberately denies himself the object, and thus habituates himself to do contentedly without it; after a time he no longer misses it, and he finds the desire for it is disappearing from his mind. At this stage he is very careful not to neglect any work which is duty because he has become indifferent to the result it brings to him, and he trains himself in discharging every duty with earnest attention, while remaining entirely indifferent to the fruits it brings forth. When he attains perfection in this, and neither desires nor dislikes any object, he ceases to generate karma; ceasing to ask anything from the earth or from Devachan, he is not drawn to either; he wants nothing that either can give him, and all links between himself and them are broken off. This is the ceasing of individual karma, so far as the generation of new karma is concerned.

But the soul has to get rid of old chains as well as to cease from the forging of new, and these old chains must either be allowed to wear out gradually or must be broken deliberately. For this breaking, knowledge is necessary, a knowledge which can look back into the past, and see the causes there set going, causes which are working out their effects in the present. Let us suppose that a person, thus looking backward over his past lives, sees certain causes which will bring about an event which is still in the future; let us suppose further that these

causes are thoughts of hatred for an injury inflicted
on himself, and that they will cause suffering a year
hence to the wrong doer; such a person can intro-
duce a new cause to intermingle with the causes
working from the past, and he may counteract them
with strong thoughts of love and goodwill that will
exhaust them, and will thus prevent their bringing
about the otherwise inevitable event, which would,
in its turn, have generated new kārmic trouble.
Thus he may neutralize forces coming out of the
past by sending against them forces equal and
opposite, and may in this way " burn up his karma
by knowledge ". In similar fashion he may bring
to an end karma generated in his present life that
would normally work out in future lives.

Again, he may be hampered by liabilities contracted to other souls in the past, wrongs he has
done to them, duties he owes to them. By the use
of his knowledge he can find those souls, whether in
this world or in either of the other two, and seek
opportunities of serving them. There may be a soul
incarnated during his own life-period to whom he
owes some kārmic debt; he may seek out that soul
and pay his debt, thus setting himself free from a
tie which, left to the course of events, would have
necessitated his own reincarnation, or would have
hampered him in a future life. Strange and puzzling
lines of action adopted by occultists have sometimes

this explanation—the man of knowledge enters into close relations with some person who is considered by the ignorant bystanders and critics to be quite outside the companionships that are fitting for him; but that occultist is quietly working out a kārmic obligation which would otherwise hamper and retard his progress.

Those who do not possess knowledge enough to review their past lives may yet exhaust many causes that they have set going in the present life; they can carefully go over all that they can remember, and note where they have wronged any or where any has wronged them, exhausting the first cases by pouring out thoughts of love and service, and performing acts of service to the injured person, where possible on the physical plane also; and in the second cases sending forth thoughts of pardon and goodwill. Thus they diminish their kārmic liabilities and bring near the day of liberation.

Unconsciously, pious people who obey the precept of all great Teachers of religion to return good for evil are exhausting karma generated in the present that would otherwise work out in the future. No one can weave with them a bond of hatred if they refuse to contribute any strands of hatred to the weaving, and persistently neutralize every force of hatred with one of love. Let a soul radiate in every direction love and compassion, and thoughts of hatred can find nothing to which they can attach themselves. " The Prince of this world cometh and hath nothing in me." All great Teachers knew the law and based on it Their precepts, and those who through reverence and devotion to Them obey Their directions profit under the law, although they know nothing of the details of its working. An ignorant man who carries out faithfully the instructions given him by a scientist can obtain results by his working with the laws of Nature, despite his ignorance of them and the same principle holds good in worlds beyond the physical. Many who have not time to study, and who perforce accept on the authority of experts rules which guide their daily conduct in life, may thus unconsciously be discharging their kārmic liabilities.

In countries where reincarnation and karma are taken for granted by every peasant and labourer, the belief spreads a certain quiet acceptance of inevitable troubles that conduces much to the calm and contentment of ordinary life. A man overwhelmed by misfortunes rails neither against God nor against his neighbours, but regards his troubles as the results of his own past mistakes and ill-doings. He accepts them resignedly and makes the best of them, and thus escapes much of the worry and anxiety with which those who know not the law aggravate troubles already sufficiently heavy. He realizes that his future lives depend on his own exertions, and that the law which brings him pain will bring him joy just as inevitably if he sows the seed of good. Hence a certain large patience and a philosophic view of life, tending directly to social stability and to general contentment. The poor and ignorant do not study profound and detailed metaphysics, but they grasp thoroughly these simple principles—that every man is reborn on earth time after time, and that each successive life is moulded by those that precede it. To them rebirth is as sure and as inevitable as the rising and setting of the sun; it is part of the course of Nature, against which it is idle to repine or to rebel. When Theosophy has restored these ancient truths to their rightful place in western thought, they will gradually work their way among all classes of society in Christendom, spreading understanding of the nature of life and acceptance of the result of the past. Then too will vanish the restless discontent which arises chiefly from the impatient and hopeless feeling that life is unintelligible, unjust, and unmanageable, and it will be replaced by the quiet strength and patience which come from an illumined intellect and a knowledge of the law, and which characterize the reasoned and balanced activity of those who feel that they are building for eternity.

CHAPTER X

THE LAW OF SACRIFICE

THE study of the Law of Sacrifice follows naturally on the study of the Law of Karma; and the understanding of the former, it was once remarked by a Master, is as necessary for the world as the understanding of the latter. By an act of Self-Sacrifice the LOGOS became manifest for the emanation of the universe, by sacrifice the universe is maintained and by sacrifice man reaches perfection.[1] Hence every religion that springs from the Ancient Wisdom has sacrifice as a central teaching, and some of the profoundest truths of occultism are rooted in the law of sacrifice.

An attempt to grasp, however feebly, the nature of the sacrifice of the LOGOS may prevent us from falling into the very general mistake that sacrifice is an essentially painful thing; whereas the very

[1] The Hindus will remember the opening words of the *Brihad-āranyakopanishad*, that the dawn is in sacrifice; the Zoroastrian will recall how Ahura-Mazda came forth from an act of sacrifice; the Christian will think of the Lamb—the symbol of the LOGOS—slain from the foundation of the world.

essence of sacrifice is a voluntary and glad pouring forth of life that others may share in it; and pain only arises when there is discord in the nature of the sacrifice, between the higher whose joy is in giving and the lower whose satisfaction lies in grasping and in holding. It is that discord alone that introduces the element of pain, and in the supreme Perfection, in the Logos, no discord could arise; the One is the perfect chord of Being, of infinite melodious concords, all turned to a single note, in which Life and Wisdom and Bliss are blended into one keynote of Existence.

The sacrifice of the Logos lay in His voluntarily circumscribing His infinite life in order that He might manifest. Symbolically, in the infinite ocean of light, with centre everywhere and with circumference nowhere, there arises a full-orbed sphere of living light, a Logos, and the surface of the sphere is His will to limit Himself that He may become manifest, His veil [1] in which He incloses Himself that within it a universe may take form. That for which the sacrifice is made is not yet in existence; its future being lies in the "thought" of the Logos alone; to Him it owes its conception and will own its manifold life. Diversity could not arise in the

[1] This is the Self-limiting power of the LOGOS, His Māyā, the limiting principle by which all forms are brought forth. His Life appears as "Spirit", His Māyā as "matter", and these are never disjoined during manifestation.

" partless Brahman " save for this voluntary sacrifice of the Deity taking on Himself form in order to
emanate myriad forms, each dowered with a spark
of His life and therefore with the power of evolving
into His image. " The primal sacrifice that causes
the birth of beings is named action (karma)," [1] it is
said; and this coming forth into activity from the
bliss of the perfect repose of self-existence has ever
been recognized as the sacrifice of the LOGOS. That
sacrifice continues throughout the term of the
universe, for the life of the LOGOS is the sole support
of every separated " life ", and He limits His life in
each of the myriad forms to which He gives birth,
bearing all the restraints and limitations implied in
each form. From any one of these He could burst
forth at any moment, the infinite Lord, filling the
universe with His glory; but only by sublime patience
and slow and gradual expansion can each form be
led upward until it becomes a self-dependent centre
of boundless power like Himself. Therefore does
He cabin Himself in forms, and bear all imper-
fections till perfection is attained, and His creature
is like unto Himself and one with Him, but with
its own thread of memory. Thus this pouring out
of His life into forms is part of the original sacrifice,
and has in it the bliss of the eternal Father sending
forth His offspring as separated lives, that each may

[1] *Bhagavad Gītā*, viii, 3.

evolve an identity that shall never perish, and yield its own note blended with all others to swell the eternal song of bliss, intelligence, and life. This marks the essential nature of sacrifice, whatever other elements may become mixed with the central idea; it is the voluntary pouring out of life that others may partake of it, to bring others into life and to sustain them in it till they become self-dependent, and this is but one expression of divine joy. There is always joy in the exercise of activity which is the expression of the power of the actor; the bird takes joy in the outpouring of song, and quivers with the mere rapture of the singing; the painter rejoices in the creation of his genius, in the putting into form of his idea; the essential activity of divine life must lie in giving, for there is nothing higher than itself from which it can receive; if it is to be active at all—and manifested life *is* active motion—it must pour itself out. Hence the sign of the spirit is giving, for spirit is the active divine life in every form.

But the essential activity of matter, on the other hand, lies in receiving; by receiving life-impulses it is organized into the forms; by receiving them these are maintained; on their withdrawal they fall to pieces. All its activity is of this nature of receiving, and only by receiving can it endure as a form. Therefore is it always grasping, clinging, seeking to hold for its own; the persistence of the form depends on its grasping and retentive power, and it will therefore seek to draw into itself all it can, and will grudge every fraction with which it parts. Its joy will be in seizing and holding; to it giving is like courting death.

It is very easy, from this standpoint, to see how the notion arose that sacrifice was suffering. While the divine life found its delight in exercising its activity of giving, and even when embodied in form cared not if the form perished by the giving, knowing it to be only its passing expression and the means of its separated growth; the form which felt its life-forces pouring away from it cried out in anguish, and sought to exercise its activity in holding, thus resisting the outward flow. The sacrifice diminished the life-energies the form claimed as its own; or even entirely drained them away, leaving the form to perish. In the lower world of form this was the only aspect of sacrifice cognizable, and the form found itself driven to the slaughter, and cried out in fear and agony. What wonder that men, blinded by form, identified sacrifice with the agonizing form instead of with the free life that gave itself, crying gladly: " Lo; I come to do Thy will, O God; I am content to do it." Nay, what wonder that men—conscious of a higher and a lower nature, and oft identifying their self-consciousness more with the lower than with the higher—felt the struggle of the lower nature, the form, as their own struggles and felt that *they* were accepting suffering in resignation to a higher will, and regarded sacrifice as that devout and resigned acceptance of pain. Not until man identifies himself with the life instead of with the form can the element of pain in sacrifice be gotten rid of. In a perfectly harmonized entity, pain cannot be, for the form is then the perfect vehicle of the life, receiving or surrendering with ready accord. With the ceasing of struggle comes the ceasing of pain. For suffering arises from jar, from friction, from antagonistic movements, and where the whole Nature works in perfect harmony the conditions that give rise to suffering are not present.

The law of sacrifice being thus the law of life-evolution in the universe, we find every step in the ladder is accomplished by sacrifice—the life pouring itself out to take birth in a higher form, while the form that contained it perishes. Those who look only at the perishing forms see Nature as a vast charnel-house; while those who see the deathless soul escaping to take new and higher form hear ever the joyous song of birth from the upward-springing life.

The Monad in the mineral kingdom evolves by the breaking up of its forms for the production and support of plants. Minerals are disintegrated that plant-forms may be built out of their materials; the plant draws from the soil its nutritive constituents, breaks them up, and incorporates them into its own substance. The mineral forms perish that the plant-forms may grow, and this law of sacrifice stamped on the mineral kingdom is the law of the evolution of life and form. The life passes onward and the Monad evolves to produce the vegetable kingdom, the perishing of the lower form being the condition for the appearing and the support of the higher.

The story is repeated in the vegetable kingdom, for its forms in turn are sacrificed in order that animal forms may be produced and may grow; on every side grasses, grains, trees perish for the sustenance of animal bodies; their tissues are disintegrated that the materials comprising them may be assimilated by the animal and build up its body. Again the law of sacrifice is stamped on the world, this time on the vegetable kingdom; its life evolves while its forms perish; the Monad evolves to produce the animal kingdom, and the vegetable is offered up that animal forms may be brought forth and maintained.

So far the idea of pain has scarcely connected itself with that of sacrifice, for, as we have seen in the course of our studies, the astral bodies of plants are not sufficiently organized to give rise to any acute sensations either of pleasure or of pain. But as we consider the law of sacrifice in its working in the animal kingdom, we cannot avoid the recognition of the pain there involved in the breaking up of forms. It is true that the amount of pain caused by the preying of one animal upon another in " the state of nature " is comparatively trivial in each case, but still some pain occurs. It is also true that man, in the part he has played in helping to evolve animals, has much aggravated the amount of pain, and has strengthened instead of diminishing the predatory instincts of carnivorous animals; still, he did not implant those instincts, though he took advantage of them for his own purposes, and innumerable varieties of animals, with the evolution of which man has had directly nothing to do, prey upon each other, the forms being sacrificed to the support of other forms, as in the mineral and vegetable kingdoms. The struggle for existence went on long before man appeared on the scene, and accelerated the evolution alike of life and of forms, while the pains accompanying the destruction of forms began the long task of impressing on the evolving Monad the transitory nature of all forms, and the difference between the forms that perished and the life that persisted.

The lower nature of man was evolved under the same law of sacrifice as ruled in the lower kingdoms.

But with the outpouring of divine Life which gave the human Monad came a change in the way in which the law of sacrifice worked as the law of life. In man was to be developed the will, the self-moving, self-initiated energy, and the compulsion which forced the lower kingdoms along the path of evolution could not therefore be employed in his case, without paralyzing the growth of this new and essential power. No mineral, no plant, no animal was asked to accept the law of sacrifice as a voluntarily chosen law of life. It was imposed upon them from without, and it forced their growth by a necessity from which they could not escape. Man was to have the freedom of choice necessary for the growth of a discriminative and self-conscious intelligence, and the question arose: " How can this creature be left free to choose, and yet learn to choose to follow the law of sacrifice, while yet he is a sensitive organism, shrinking from pain, and pain is inevitable in the breaking up of sentient form? "

Doubtless, aeons of experience, studied by a creature becoming ever more intelligent, might have finally led man to discover that the law of sacrifice is the fundamental law of life; but in this, as in so much else, he was not left to his own unassisted efforts. Divine Teachers were there at the side of man in his infancy, and they authoritatively

21

proclaimed the law of sacrifice, and incorporated it in a most elementary form in the religions by which They trained the dawning intelligence of man. It would have been useless to have suddenly demanded from these child-souls that they should surrender without return what seemed to them to be the most desirable objects, the objects on the possession of which their life in form depended. They must be led along a path which would lead gradually to the heights of voluntary self-sacrifice. To this end they were first taught that they were not isolated units, but were parts of a larger whole, and that their lives were linked to other lives both above and below them. Their physical lives were supported by lower lives, by the earth, by plants; they consumed these, and in thus doing they contracted a debt which they were bound to pay. Living on the sacrificed lives of others, they must sacrifice in turn something which should support other lives; they must nourish even as they were nourished; taking the fruits produced by the activity of the astral entities that guide physical Nature, they must recruit the expended forces by suitable offerings. Hence have arisen all the sacrifices to these forces—as science calls them,—to these intelligences guiding physical order, as religions have always taught. As fire quickly disintegrated the dense physical, it quickly restored the ethertic particles of the burnt offerings to the ethers; thus the astral particles were easily set free to be assimilated by the astral entities concerned with the fertility of the earth and the growth of plants. Thus the wheel of production was kept turning, and man learned that he was constantly incurring debts to Nature which he must as constantly discharge. Thus the sense of obligation was implanted and nurtured in his mind, and the duty that he owed to the whole, to the nourishing mother Nature, became impressed on his thought. It is true that this sense of obligation was closely connected with the idea that its discharge was necessary for his own welfare, and that the wish to continue to prosper moved him to the payment of his debt. He was but a child-soul, learning his first lessons, and this lesson of the interdependence of lives, of the life of each depending on the sacrifice of others, was of vital importance to his growth. Not yet could he feel the divine joy of giving; the reluctance of the form to surrender aught that nourished it had first to be overcome, and sacrifice became identified with this surrender of something valued, a surrender made from a sense of obligation and the desire to continue prosperous.

The next lesson removed the reward of sacrifice to a region beyond the physical world. First, by a sacrifice of material goods material welfare was to be secured. Then the sacrifice of material goods was to bring enjoyment in heaven, on the other side of death. The reward of the sacrificer was of a higher kind, and he learned that the relatively permanent might be secured by the sacrifice of the relatively transient—a lesson that was important as leading to discriminative knowledge. The clinging of the form to physical objects was exchanged for a clinging to heavenly joys. In all exoteric religions we find this educative process resorted to by the Wise Ones—too wise to expect from child-souls the virtue of unrewarded heroism, and content, with a sublime patience, to coax their wayward charges slowly along a pathway that was a thorny and stony one to the lower nature. Gradually men were induced to subjugate the body, to overcome its sloth by the regular daily performance of religious rites, often burdensome in their nature, and to regulate its activities by directing them into useful channels; they were trained to conquer the form and to hold it in subjection to the life, and to accustom the body to yield itself to works of goodness and charity in obedience to the demands of the mind, even while that mind was chiefly stimulated by a desire to enjoy reward in heaven. We can see among the Hindus, the Persians, the Chinese, how men were taught to recognize their manifold obligations; to make the body yield dutiful sacrifice of obedience and reverence to ancestors, to parents, to elders; to bestow charity with courtesy; and to show kindness to all. Slowly men were helped to evolve both heroism and self-sacrifice to a high degree, as witness the martyrs who joyfully flung their bodies to torture and death rather than deny their faith or be false to their creed. They looked indeed for a " crown of glory " in heaven as a recompense for the sacrifice of the physical form, but it was much to have overcome the clinging to that physical form, and to have made the invisible world so real that it outweighed the visible.

The next step was achieved when the sense of duty was definitely established; when the sacrifice of the lower to the higher was seen to be " right ", apart from all question of a reward to be received in another world; when the obligation owed by the part to the whole was recognized, and the yielding of service by the form that existed by the service of others was felt to be justly due without any claim to wages being established thereby. Then man began to perceive the law of sacrifice as the law of life, and voluntarily to associate himself with it; and he began to learn to disjoin himself in idea from the form he dwelt in and to identify himself with the evolving life. This gradually led him to feel a certain indifference to all the activities of form, save as they consisted in " duties that ought to be done ", and to regard all of them as mere channels for the life-activities that were due to the world, and not as activities performed by him with any desire for their results. Thus he reached the point already noted, when karma attracting him to the three worlds ceased to be generated, and he turned the wheel of existence because it ought to be turned, and not because its revolution brought any desirable object to himself.

The full recognition of the law of sacrifice, however, lifts man beyond the mental plane—whereon duty is recognized as duty, as " what ought to be done because it is owed "—to that higher plane of Buddhi where all selves are felt as one, and where all activities are poured out for the use of all, and not for the gain of a separated self. Only on that plane is the law of sacrifice *felt* as a joyful privilege, instead of only recognized intellectually as true and just. On the buddhic plane man clearly sees that life is one, that it streams out perpetually as the free outpouring of the love of the LoGos, that life holding itself separate is a poor and a mean thing at best, and an ungrateful one to boot. There the whole heart rushes upwards to the LoGos in one strong surge of love and worship, and gives itself in joyfullest self-surrender to be a channel of His life and love to the world. To be a carrier of His light, a messenger of His compassion, a worker in His realm—that appears as the only life worth living; to hasten human evolution, to serve the Good Law, to lift part of the heavy burden of the world—that seems to be the very gladness of the Lord Himself.

From this plane only can a man act as one of the Saviours of the world, because on it he is one with the selves of all. Identified with humanity where it is one, his strength, his love, his life, can flow downwards into any or into every separated self. He has become a spiritual force, and the available spiritual energy of the world-system is increased by the pouring into it of his life. The forces he used to expend on the physical, astral, and mental planes, seeking things for his separated self, are now all gathered up in one act of sacrifice, and, transmuted thereby into spiritual energy, they pour down upon the world as spiritual life. This transmutation is wrought by the motive which determines the plane on which the energy is set free. If a man's motive be the gain of physical objects, the energy liberated works only on the physical plane; if he desire astral objects, he liberates energy on the astral plane; if he seek mental joys, his energy functions on the mental plane; but if he sacrifice himself to be a channel of the Logos, he liberates energy on the spiritual plane, and it works everywhere with the potency and keenness of a spiritual force. For such a man action and inaction are the same; for he does everything while doing nothing, he does nothing while doing everything. For him, high and low, great and small are the same; he fills any place that needs filling, and the Logos is alike in every place and in every action. He can flow into any form, he can work along any line, he knows not any longer choice or difference; his life by sacrifice has been made one with the life of the Logos—he sees God in everything and everything in God. How then can place or form make to him any difference? He no longer identifies himself with form, but is self-conscious Life. " Having nothing, he possesseth all things "; asking for nothing, everything flows into him. His life is bliss, for he is one with his Lord, who is Beatitude; and, using form for service without attachment to it, " he has put an end to pain ".

Those who grasp something of the wonderful possibilities which open out before us as we voluntarily associate ourselves with the law of sacrifice will wish to begin that voluntary association long ere they can rise to the heights just dimly sketched. Like other deep spiritual truths, it is eminently practical in its application to daily life, and none who feel its beauty need hesitate to begin to work with it. When a man resolves to begin the practice of sacrifice, he will train himself to open every day with an act of sacrifice, the offering of himself, ere the day's work begins, to Him to whom he gives his life; his first waking thought will be this dedication of all his power to his Lord. Then each thought, each word, each action in daily life will be done as a sacrifice—not for its fruit, not even as duty, but as the way in which, at the moment, his Lord can be served. All that comes will be accepted as the expression of His will; joys, troubles, anxieties, successes, failures, all to him are welcome as marking out his path of service; he will take each happily as it comes and offer it as a sacrifice; he will lose each happily as it goes, since its going shows that his Lord has no longer need for it. Any powers he has he gladly uses for service; when they fail him, he takes their failure with happy equanimity; since they are no longer available he cannot give them. Even suffering that springs from past causes not yet exhausted can be changed into a voluntary sacrifice by welcoming it; taking possession of it by willing it, a man may offer it as a gift, changing it by this motive into a spiritual force. Every human life offers countless opportunities for this practice of the law of sacrifice, and every human life becomes a power as these opportunities are seized and utilized. Without any expansion of his waking consciousness, a man may thus become a worker on the spiritual planes, liberating energy there which pours down into the lower worlds.

His self-surrender here in the lower consciousness, imprisoned as it is in the body, calls out responsive thrills of life from the buddhic aspect of the Monad which is his true Self, and hastens the time when that Monad shall become the spiritual Ego, self-moved and ruling all his vehicles, using each of them at will as needed for the work that is to be done. In no way can progress be made so rapidly, and the manifestation of all the powers latent in the Monad be brought about so quickly, as by the understanding and the practice of the law of sacrifice. Therefore was it called by a Master, " The Law of evolution for the man ". It has indeed profounder and more mystic aspects than any touched on here, but these will unveil themselves without words to the patient and loving heart whose life is all a sacrificial offering. There are things that are heard only in stillness; there are teachings that can be uttered only by " the Voice of the Silence ". Among these are the deeper truths rooted in the law of sacrifice.

but one grade in evolution in the linked lives that
stretch from the elemental essence onwards to the
manifested God.

of the embryonic soul in the spiritually
advanced, through the stages of evolving consciousness from the life of the life of thought.

CHAPTER XI

MAN'S ASCENT

So stupendous is the ascent up which some men
have climbed, and some are climbing, that when we
scan it by an effort of the imagination we are apt to
recoil, wearied in thought by the mere idea of that
long journey. From the embryonic soul of the
primitive man to the liberated and triumphant perfected spiritual soul of the divine man—it seems
scarcely credible that the one can contain in it all
that is expressed in the other, and that the difference
is but a difference in evolution, that one is only at
the beginning and the other at the end of man's
ascent. Below the one stretch the long ranks of
the sub-human—the animals, vegetables, minerals,
elemental essence; above the other stretch the infinite gradations of the superhuman—the Chohans,
Manus, Buddhas, Builders, Lipikas; who may name
or number the hosts of the mighty Ones? Looked at
thus, as a stage in a yet vaster life, the many steps
within the human kingdom shrink into a narrower
compass, and man's ascent is seen as comprising

but one grade in evolution in the linked lives that stretch from the elemental essence onwards to the manifested God.

We have traced man's ascent from the appearance of the embryonic soul to the state of the spiritually advanced, through the stages of evolving consciousness from the life of sensation to the life of thought. We have seen him re-tread the cycle of birth and death in the three worlds, each world yielding him its harvest and offering him opportunities for progress. We are now in a position to follow him into the final stages of his human evolution, stages that lie in the future for the vast bulk of our humanity, but that have already been trodden by its eldest children, and that are being trodden by a slender number of men and women in our own day.

These stages have been classified under two headings—the first are spoken of as constituting "the probationary Path", while the later ones are included in "the Path proper" or "the Path of discipleship". We will take them in their natural order.

As a man's intellectual, moral, and spiritual nature develops, he becomes more and more conscious of the purpose of human life, and more and more eager to accomplish that purpose in his own person. Repeated longings for earthly joys, followed by full possession and by subsequent weariness, have gradually taught him the transient and unsatisfactory nature of earth's best gifts; so often has he striven for, gained, enjoyed, been satiated, and finally nauseated, that he turns away discontented from all that earth can offer. "What doth it profit?" sighs the wearied soul. "All is vanity and vexation. Hundreds, yea, thousands of times have I possessed, and finally have found disappointment even in possession. These joys are illusions, as bubbles on the stream, airy-coloured, rainbow-hued, but bursting at a touch. I am athirst for realities; I have had enough of shadows; I pant for the eternal and the true, for freedom from the limitations that hem me in, that keep me a prisoner amid these changing shows."

This first cry of the soul for liberation is the result of the realization that, were this earth all that poets have dreamed it, were every evil swept away, every sorrow put an end to, every joy intensified, every beauty enhanced, were everything raised to its point of perfection, he would still be aweary of it, would turn from it void of desire. It has become to him a prison, and, let it be decorated as it may, he pants for the free and limitless air beyond its inclosing walls. Nor is heaven more attractive to him than earth; of that too he is aweary; its joys have lost their attractiveness, even its intellectual and emotional delights no longer satisfy. They also

" come and go, impermanent ", like the contacts of the senses; they are limited, transient, unsatisfying. He is tired of the changing; from very weariness he cries out for liberty.

Sometimes this realization of the worthlessness of earth and heaven is at first but as a flash in consciousness, and the external worlds reassert their empire and the glamour of their illusive joys again laps the soul into content. Some lives even may pass, full of noble work, and unselfish achievement, of pure thoughts and lofty deeds, ere this realization of the emptiness of all that is phenomenal becomes the permanent attitude of the soul. But sooner or later the soul once and for ever breaks with the earth and heaven as incompetent to satisfy his needs, and this definite turning away from the transitory, this definite will to reach the eternal, is the gateway to the probationary Path. The soul steps off the highway of evolution to breast the steeper climb up the mountain-side, resolute to escape from the bondage of earthly and heavenly lives, and to reach the freedom of the upper air.

The work which has to be accomplished by the man who enters on the probationary Path is entirely mental and moral; he has to bring himself up to the point at which he will be fit to " meet his Master face to face "; but the very words " his Master ", need explanation. There are certain great Beings belonging to our race who have completed Their human evolution, and to whom allusion has already been made as constituting a Brotherhood, and as guiding and forwarding the development of the race. These Great Ones, the Masters, voluntarily incarnate in human bodies in order to form the connecting link between human and superhuman beings, and They permit those who fulfil certain conditions to become Their disciples, with the object of hastening their evolution and thus qualifying themselves to enter the great Brotherhood, and to assist in Its glorious and beneficent work for man.

The Masters ever watch the race, and mark any who by the practice of virtue, by unselfish labour for human good, by intellectual effort turned to the service of man, by sincere devotion, piety, and purity, draw ahead of the mass of their fellows, and render themselves capable of receiving spiritual assistance beyond that shed down on mankind as a whole. If an individual is to receive special help he must show special receptivity. For the Masters are the distributors of the spiritual energies that help on human evolution, and the use of these for the swifter growth of a single soul is only permitted when that soul shows a capacity for rapid progress and can thus be quickly fitted to become a helper of the race, returning to it the aid that had been afforded to himself. When a man by his own efforts, utilizing to the full all the general help coming to him through religion and philosophy, has struggled onwards to the front of the advancing human wave and when he shows a loving, selfless, helpful nature, then he becomes a special object of attention to the watchful Guardians of the race, and opportunities are put in his way to test his strength and call forth his intuition. In proportion as he successfully uses these, he is yet further helped, and glimpses are afforded to him of the true life, until the unsatisfactory and unreal nature of mundane existence presses more and more on the soul, with the result already mentioned—the weariness which makes him long for freedom and brings him to the gateway of the probationary Path.

His entrance on his Path places him in the position of a disciple or chela, on Probation, and some one Master takes him under His care, recognizing him as a man who has stepped out of the highway of evolution, and seeks the Teacher who shall guide his steps along the steep and narrow path which leads to liberation. That Teacher is awaiting him at the very entrance of the Path, and even though the neophyte knows not his Teacher, his Teacher knows him, sees his efforts, directs his steps, leads him into the conditions that best subserve his progress, watching over him with the tender solicitude of a mother, and with the wisdom born of perfect insight. The road may seem lonely and dark, and the young disciple may fancy himself deserted, but a " friend who sticketh closer than a brother " is ever at hand, and the help withheld from the senses is given to the soul.

There are four definite " qualifications " that the probationary chelā must set himself to acquire, that are by the wisdom of the great Brotherhood laid down as the conditions of full discipleship. They are not asked for in perfection, but they must be striven for and partially possessed ere Initiation is permitted. The first of these is the discrimination between the real and the unreal which has been already dawning on the mind of the pupil, and which drew him to the Path on which he has now entered; the distinction grows clear and sharply defined in his mind, and gradually frees him to a great extent from the fetters which bind him, for the second qualification, indifference to external things, comes naturally in the wake of discrimination, from the clear perception of their worthlessness. He learns that the weariness which took all the savour out of life was due to the disappointments constantly arising from his search for satisfaction in the unreal, when only the real can content the soul; that all forms are unreal and without stability, changing ever under the impulses of life, and that

22

nothing is real but the one Life that we seek for and love unconsciously under its many veils. This discrimination is much stimulated by the rapidly changing circumstances into which a disciple is generally thrown, with the view of pressing on him strongly the instability of all external things. The lives of a disciple are generally lives of storm and stress, in order that the qualities which are normally evolved in a long succession of lives in the three worlds may in him be forced into swift growth and quickly brought to perfection. As he alternates rapidly from joy to sorrow, from peace to storm, from rest to toil, he learns to see in the changes the unreal forms, and to feel through all a steady unchanging life. He grows indifferent to the presence or the absence of things that thus come and go, and more and more he fixes his gaze on the changeless reality that is ever present.

While he is thus gaining in insight and stability he works also at the development of the third qualification—the six mental attributes that are demanded from him ere he may enter on the Path itself. He need not possess them all perfectly, but he must have them all partially present at least ere he will be permitted to pass onward. First he must gain control over his thoughts, the progeny of the restless, unruly mind, hard to curb as the wind.[1]

[1] *Bhagavad Gītā*, vi, 34.

Steady, daily practice in meditation, in concentration, had begun to reduce this mental rebel to order ere he entered on the probationary Path, and the disciple now works with concentrated energy to complete the task, knowing that the great increase in thought-power that will accompany his rapid growth will prove a danger both to others and to himself unless the developing force be thoroughly under his control. Better give a child dynamite as a plaything, than place the creative powers of thought in the hands of the selfish and the ambitious. Secondly, the young chelā must add outward self-control to inner, and must rule his speech and his actions as rigidly as he rules his thoughts. As the mind obeys the soul, so must the lower nature obey the mind. The usefulness of the disciple in the outer world depends as much on the pure and noble example set by his visible life, as his usefulness in the inner world depends on the steadiness and strength of his thoughts. Often is good work marred by carelessness in this lower part of human activity, and the aspirant is bidden strive towards an ideal, perfect in every part, in order that he may not later, when treading the Path, stumble in his own walk and cause the enemy to blaspheme.

As already said, perfection in anything is not demanded at this stage, but the wise pupil strives towards perfection, knowing that at his best he is still far away from his ideal. Thirdly, the candidate for full discipleship seeks to build into himself the sublime and far-reaching virtue of tolerance— the quiet acceptance of each man, each form of existence, as it is, without demand that it should be something other, shaped more to his own liking. Beginning to realize that the one Life takes on countless limitations, each right in its own place and time, he accepts each limited expression of the Life without wishing to transform it into something else; he learns to revere the wisdom which planned this world and which guides it, and to view with wide-eyed serenity the imperfect parts as they slowly work out their partial lives. The drunkard, learning his alphabet of the suffering caused by the dominance of the lower nature, is doing as usefully in his own stage as is the saint in his, completing his last lesson in earth's school, and no more can justly be demanded from either than he is able to perform. One is in the kindergarten stage, learning by object-lessons, while the other is graduating, ready to leave his university; both are right for their age and their place, and should be helped and sympathized with *in their place*. This is one of the lessons of what is known in occultism as " tolerance ". Fourthly must be developed endurance, the endurance that cheerfully bears all and resents nothing,

going straight onwards unswervingly to the goal.
Nothing can come to him but by the Law, and he
knows the Law is good. He understands that the
rocky pathway that leads up the mountain-side
straight to the summit cannot be as easy to his feet
as the well-beaten winding highway. He realizes
that he is paying in a few short lives all the kārmic
obligations accumulated during his past, and that
the payments must be correspondingly heavy. The
very struggles into which he is plunged develop in
him the fifth attribute, faith—faith in his Master
and in himself, a serene strong confidence that is
unshakable. He learns to trust in the wisdom, the
love, the power of his Master, and he is beginning
to realize—not only to say he believes in—the
Divinity within his own heart, able to subdue all
things to Himself. The last mental requisite,
balance, equilibrium, grows up to some extent
without conscious effort during the striving after
the preceding five. The very setting of the will to
tread the Path is a sign that the higher nature is
opening out, and that the external world is definitely
relegated to a lower place. The continuous efforts
to lead the life of discipleship disentangle the soul
from any remaining ties that may knit it to the
world of sense, for the withdrawal of the soul's
attention from lower objects gradually exhausts the
attractive power of those objects. They " turn

away from an abstemious dweller in the body ", [1] and soon lose all power to disturb this balance. Thus he learns to move amid them undisturbed, neither seeking nor rejecting any. He also learns balance amid mental troubles of every kind, amid alternations of mental joy and mental pain, this balance being further taught by the swift changes already spoken of through which his life is guided by the ever-watchful care of his Master.

These six mental attributes being in some measure attained, the probationary chelā needs further but the fourth qualification, the deep intense longing for liberation, that yearning of the soul towards union with the Deity that is the promise of its own fulfilment. This adds the last touch to his readiness to enter into full discipleship, for once that longing has definitely asserted itself, it can never again be eradicated, and the soul that has felt it can never again quench his thirst at earthly fountains; their waters will ever taste flat and vapid when he sips them, so that he will turn away with ever-deepening longing for the true water of life. At this stage he is " the man ready for Initiation ", ready to definitely " enter the stream " that cuts him off forever from the interests of earthly life save as he can serve his Master in them and help forward the evolution of the race. Henceforth his life

[1] *Bhagavad Gītā*, ii, 59.

is not to be the life of separateness; it is to be offered up on the altar of humanity, a glad sacrifice of all he is, to be used for the common good.[1]

During the years spent in evolving the four qualifications, the probationary chelā will have been advancing in many other respects. He will have been receiving from his Master much teaching, teaching usually imparted during the deep sleep of

---

[1] The student will be glad to have the technical names of these stages in Sanskrit and Pāli, so that he may be able to follow them out in more advanced books:

SANSKRIT (used by Hindus)		PĀLI (used by Buddhists)	
1. VIVEKA:	discrimination between the real and the unreal	1. MANODVĀ-RAVAJJANA:	the opening of the doors of the mind; a conviction of the impermanence of the earthly.
2. VAIRĀGYA:	indifference to the unreal, the transitory.	2. PARIKAM-MA:	preparation for action; indifference to the fruits of action.
3. SHAT-SAMPATTI	*Sama*: control of thought. *Dama*: control of conduct. *Uparati*: tolerance. *Titiksha*: endurance. *Śraddhā*: faith. *Samādhāna*: balance.	3. UPACHĀ-RO:	attention or conduct; divided under the same headings as in the Hindu.
4. MUMUK-SHATWA:	desire for liberation.	4. ANULOMA:	direct order or succession, its attainment following on the other three.

The man is then the ADHIKĀRI. The man is then the GOTRA-BHU

the body; the soul, clad in his well-organized astral body, will have become used to it as a vehicle of consciousness, and will have been drawn to his Master to receive instruction and spiritual illumination. He will further have been trained in meditation, and this effective practice outside the physical body will have quickened and brought into active exercise many of the higher powers; during such meditation he will have reached higher regions of being, learning more of the life of the mental plane. He will have been taught to use his increasing powers in human service, and during many of the hours of sleep for the body he will have been working diligently on the astral plane, aiding the souls that have passed on to it by death, comforting the victims of accidents, teaching any less instructed than himself, and in countless ways helping those who needed it, thus in humble fashion aiding the beneficent work of the Masters, and being associated with Their sublime Brotherhood as a co-labourer in a however modest and lowly degree.

Either on the probationary Path or later, the chelā is offered the privilege of performing one of those acts of renunciation which mark the swifter ascent of man. He is allowed " to renounce Devachan ", that is, to resign the glorious life in the heavenly places that awaits him on his liberation from the physical world, the life which in his case would mostly be spent in the middle arūpa world in the company of the Masters, and in all the sublime joys of the purest wisdom and love. If he renounce this fruit of his noble and devoted life, the spiritual forces that would have been expended in his Devachan are set free for the general service of the world,. and he himself remains in the astral region to await a speedy rebirth upon earth. His Master in this case selects and presides over his reincarnation, guiding him to take birth amid conditions conducive to his usefulness in the world, suitable for his own further progress and for the work required at his hands. He has reached the stage at which every individual interest is subordinated to the divine work, and in which his will is fixed to serve in whatever way may be required of him. He therefore gladly surrenders himself into the hands he trusts, accepting willingly and joyfully the place in the world in which he can best render service, and perform his share of the glorious work of aiding the evolution of humanity. Blessed is the family into which a child is born tenanted by such a soul, a soul that brings with him the benediction of the Master and is ever watched and guided, every possible assistance being given him to bring his lower vehicles quickly under control. Occasionally, but rarely, a chelā may reincarnate in a body that has passed through infancy and extreme youth as the tabernacle of a less progressed Ego; when an Ego comes to the earth for a very brief life-period, say for some fifteen or twenty years, he will be leaving his body at the time of dawning manhood, when it has passed through the time of early training and is rapidly becoming an effective vehicle for the soul. If such a body be a very good one, and some chelā be awaiting a suitable reincarnation, it will often be watched during its tenancy by the Ego for whom it was originally builded, with the view of utilizing it when he has done with it; when the life-period of that Ego is completed, and he passes out of the body into Kāmaloka on his way to Deva-chan, his cast-off body will be taken possession of by the waiting chelā, a new tenant will enter the deserted house, and the apparently dead body will revive. Such cases are unusual, but are not unknown to occultists, and some references to them may be found in occult books.

Whether the incarnation be normal or abnormal, the progress of the soul, of the chelā himself, continues, and the period already spoken of is reached when he is " ready for Initiation "; through that gateway of Initiation he enters, as a definitely accepted chelā, on the Path. This Path consists of four distinct stages, and the entrance into each is guarded by an Initiation. Each Initiation is accompanied by an expansion of consciousness which gives what is called "the key of knowledge" belonging to the stage to which it admits, and this key of knowledge is also a key of power, for truly is knowledge power in all the realms of Nature. When the chelā has entered the Path he becomes what has been called " the houseless man ",[1] for he no longer looks on earth as his home, he has no abiding-place here, to him all places are welcome wherein he can serve his Master. While he is on this stage of the Path there are three hindrances to progress, technically called " fetters ", which he has to get rid of, and now —as he is rapidly to perfect himself—it is demanded from him that he shall entirely eradicate faults of character, and perform completely the task belonging to his condition. The three fetters that he must loose from his limbs ere he can pass the second Initiation are: the illusion of the personal self, doubt, and superstition. The personal self must be felt in consciousness as an illusion, and must lose forever its power to impose itself on the soul as a reality. He must feel himself one with all, all must live and breathe in him and he in all. Doubt must be destroyed, but by knowledge, not by crushing out; he must know reincarnation and karma and

---

[1] The Hindu calls this stage that of the Parivrājaka, the wanderer; the Buddhist calls it that of the Srotāpatti, he who has reached the stream. The chelā is thus designated after his first Initiation and before his second.

the existence of the Masters as facts; not accepting them as intellectually necessary, but knowing them as facts in Nature that he has himself verified, so that no doubt on these heads can ever again rise in his mind. Superstition is escaped as the man rises into a knowledge of realities, and of the proper place of rites and ceremonies in the economy of Nature; he learns to use every means and to be bound by none. When the chelā has cast off these fetters—sometimes the task occupies several lives, sometimes it is achieved in part of a single life—he finds the second Initiation open to him, with its new " key of knowledge " and its widened horizon. The chelā now sees before him a swiftly shortening span of compulsory life on earth, for when he has reached this stage he must pass through his third and fourth Initiations in his present life or in the next.[1]

In this stage he has to bring into full working order the inner faculties, those belonging to the subtle bodies, for he needs them for his service in the higher realms of being. If he has developed them previously, this stage may be a very brief one, but he may pass through the gateway of death once more ere he is ready to receive his third Initiation, to become " the Swan ", the

[1] The chelā on the second stage of the Path is for the Hindu the Kuṭīcchaka, the man who builds a hut; he has reached a place of peace. For the Buddhist he is the Sakridāgāmin, the man who receives birth but once more.

individual who soars into the empyrean, that wond-
rous Bird of Life whereof so many legends are related.[1] On this third stage of the Path the chelā casts
off the fourth and fifth fetters, those of desire and
aversion; he sees the One Self in all, and the outer
veil can no longer blind him, whether it be fair or
foul. He looks on all with an equal eye; that fair
bud of tolerance that he cherished on the probationary Path now flowers out into an all-embracing
love that wraps everything within its tender embrace.
He is "the friend of every creature", the "lover of
all that lives" in a world where all things live. As
a living embodiment of divine love, he passes swiftly
onwards to the fourth Initiation, that admits him
to the last stage of the Path, where he is "beyond
the Individual", the worthy, the venerable.[2] Here
he remains at his will, casting off the last five fetters
that still bind him with threads, however fragile,
and keep him back from liberation. He throws
off all clinging to life in form, and then all longing
for formless life; these are chains and he must be
chainless; he may move through the three worlds,
but not a shred of theirs must have power to hold
him; the splendours of the "formless world" must

---

[1] The Hamsa, he who realizes "I am THAT", in the Hindu
terms; Anāgāmin, the man who receives birth no more, in the
Buddhist.

[2] The Hindu calls him the Paramahamsa, beyond the "I"; the
Buddhist names him the Arhat, the worthy.

charm him no more than the concrete glories of the worlds of form.[1] Then—mightiest of all achievements—he casts off the last fetter of separateness, the " I-making " faculty [2] which realizes itself as apart from others, for he dwells ever on the plane of unity in his waking consciousness, on the buddhic plane where the Self of all is known and realized as one. This faculty was born with the soul, is the essence of individuality, and it persists till all that is valuable in it is worked into the Monad, and it can be dropped on the threshold of liberation, leaving its priceless result to the Monad, that sense of individual identity which is so pure and fine that it does not mar the consciousness of oneness. Easily then drops away aught that could respond to ruffling contacts, and the chelā stands robed in that glorious vesture of unchanging peace that naught can mar. And the casting away of that same " I-making " faculty has cleared away from the spiritual vision the last clouds that could dim its piercing insight, and in the realization of unity, ignorance [3]—the limitation that gives birth to all separateness—falls away, and the man is perfect, is free.

[1] See Chapter IV, " The Mental Plane ".

[2] Ahamkāra, generally given as Māna, pride, since pride is the subtlest manifestation of the " I " as distinct from others.

[3] Avidyā, the first illusion and the last, that which makes the separated worlds—the first of the Nidānas—and that which drops off when liberation is attained.

Then has come the ending of the Path, and the ending of the Path is the threshold of Nirvāna. Into that marvellous state of consciousness the chelā has been wont to pass out of the body while he has been traversing the final stage of the Path; now, when he crosses the threshold, the nirvānic consciousness becomes his normal consciousness, for Nirvāna is the home of the liberated Self.[1] He has completed man's ascent, he touches the limit of humanity; above him there stretch hosts of mighty Beings, but they are Superhuman; the crucifixion in flesh is over, the hour of liberation has struck, and the triumphant " It is finished! " rings from the conqueror's lips. See! he has crossed the threshold, he has vanished into the light nirvānic, another son of earth has conquered death. What mysteries are veiled by that light supernal we know not; dimly we feel that the Supreme Self is found, that lover and Beloved are one. The long search is over, the thirst of the heart is quenched forever, he has entered into the joy of his Lord.

But has earth lost her child, is humanity bereft of her triumphant son? Nay! He has come forth from the bosom of the light, and He standeth again on the threshold of Nirvāna, Himself seeming the very embodiment of that light, glorious beyond all telling,

---

[1] The Jīvanmukta, the liberated life, of the Hindu; the Asekha, he who has no more to learn, of the Buddhist.

a manifested Son of God. But now His face is
turned to earth, His eyes beam with divinest compassion on the wandering sons of men, His brethren
after the flesh; He cannot leave them comfortless,
scattered as sheep without a shepherd. Clothed in
the majesty of a mighty renunciation, glorious with
the strength of perfect wisdom and " the power of
an endless life ", He returns to earth to bless and
guide humanity, Master of the Wisdom, kingly
Teacher, divine Man.

Returning thus to earth, the Master devotes Himself to the service of humanity with mightier forces
at His command than He wielded while He trod
the Path of discipleship; He has dedicated Himself
to the helping of man, He bends all the sublime
powers that He holds to the quickening of the
evolution of the world. He pays to those who are
approaching the Path the debt He contracted in the
days of His own cheláship, guiding, helping, teaching them as He was guided, helped, and taught
before.

Such are the stages of man's ascent, from the
lowest savagery to divine manhood. To such goal
is humanity climbing, to such glory shall the race
attain.

CHAPTER XII

BUILDING A KOSMOS

IT is not possible, at our present stage of evolution, to do more than roughly indicate a few points in the vast outline of the kosmic scheme in which our globe plays its little part. By a " kosmos " is here meant a system which seems, from our standpoint, to be complete in itself, arising from a single Logos, and sustained by His Life. Such a system is our solar system, and the physical sun may be considered to be the lowest manifestation of the Logos when acting as the centre of His kosmos; every form is indeed one of His concrete manifestations, but the sun is His lowest manifestation as the life-giving, invigorating, all-pervading, all-controlling, regulative, co-ordinating central power.

Says an occult commentary: Sūrya (the sun),

in its visible reflection, exhibits the first or lowest state of the seventh, the highest state of the Universal PRESENCE, the pure of the pure; the first manifested Breath of the ever unmanifested SAT (Be-ness). All the central physical or objective Suns are in their

23

substance the lowest state of the first Principle of the
BREATH,[1]

are, in short, the lowest state of the " Physical
Body " of the Logos.

All physical forces and energies are but transmu-
tations of the life poured forth by the sun, the Lord
and Giver of life to His system.   Hence in many
ancient religions the sun has stood as the symbol of
the Supreme God—the symbol, in truth, the least
liable to misconstruction by the ignorant.

Mr. Sinnett well says:

The solar system is indeed an area of Nature including more than any but the very highest beings
whom our humanity is capable of developing are in
a position to investigate. Theoretically we may feel
sure—as we look up into the heavens at night—that
the whole solar system itself is but a drop in the ocean
of the kosmos, but that drop is in its turn an ocean
from the point of view of the consciousness of such
half-developed beings within it as ourselves, and we
can only hope at present to acquire vague and shadowy
conceptions of its origin and constitution. Shadowy,
however, though these may be, they enable us to assign
the subordinate planetary series, in which our own
evolution is carried on, to its proper place in the
system of which it is a part, or at all events to get
a broad idea of the relative magnitude of the whole
system, of our planetary chain, of the world in which
we are at present functioning, and of the respective
periods of evolution in which as human beings we are
interested.[2]

[1] The Secret Doctrine, I, 309, 1893 Edn.; I, 330, Adyar Edn.
[2] The System To Which We Belong, p. 4.

For in truth we cannot grasp our own position intellectually without some idea—however vague it may be—of our relation to the whole; and while some students are content to work within their own sphere of duty and to leave the wider reaches of life until they are called to function in them, others feel the need of a far-reaching scheme in which they have their place, and take an intellectual delight in soaring upwards to obtain a bird's-eye view of the whole field of evolution. This need has been recognized and met by the spiritual Guardians of humanity in the magnificent delineation of the kosmos from the standpoint of the occultist traced by Their pupil and messenger, H. P. Blavatsky, in *The Secret Doctrine*, a work that will become ever more and more enlightening as students of the Ancient Wisdom themselves explore and master the lower levels of our evolving world.

The appearance of the Logos, we are told, is the herald of the birth-hour of our kosmos.

When He is manifest, all is manifested after Him; by His manifestation this All becomes manifest.[1]

With Himself He brings the fruits of a past kosmos—the mighty spiritual Intelligences who are to be His co-workers and agents in the universe now to be built. Highest of these are " the Seven ", often Themselves spoken of as Logoi, since each in His

[1] *Mundakopanishad*, II, ii, 10.

place is the centre of a distinct department in the kosmos, as the LOGOS is the centre of the whole. The commentary before quoted says:

> The seven Beings in the Sun are the Seven Holy Ones, Self-born from the inherent power in the matrix of Mother-substance. . . . The energy from which they sprang into conscious existence in every Sun is what some people call Vishnu, which is the Breath of the Absoluteness. We call it the one manifested Life— itself a reflection of the Absolute.[1]

This " one manifested Life " is the LOGOS, the manifested God.

From this primary division our kosmos takes its sevenfold character, and all subsequent divisions in their descending order reproduce this seven-keyed scale. Under each of the seven secondary Logoi come the descending hierarchies of Intelligences that form the governing body of His kingdom; among These we hear of the Lipika, who are the Recorders of the karma of that kingdom and of all entities therein; of the Mahārājas or Devarājas, who superintend the working out of kārmic law; and of the vast hosts of the Builders, who shape and fashion all forms after the Ideas that dwell in the treasure-house of the LOGOS, in the Universal Mind, and that pass from Him to the Seven, each of whom plans out His own realm under that su- preme direction and all-inspiring life, giving to it, at

[1] *The Secret Doctrine*, I. 310, 1839 Edn.; I, 331, Adyar Edn.

the same time, His own individual colouring. H. P. Blavatsky calls these Seven Realms that make up the solar system the seven Laya centres; she says:

> The seven Laya centres are the seven Zero points, using the term Zero in the same sense that chemists do, to indicate a point at which, in Esotericism, the scale of reckoning of differentiation begins. From the Centres—beyond which Esoteric philosophy allows us to perceive the dim metaphysical outlines of the " Seven Sons " of Life and Light, the seven Logoi of the Hermetic and all other philosophies—begins the differentiation of the elements which enter into the constitution of our Solar System.[1]

This realm is a planetary evolution of a stupendous character, the field in which are lived out the stages of a life of which a physical planet, such as Venus, is but a transient embodiment. We may speak of the Evolver and Ruler of this realm as a planetary Logos, so as to avoid confusion. He draws from the matter of the solar system, outpoured from the central Logos Himself, the crude materials He requires, and elaborates them by His own life-energies, each planetary Logos thus specializing the matter of His realm from a common stock.[2] The atomic state in each of the seven planes of His kingdom being identical with the matter of a subplane of the whole solar system, continuity is thus

[1] *The Secret Doctrine*, I, 162, 1893 Edn.; I, 195, Adyar Edn.

[2] See in Chapter I, " The Physical Plane ", the statement on the evolution of matter.

established throughout the whole. As H. P. Blavatsky remarks, atoms change "their combining
equivalents on every planet", the atoms themselves
being identical, but their combinations differing.
She goes on:

> Not alone the elements of our planets, but even
> those of all its sisters in the solar system, differ as
> widely from each other in their combinations, as from
> the cosmic elements beyond our solar limits. . . . Each
> atom has seven planes of being, or existence, we are
> taught,[1]

—the sub-planes, as we have been calling them, of
each great plane.

On the three lower planes of His evolving realm
the planetary Logos establishes seven globes or
worlds, which for convenience sake, following the
received nomenclature, we will call globes A, B, C,
D, E, F, G. These are the

> Seven small wheels revolving, one giving birth to
> the other,

spoken of in Stanza vi of the *Book of Dzyan*:

> He builds them in the likeness of older wheels,
> placing them on the imperishable centres.[2]

Imperishable, since each wheel not only gives
birth to its successor, but is also itself reincarnated
at the same centre, as we shall see.

---

[1] *The Secret Doctrine*, I, 166, 174, 1893 Edn.; I, 199, 205, Adyar
Edn.

[2] *Ibid.*, I, 64, 1893 Edn.; I, 97, Adyar Edn.

These globes may be figured as disposed in three pairs on the arc of an ellipse, with the middle globe at the mid-most and lowest point; for the most part globes A and G—the first and seventh—are on the arūpa levels of the mental plane; globes B and F—the second and sixth—are on the rūpa levels; globes C and E—the third and fifth—are on the astral plane; globe D—the fourth—is on the physical plane. These globes are spoken of by H. P. Blavatsky as " graduated on the four lower planes of the World of Formation ",[1] *i.e.*, the physical and astral planes, and the two subdivisions of the mental (rūpa and arūpa). They may be figured:[2]

arūpa	(A) (G)	*archetypal*
rūpa	(B) (F)	*creative or intellectual* }
astral	(C) (E)	*formative*
physical	(D)	*physical*

This is the typical arrangement, but it is modified at certain stages of evolution. These seven globes

[1] *The Secret Doctrine*, I, 176, 1893 Edn.; I, 207, Adyar Edn.
[2] *Ibid.*, I, 221, 1893 Edn.; I, 249, Adyar Edn.; the note is important that the archetypal world is not the world as it existed in the mind of the planetary Logos, but the first model which was made.

form a planetary ring or chain, and—if for a moment we regard the planetary chain as a whole, as, so to say, an entity, a planetary life or individual —that chain passes through seven distinct stages in its evolution; the seven globes as *a whole* form its planetary body, and this planetary body disintegrates and is re-formed seven times during the planetary life. The planetary chain has seven incarnations, and the results obtained in one are handed on to the next.

Every such chain of worlds is the progeny and creation of another lower and dead chain—its reincarnation, so to say.[1]

These seven incarnations [2] make up "planetary evolution", the realm of a planetary Logos. As there are seven planetary Logoi, it will be seen that seven of these planetary evolutions, each distinct from the others, make up the solar system.[3] In an occult commentary this coming forth of the seven Logoi from the One, and of the seven successive chains of seven globes each, is described:

From one light, seven lights; from each of the seven, seven times seven.[4]

Taking up the incarnations of the chain, the manvantaras, we learn that these also are subdivisible

---

[1] *The Secret Doctrine*, I, 176, 1893 Edn.; I, 207, Adyar Edn.
[2] Technically called " manvantaras ".
[3] Mr. Sinnett calls these " seven schemes of evolution ".
[4] *The Secret Doctrine*, I, 147, 1893 Edn.; I, 180, Adyar Edn.

into seven stages; a wave of life from the planetary Logos is sent round the chain, and seven of these great life-waves, each one technically spoken of as " a round ", complete a single manvantara. Each globe has thus seven periods of activity during a manvantara, each in turn becoming the field of evolving life.

Looking at a single globe we find that during the period of its activity seven root-races of a humanity evolve on it, together with six other non-human kingdoms interdependent on each other. As these seven kingdoms contain forms at all stages of evolution, as all have higher reaches stretching before them, the evolving forms of one globe pass to another to carry on their growth when the period of activity of the former globe comes to an end, and go on from globe to globe to the end of that round; they further pursue their course round after round to the close of the seven rounds or manvantaras; they once again climb onward through manvantara after manvantara till the end of the reincarnations of their planetary chain is reached, when the results of that planetary evolution are gathered up by the planetary Logos. Needless to say that scarcely anything of this evolution is known to us; only the salient points in the stupendous whole have been indicated by the Teachers.

Even when we come to the planetary evolution in which our own world is a stage, we know nothing of the processes through which its seven globes evolved during its first two manvantaras; and of its third manvantara we only know that the globe which is now our moon was globe D of that planetary chain. This fact, however, may help us to realize more clearly what is meant by these successive reincarnations of a planetary chain. The seven globes which formed the lunar chain passed in due course through their sevenfold evolution; seven times the life-wave, the Breath of the planetary Logos, swept round the chain, quickening in turn each globe into life. It is as though that Logos in guiding His kingdom turned His attention first to globe A, and thereon brought into successive existence the innumerable forms that in their totality make up a world; when evolution had been carried to a certain point, He turned His attention to globe B, and globe A slowly sank into a peaceful sleep. Thus the life-wave was carried from globe to globe, until one round of the circle was completed by globe G finishing its evolution; then there succeeded a period of rest,[1] during which the external evolutionary activity ceased. At the close of this period external evolution recommenced, starting on its second round and beginning as before on globe A.

[1] Technically called a pralaya.

The process is repeated six times, but when the seventh, the last round, is reached, there is a change. Globe A, having accomplished its seventh life-period, gradually disintegrates, and the imperishable laya centre state supervenes; from that, at the dawn of the succeeding manvantara a new globe A is evolved—like a new body—in which the " principles " of the preceding planet A take up their abode. This phrase is only intended to convey the idea of a relation between globe A of the first manvantara and globe A of the second, the nature of that connection remains hidden.

Of the connection between globe D of the lunar manvantara—our moon—and globe D of the terrene manvantara—our earth—we know a little more, and Mr. Sinnett has given a convenient summary of the slender knowledge we possess in *The System To Which We Belong*. He says:

The new earth nebula was developed round a centre bearing pretty much the same relation to the dying planet that the centres of the earth and moon bear to one another at present. But in the nebulous condition this aggregation of matter occupied an enormously greater volume than the solid matter of the earth now occupies. It stretched out in all directions so as to include the old planet in its fiery embrace. The temperature of a new nebula appears to be considerably higher than any temperatures we are acquainted with, and by this means the old planet was superficially heated afresh in such a manner that all atmosphere, water, and volatilizable matter upon

it was brought into the gaseous condition and so became amenable to the new centre of attraction set up
at the centre of the new nebula. In this way the air
and seas of the old planet were drawn over into the
constitution of the new one, and thus it is that the
moon in its present state is an arid, glaring mass, dry
and cloudless, no longer habitable, and no longer
required for the habitation of any physical beings.
When the present manvantara is nearly over, during
the seventh round, its disintegration will be completed
and the matter which it still holds together will resolve
into meteoric dust.[1]

In the third volume of *The Secret Doctrine*, in
which are printed some of the oral teachings given
by H. P. Blavatsky to her more advanced pupils,
it is stated:

At the beginning of the evolution of our globe,
the moon was much nearer to the earth, and larger
than it is now. It has retreated from us, and shrunk
much in size. (The moon gave all her principles to
the earth.) . . . A new moon will appear during the
seventh round, and our moon will finally distintegrate
and disappear.[2]

Evolution during the lunar manvantara produced
seven classes of beings, technically called Fathers,
or Pitris, since it was they who generated the beings
of the terrene manvantara. These are the Lunar
Pitris of *The Secret Doctrine*. More developed than
these were two other classes—variously called Solar
Pitris, Men, Lower Dhyānis—too far advanced to

[1] *Op. cit.*, p. 10.

[2] *Op. cit.*, III, 562, 1893 Edn.; V, 535, Adyar Edn.

enter on the terrene evolution in its early stages, but requiring the aid of later physical conditions for their future growth. The higher of these two classes consisted of individualized animal-like beings, creatures with enbryonic souls, *i.e.*, they had developed the causal body; the second were approaching its formation. Lunar Pitris, the first class, were at the beginning of that approach showing mentality, while the second and third had only developed the kāmic principle. These seven classes of Lunar Pitris were the product the lunar chain handed on for further development to the terrene, the fourth reincarnation of the planetary chain. As Monads —with the mental principle present in the first, the kāmic principle developed in the second and third classes, this germinal in the fourth, only approaching the germ stage in the still less developed fifth, and imperceptible in the sixth and seventh—these entities entered the earth-chain, to ensoul the elemental essence and the forms shaped by the Builders.[1]

The nomenclature adopted by me is that of *The Secret Doctrine*. In the valuable paper by Mrs. Sinnett and Mr. Scott-Elliot on the *Lunar Pitris*, H. P. B.'s " Lower Dhyānis ", that incarnate in the

[1] H. P. Blavatsky, in *The Secret Doctrine*, does not include those whom Mrs. Sinnett calls first- and second-class Pitris in the " monads from the lunar chain "; she takes them apart as " men ", as " Dhyān Chohans ". Compare I, 197, 207, 211, 1893 Edn.; I, 227, 236, 239, Adyar Edn.

third and fourth rounds, are taken as the first and second classes of Lunar Pitris; their third class is therefore H. P. B.'s first class, their fourth class her second, and so on. There is no difference in the statement of facts, only in nomenclature, but this difference of nomenclature may mislead the student if it be not explained. As I am using H. P. B.'s nomenclature, my fellow-students of the London Lodge and the readers of their " Transaction " will need to remember that my first is their third, and so on sequentially.

The " Builders " is a name including innumerable Intelligences, hierarchies of beings of graduated consciousness and power, who on each plane carry out the actual building of forms. The higher direct and control, while the lower fashion the materials after the models provided. And now appears the use of the successive globes of the planetary chain. Globe A is the archetypal world, on which are built the models of the forms that are to be elaborated during the round; from the mind of the planetary Logos the highest Builders take the archetypal Ideals, and guide the Builders on the arūpa levels as they fashion the archetypal forms for the round. On globe B these forms are reproduced in varied shapes in mental matter by a lower rank of Builders, and are evolved slowly along different lines, until they are ready to receive an infiltration of denser

matter; then the Builders in astral matter take up
the task, and on globe C fashion astral forms, with
details more worked out; when the forms have been
evolved as far as the astral conditions permit, the
Builders of globe D take up the task of form-shaping
on the physical plane, and the lowest kinds of matter
are thus fashioned into appropriate types, and the
forms reach their densest and most complete
condition.

From this middle point onwards the nature of the
evolution somewhat changes: hitherto the greatest
attention had been directed to the building of the
form; on the ascending arc the chief attention is
directed to using the form as a vehicle of the
evolving life and on the second half of the evolution
on globe D, and on globes E and F the consciousness expresses itself first on the physical and then
on the astral and lower mental planes through the
equivalents of the forms elaborated on the descending arc. On the descending arc the Monad
impresses itself as best it may *on* the evolving forms,
and these impressions appear vaguely as impressions, intuitions, and so on; on the ascending
arc the Monad expresses itself *through* the forms
as their inner ruler. On globe G the perfection
of the round is reached, the Monad inhabiting
and using as its vehicles the archetypal forms of
globe A.

During all these stages the Lunar Pitris have acted as the souls of the forms, brooding over them, later inhabiting them. It is on the first-class Pitris that the heaviest burden of the work falls during the first three rounds. The second- and third- class Pitris flow into the forms worked up by the first; the first prepare these forms by ensouling them for a time and then pass on, leaving them for the tenancy of the second and third classes. By the end of the first round the archetypal forms of the mineral would have been brought down, to be elaborated through the succeeding rounds, till they reach their densest state in the middle of the fourth round. " Fire " is the " element " of this first round.

In the second round the first-class Pitris continue their human evolution, only touching the lower stages as the human foetus still touches them to-day, while the second class, at the close of the round, have reached the incipient human stage. The great work of the round is bringing down the archetypal forms of vegetable life, which will reach their perfection in the fifth round. " Air " is the second round " element ".

In the third round the first-class Pitris become definitely human in form; though the body is jelly-like and gigantic, it is yet, on globe D, compact enough to begin to stand upright; he is ape-like and is covered with hairy bristles. The third-class

Pitris reach the incipient human stage. Second-class solar Pitris make their first appearance on Globe D in this round, and take the lead in human evolution. The archetypal forms of animals are brought down to be elaborated into perfection by the end of the sixth round, and " water " is the characteristic " element ".

The fourth round, the middle one of the seven that make up the terrene manvantara, is distinguished by bringing to globe A the archetypal forms of humanity, this round being as distinctively human as its predecessors were respectively animal, vegetable, and mineral. Not till the seventh round will these forms be all fully realized by humanity, but the possibilities of the human form are manifested in archetypal in the fourth. " Earth " is the " element " of this round, the densest, the most material. The first-class solar Pitris may be said to hover round globe D more or less in this round during its early stages of activity, but they do not definitely incarnate until after the third great out-pouring of life from the planetary Logos in the middle of the third race, and then only slowly, the number increasing as the race progresses, and multitudes incarnating in the early fourth race.

The evolution of humanity on our earth, globe D, offers in a strongly marked form the continual sevenfold diversity already often alluded to. Seven

24

races of men had already shown themselves in the
third round, and in the fourth these fundamental
divisions became very clear on globe C, where seven
races, each with sub-races, evolved. On globe D,
humanity begins with a First Race—usually called
a Root-Race—at seven different points, " seven of
them, each on his lot ".[1] These seven types side by
side, not successive, make up the first root-race,
and each again has its own seven sub-races. From
the first root-race—jelly-like amorphous creatures—
evolves the second root-race with forms of more
definite consistency, and from it the third, ape-like
creatures that become clumsy gigantic men. In
the middle of the evolution of this third root-race,
called the Lemurian, there come to earth—from
another planetary chain, that of Venus, much
farther advanced in its evolution—members of its
highly evolved humanity, glorious Beings, often
spoken of as Sons of the Fire, from Their radiant
appearance, a lofty order among the Sons of Mind.[2]
They take up Their abode on earth, as the Divine
Teachers of the young humanity, some of Them
acting as channels for the third outpouring and
projecting into animal man the spark of monadic
life which forms the causal body. Thus the first,

[1] *Stanzas of Dzyan*, 3, 13.   *The Secret Doctrine*, II, 18, 1893 Edn.;
III, 29, Adyar Edn.

[2] *Mānasaputra*. This vast hierarchy of self-conscious Intelligences embraces many orders.

second, and third classes of Lunar Pitris become individualized—the vast bulk of humanity. The two classes of solar Pitris, already individualized—the first ere leaving the lunar chain and the second later—form two low orders of the Sons of Mind; the second incarnate in the third race at its middle point, and the first come in later, for the most part in the fourth race, the Atlantean. The fifth, or Aryan race, now leading human evolution, was evolved from the fifth sub-race of the Atlantean, the most promising families being segregated in Central Asia, and the new race-type evolved, under the direct superintendence of a Great Being, technically called a Manu. Emerging from Central Asia the first sub-race settled in India, south of the Himālayas, and in their four orders of teachers,[1] warriors, merchants, and workmen, became the dominant race in the vast Indian peninsula, conquering the fourth-race and third-race nations who then inhabited it.

At the end of the seventh race of the seventh round, i.e., at the close of our terrene manvantara, our chain will hand on to its successor the fruits of its life; these fruits will be perfected divine men, Buddhas, Manus, Chohans, Masters, ready to take up the work of guiding evolution under direction of the planetary Logos, with hosts of less evolved

---

[1] Brāhmanas, Kshattriyas, Vaishyas and Shūdras.

entities of every grade of consciousness, who still need physical experience for the perfecting of their divine possibilities. The fifth, sixth, and seventh manvantaras of our chain are still in the womb of the future after this fourth one has closed, and then the planetary Logos will gather up into Himself all the fruits of evolution, and with His children enter on a period of rest and bliss. Of that high state we cannot speak; how at this stage of our evolution could we dream of its unimaginable glory! Only we dimly know that our glad spirits shall " enter into the joy of the Lord ", and, resting in Him, shall see stretching before them boundless ranges of sublime life and love, heights and depths of power and joy, limitless as the One Existence, inexhaustible as the One that is.

PEACE TO ALL BEINGS

INDEX

25